★ ★ ★ ★ ★ ★ ★ ★ ★ ★ ★ ★ ★ ★ ★ ★ ★ ★ ★

Lifetime Physical Fitness: Assessments, Concepts, Prescriptions

Fourth Edition

★ ★ ★ ★ ★ ★ ★ ★

Virginia Politano, Ph.D.
Lewis Bowling, M.S.
T. J. Tipper, M.S.

Department of Physical Education and Recreation
North Carolina Central University
Durham, NC

KENDALL/HUNT PUBLISHING COMPANY
4050 Westmark Drive   Dubuque, Iowa 52002

Cover and interior photos provided by author.

Contents

3. Cardiorespiratory Fitness   45

Carey Hughley and Virginia Politano

4. Muscle Strength and Muscle Endurance   87

Lewis Bowling

5. Flexibility   107

T. J. Tipper

6. Body Composition and Weight Management   127

Virginia Politano

7. Nutrition 149

Virginia Politano

Preface

The purpose of this book is to introduce you to the world of physical fitness and to help you to change your lifestyle. Americans can substantially improve their health and quality of life by including a moderate amount of physical activity in their daily lives. The person does not have to be in training for anything in order to derive benefits from physical activity. Making physical activity a part of a lifestyle change will make a difference in the health and fitness of all people.

As in previous editions, the book addresses the areas of cardiorespiratory endurance, muscular strength and endurance, flexibility, and body composition. Intended for an introductory college fitness course, *Lifetime Physical Fitness* focuses on how to achieve a moderate level of fitness and to provide information to help you make an informed decision about lifestyle changes.

The fourth edition contains new content that builds upon the previous editions but contains new information as well:

★ New chapter on nutrition with the new food label, nutrients, daily recommended requirements, and updated information on other areas of nutrition

★ New tables and figures

★ New labs for weight management and nutrition

★ New information on maximum heart rate, exercise dose, stretching exercises, and contraindicated exercises

★ More pictures and tables

★ ACSM physical activity guidelines

Lifetime Physical Fitness offers a comprehensive look at physical fitness with a simple, workable approach to a healthy lifestyle.

Becoming Physically Active: An Introduction

Objectives

After completing this chapter, you will be able to do the following:

★ Define the terms fitness, physical fitness, and health-related fitness.

★ Determine why physical fitness is important.

★ List and define the health-related components of physical fitness.

★ List the Healthy People 2000 goals for the nation.

★ Describe the benefits of a physical fitness program.

★ Explain the importance of a regular exercise program.

★ Describe the Surgeon General's Report on Physical Activity and Health.

★ *The Surgeon General's Report on Physical Activity and Health (1996) summarized existing research showing the benefits of physical activity in preventing disease. It was reported that all Americans could greatly improve their quality of life and health by participating in moderate amounts of physical activity. Moderate physical activity performed 3–4 times a week can reduce the risk of dying from heart disease, diabetes, and high blood pressure. Physical activity does not have to be strenuous to be beneficial. Moderate amounts of daily physical activity are recommended for young adults. This could be performed in longer sessions of moderately intense activities such as brisk walking for 30 minutes or for shorter intense sessions of jogging for 15–20 minutes.*

Tips for Strengthening Your Note Taking Skills

Tip 1

Organize and plan your approach to note taking. What will you write with?

Come to class prepared. Have a pen or pencil to write with. Black ink is usually best because it is a dark color which is easy to see and does not fade into the page. Ink lasts longer than pencil markings. A student is more receptive to studying when the ink is readable, not very light and fading.

What will you write on? Where will you keep your notes?

Have a separate spiral notebook for each subject area. Leave the front pages clean so that you may develop a table of contents for your notes as the semester develops. Number all other pages in the notebook so that you will have an orderly progression to your notes. If it is more comfortable, use a sectioned ring binder to which you can add loose-leaf pages for each subject. Again, keep a separate loose-leaf for each subject.

Leave space in your notes to add information and explanatory details.

Tip 2

Take an active role in note taking. Be an *active listener.*

Set up questions to keep yourself in the lead. Turn your reading and your instructor's lecture titles or opening sentences into questions. These are not questions that you ask your instructor, but ones around which you plan your listening. Make up your own questions, then listen for the answers.

Pay attention to the instructor's organization, and his or her major points. Then jot down the basic ideas as you grasp them. Get in the habit of listening for major points and conclusions. Identify main ideas and the connections among them. Identify those general assertions that must be supported by specific comments. Identify the specific information (supporting details). Information presented to you in a series or a sequence is frequently worthy of note, (e.g.: "There are four reasons this occurs, . . ."). Active listeners pay attention to what they hear and try to make sense of it.

Ignore distractions that compete for your attention. Keep your focus on the material the lecturer is presenting.

Tip 3

Develop your own abbv. for commonly used wds.

Your own shorthand style will save time and make sense later when you are reviewing your notes. For example, psychology may be abbreviated as psy. You are already familiar with many abbreviations: days of the week, months of the year, states, college courses, etc. You also have many abbreviations you can use from your math studies, $=$ (equal to); $>$ (greater than); $<$ (less than).

There are times when you shouldn't use shorthand. When you are given a precise definition, you will want to make sure you record exactly what is presented. This is also true when you are given a formula or an example of an application of the formula.

Tip 4

Identify the main ideas.

Lecturers sometimes announce the purpose of a class lecture or offer an outline, thereby providing you with the skeleton of main ideas and details. Use this information to structure your notes, identifying the major points and the details that support them.

During the lecture, there are many clues which indicate that some of what is said is more important than other information. Some lecturers change their tone of voice, stamp the podium, or repeat themselves at each key idea. If your instructor emphasizes the same information repeatedly, it should become obvious to you that the instructor feels this information is important. Chances are good that you will see these topics again on the exam.

Some lecturers ask questions to promote classroom discussion. This is a clue to what the lecturer believes is important. Identify the theme of the question.

Tip 5

Bring your textbooks to class as supportive material.

Many instructors refer in their lectures to information in the textbook. Sometimes they will ask you to do an exercise from the text, or review the interpretation of a graph or visuals accompanying data presentation. Some instructors lecture on material contained in the book and supplement this material. If you have your text in class, you will be able to follow along and note important material.

Tip 6

Make a personal commitment to learn and use good note taking skills. Assume personal responsibility.

A positive frame of mind will strengthen your motivation to be an active listener. Assume that you will learn something useful, that you will expand your knowledge, and that your understanding of the course will increase.

Tip 7

Write down what the instructor puts on the board.

If a professor takes the time to write points on the board, you need to give that information special consideration.

Tip 8

Write down and use the dictionary to learn unfamiliar words.

Ask the instructors in class what unfamiliar words mean. Use these new words in your vocabulary.

Tip 9

Be an active participant.
Summarize statements of information presented in the lecture in your notes or to the class-at-large. **Take notes with a purpose.**

Don't be afraid to ask questions. If you don't understand some of the material, it's very likely that your classmates have similar concerns.

When you realize that you have missed an important point, ask the instructor to repeat it. If you don't understand what is being said and

need time to dwell on it, leave a space in your notes and put a question mark (?) in this place. Fill this void in your notes by asking a classmate or the professor prior to the next class session.

You may find graphs, charts, and drawings to be helpful. When these are used to illustrate a point, make your own sketch of what the instructor has presented.

Tip 10

Do not rely on a tape recorder for note taking.
If you use a tape recorder, do not allow this crutch to encourage you to become a passive learner. You still need to write the main points the instructor is lecturing on.

Tip 11

Recall
Create a recall column in your notes. This remains blank while you take notes during class. It is, however, used within 24 hours of the note taking to review and integrate (synthesize) your learning of the material. Write the main ideas and key information covered in the notes in the recall column.

Tip 12

Recite
Use key words or phrases highlighted in the recall column to recall and recite out loud what you understand from the class notes. This summarization of your notes can then be used to prepare for test-taking.

Tip 13

Review
Before lectures begin, review notes from the previous day. This is a "warm-up" to help your mind focus on the material to be covered and to prepare you to think critically during the lecture.

Notes are to be used frequently. Within 24 hours after the lecture, go through your notes and complete any information which might have been recorded hastily or with the intention that you would provide more detail after class. During this quick trip through your notes, make sure concepts are clear and understandable. If not, read your book; check your notes against the text, especially if you missed some main points while writing them down; speak with other students; or check with your instructor. You may also bring these questions up with the professor at the beginning of the next class.

Compare notes with other students and discuss for better retention and understanding.

Work on condensing many thoughts, ideas, or facts into a few words or phrases which will be meaningful to you at a later date.

Tip 14

Find out who's the best note taker in your class.

Compare notes, borrow notes, restructure notes. Should you miss a class, make copies of these notes.

Tip 15

Build test questions from your notes.

Once you have identified the key points in a lecture, you can identify exam answers by making up your own set of exam questions. This is exactly what the instructor does in making up an exam, giving most of the same questions— and the answers, too. In a study conducted at one eastern college, a group of students was asked to use this study method. It was found that up to 80 percent of the actual exam questions were among the key point questions the students had made up ahead of time. The grades of these students were 10 points higher than students not using this method of study (Olney, 1991).

After you have developed all of your questions, use your notes to highlight the answers for each question. If you find an answer is incomplete in your notes, fill in the necessary detail. You may want to transfer questions and their answers to note cards for easy and "portable" review.

Tip 16

Apply your note taking skills as you study and mark your books.

Use your pencil as you read.

Underline important points.

Write notes in the margins.

Draw arrows connecting important material.

Circle material you want to focus on.

Find a system of marking your textbook that is right for you.

These activities help you to be actively involved in note taking. Activity such as this forces you to focus on the material and to concentrate.

Active reading and note taking helps you consciously to search for what is important. Your markings serve a similar purpose to the recall column while the underlined text provides supporting detail.

The benefits of good note taking are many. Increased immediate learning, longer attention span, more interest in the material, an enhanced ability to apply the material in many situations, better retention, and improved notes for later study.

It does take time and self-discipline to use a note taking study system. As you progress in college, you will be forming new habits with regard to your listening skills, improve and monitor your attitude when attending a lecture, adjust where you write information on a sheet of paper, and cultivate a new standard of note taking that ensures you have studied and used your notes well.

Who Is Exercising?

According to the Surgeon General's Report nearly one-half of America's young adults are not vigorously active on a regular basis and men are more likely to be more active than women. Inactivity is more common among females than males and among black females than white females. Men tend to engage in a wider range of sports and fitness activities while women tend to engage in various forms of aerobics (i.e., dance aerobics, water aerobics, walking). Although women are becoming more active they tend to be more physically inactive than men. More than 60% of adults in the United States do not engage in the recommended amount of physical activity. Approximately 25% of all adults in the United States are not active and adults tend to accept a more sedentary lifestyle. Perhaps most tragic is the fact that 50% of young people between 12 and 21 years of age do not engage in regular vigorous or even moderate physical activity. At least 1 in 4 adults do not exercise during their daily

	Moderate Intensity*	High Intensity** (Exercise)
Overall	20%	14%
By Gender		
Men	21	13
Women	19	16
By Ethnicity		
White	21	15
African American	15	9
Hispanic American	20	12

*A minimum of 5 days per week for at least 30 minutes per session.
**A minimum of 3 days per week for a minimum of 20 minutes.
Source: U.S. Department of Health and Human Services. *Physical Activity and Health: A Report of the Surgeon General* (Atlanta: Centers for Disease Control and Prevention, National Center for Chronic Disease Prevention and Healthy Promotion, 1996).

Figure 1.0   Percent of Total U.S. Adult Population That Regularly Participates in Physical Activity

Table 1.0   Patterns and Trends in Physical Activity

Adults
★ Approximately 37% of adults engage in vigorous physical activity (3–5 times per week for at least 20–30 minutes)
★ 25% of adults do not participate in physical activity
★ Physical inactivity is more prevalent among women, among blacks and Hispanics, among older adults and among the less affluent

Adolescents and Young Adults
★ One-half of American young people regularly participate in vigorous physical activity
★ One-fourth of young people engage in light to moderate activity every day
★ 14% report no physical activity. Inactivity is more common among females (14%) than males (7%) and among black females (21%) than white females (12%)
★ Participation in all types of physical activity declines with age

Persons with Disabilities
★ Less likely to engage in regular moderate physical activity

U.S. Department of Health and Human Services. (1996). *Physical activity and health: A report of the Surgeon General.* Atlanta, GA: U.S. Department of Health and Human Services.

Patterns and Trends in Physical Activity

★ Three out of 10 young adults are physically active on a regular basis.

★ Males are more likely to exercise than females.

★ Individuals with a higher level of education are more likely to exercise than those with less than a high school education.

★ Low income individuals are less likely to engage in physical activity than those with a higher income.

Why Choose to Be Active?

Studies have shown that at least half of college students, on any college campus, are sedentary. A national study showed that only 33% of the college students exercised at the American College of Sports Medicine (ACSM) recommended levels. The study also indicated

lives. As society becomes older, this becomes a major concern (see Table 1.0). However, when polled, 90% of the adults in the United States expressed that "good health" was a major concern. The report indicated that moderate physical activity could prevent premature health risks.

Table 1.1 Effects of Physical Activity on Disease and Health

★ Reduces the risk of premature death
★ Decreases the risk of cardiovascular disease
★ Lowers the risk of developing diabetes
★ Reduces the risk of high blood pressure and reduces blood pressure in individuals who have high blood pressure
★ Helps reduce body fat
★ Helps build and maintain healthy bones, muscles, and joints
★ Improves health-related quality of life by promoting psychological well-being
★ Reduces the risk of developing colon cancer
★ Reduces feelings of depression and anxiety
★ Helps older adults become stronger and better able to move about without falling

U.S. Department of Health and Human Services. (1996). *Physical activity and health: A report of the Surgeon General.* Atlanta, GA: U.S. Department of Health and Human Services

that 35% of college students were overweight (Douglas et. al., 1997).

Most people will acknowledge the need for physical activity but few do anything about it. Physical activity does not require special equipment or a lot of money. Physical activity is anything you want it to be, when you are not sitting or lying down. Besides the well-known activities such as jogging, swimming, cycling, and aerobic dance, physical activity includes yoga, kickboxing, walking, gardening, martial arts training, and tai chi ch'uan. For example, walking strengthens muscles, expends energy, and increases aerobic capacity. When one has physical activity in his or her life, other healthy behaviors will follow (smoking cessation, stress reduction). There are many benefits of exercise; however, if these benefits do not convince you to become physically active, think of it as setting aside time for you.

There are many decisions to be made during a lifetime and these decisions are by no means easy. Making a choice to include physical activity in one's daily routine is a decision that will not show an immediate impact. The quality and quantity of the future depends on habits begun today. Aside from heredity, the two factors that most affect well-being are physical activity and diet. Lack of exercise and low levels of fitness are important disease risk factors. The effects of physical activity on disease and health are outlined in Table 1.1. It is not necessary to do volumes of exercise to produce significant improvement in health. As stated earlier in the chapter,

moderate exercise and fitness levels offer considerable health benefits. Activity does not need to be quantified, measured, or monitored. It simply needs to be performed, appreciated, and enjoyed. It is important that people strive to be physically active at least 30 minutes per day. The Surgeon General's Report defines physical activity as using 150 calories of energy per day (1,000 calories per week).

Effects of Physical Activity on Disease and Health

Are you living a physically active lifestyle? Are you enjoying the many benefits from an active lifestyle? Or is your physically inactive lifestyle increasing your chances of developing health risk factors? Physical fitness and being physically active are essential for a healthy lifestyle. The positive effects from being physically active have encouraged individuals to continue to stay active. Physical fitness affects the total person and how he or she reacts to obligations and stresses. A common misconception among college students is that daily activities, such as walking leisurely to class, are adequate exercise to improve fitness and health. Including an exercise program into your daily activities can make a lifelong health improvement.

Concern about appearance is often a reason for participating in physical fitness activities. Many students choose a physical activity for the possibility of changing the way others see them and the way they see themselves. The images of the thin "buff" bodies have contributed to the obsession of weight and the association weight has with appearance. Exercise can make an individual look, feel, and function better. Some college students exercise for self-improvement and to stay healthy. Increased leisure time and the desire to look and feel young have also contributed to the reasons why people exercise. The positive effects of remaining active throughout life have encouraged many adults to continue to participate in regular physical activities. The benefit that comes from a healthy lifestyle that includes proper exercise and diet is an obvious reason for becoming physically fit. A single bout of activity has psychological effects for many individuals. The time spent on healthy behaviors (physical activity) is less time spent in unhealthy behaviors. Physical activity:

★ Improves quality of life

★ Extends longevity; protects against CHD, stroke, hypertension, obesity, diabetes, osteoporosis, and depression

★ Helps maintain independence and full functioning among the elderly

Healthy People 2010

The health goals of the nation were outlined in the Healthy People 2010 Report (2000). The national health objectives are intended to be realistic goals to improve health of all Americans. Achieving "healthy people" in healthy communities is a paramount goal of Healthy People 2010. The general goals of Healthy People 2010 are these:

★ Increase quality and years of healthy life.

★ Eliminate health disparities among Americans.

★ Increase incidence of people reporting "healthy and active days."

★ Increase access to health information and services for all people.

★ Improve health, fitness, and quality of life through daily physical activity.

★ Increase leisure-time physical activity.

Physical activity and fitness are identified as two of the priority areas in which change in lifestyle would have a positive influence on health. Table 1.2 is a summary of the fitness and physical activity objectives.

What Is Physical Fitness?

What exactly is physical fitness and why is it important? Fitness is a broad term that means different things to different people? Physical fitness is very difficult to define but is widely used by many. To many students, fitness means "getting in shape" or "good physical condition." **Fitness** is a broad term used to denote physical, mental, social, and emotional well-being. **Physical fitness** refers to the optimal functioning of the various systems of the body so as to enable the individual to engage in activities of daily living and leisure without undue fatigue. If you are physically fit, you can perform your everyday activities and still have energy to pursue other physical demands such as recreational sports and leisure activities. Being fit allows you to have energy to meet the emergencies and crisis situations whenever they occur.

Being physically fit is important to our overall health and well-being and everyone is capable of even minimal fitness levels. Physical fitness is personal and focusing on our limitations and strengths is the key to functioning

Table 1.2   Selected Healthy People 2010 Physical Activity Objectives

★ Improve fitness and quality of life for all people through regular, daily physical activity
★ Increase leisure time physical activity
★ Increase the proportion of people who do moderate daily activity for 30 minutes
★ Increase the proportion of people who do vigorous physical activity at least three times per week
★ Increase the proportion of people who do regular muscular strength and endurance exercise
★ Increase the proportion of people who do regular flexibility exercise
★ Increase the prevalence of healthy weight
★ Reduce the prevalence of overweight

U.S. Department of Health and Human Services. (2000). *Healthy people 2010 objectives: National health promotion and disease.* Washington, DC: U.S. Department of Health and Human Services.

efficiently and effectively. The same degree of physical fitness is not essential for everyone as it varies with the individual, the demands, and requirements of the specific task. The elite athlete must constantly work to improve or maintain his or her fitness level whereas the nonathlete requires less effort to maintain his or her level of physical fitness. The level of fitness you need depends on the type of tasks you perform and your potential for physical effort. Physical fitness is not entirely dependent on exercise but includes desirable health practices such as not smoking, eating correctly, and changing lifestyles. Physical fitness affects the total person. The goals of an individual's exercise program can be derived from the goals of exercising to improve sport performance and exercise that improves or maintains health-related fitness. The overall goal of a health-related fitness program is to optimize a higher quality of life and prevention of major health problems (Howley & Franks, 2003). Overall, being physically fit allows a person to work more efficiently, be healthy, and resist hypokinetic diseases which are associated with the lack of physical activity. It is well-known that good physical fitness contributes to good health and wellness. Physical fitness has been shown to be associated with reduced risk of heart disease, high blood pressure, obesity, and diabetes.

Training for Competition versus Health-Related Fitness

What is the difference? When asked why they are training, college students gave broad responses: lose weight, gain weight, sports, get in shape, and fun. Most students understand the benefits of working out for health but many go beyond the ACSM's guidelines for general health. Many times students exercise too much and too hard when beginning an exercise program. Training for competition involves a plan that progressively increases physical characteristics necessary for high intensity competition (Swanson, 2005). For example, walking 30 minutes most days of the week is a great health benefit. Does walking every day meet your individual goal to be a better soccer player? The intensity of training is different for competitive players. You may be walking at 50% of your maximum heart rate for 30 minutes but for competition the physical stress is much higher,

perhaps up to 85–95% of your maximum heart rate. It is important to understand your goals (what is the purpose of your training?).

Health-Related Components of Fitness

The five components of health-related fitness are cardiorespiratory endurance, muscular endurance, muscular strength, flexibility, and body composition. You must develop/maintain an acceptable level of health-related fitness in order for your body to function at optimal capacity and efficiency. Each of the components has a direct relationship to good health and helps reduce the risk of hypokinetic disease (Corbin et al., 2006). It is important to have a moderate level of health-related fitness components.

Cardiorespiratory Endurance

Cardiorespiratory endurance is the ability of the body to perform prolonged physical activity that requires the heart and lungs to deliver oxygen and blood to the working muscles. Efficient functioning of the lungs and

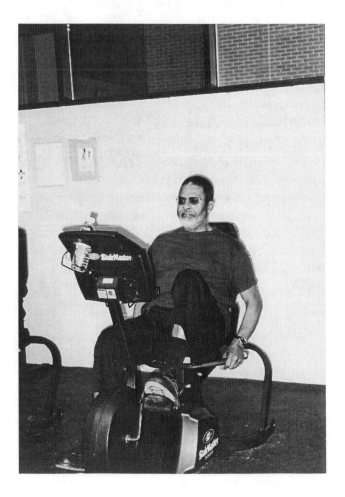

heart is required for optimal enjoyment of physical activity. The more efficient the heart and lungs, the easier it is to do aerobic activities (walking, swimming, running) for longer periods of time. A fit person can sustain physical activity for long periods of time. When the level of cardiorespiratory fitness is low, the lungs and heart have to work harder and the individual cannot sustain high intensity physical activity in an emergency. As cardiorespiratory fitness improves, the heart and lungs function more efficiently, and a more efficient heart and lungs are able to maintain effort for a longer period of time.

Cardiorespiratory endurance exercise involves the heart, the blood vessels, and the oxygen carrying capacity of the blood. Cardiorespiratory endurance is essential to overall good health and is often considered the most important health-related fitness component. Low levels of cardiorespiratory fitness are linked with heart disease. Cardiorespiratory endurance is assessed in a variety of ways, some of which are discussed in Chapter 3.

Muscular Endurance

Muscular endurance refers to the ability of a muscle or a group of muscles to continue exerting force during contraction for long periods without undue fatigue. Muscular endurance is closely related to muscular strength. Muscular endurance helps people meet the physical demands of everyday activities and is important in leisure and fitness. A fit person can continue movements for relatively long periods without undue fatigue. An example of muscular endurance is illustrated by lifting a light weight for multiple lifts or

repetitions. Most sports that are played by individuals require muscular strength in order to play longer matches, games, and so forth. Everyday activities require some level of muscular endurance, for example carrying books as you walk across campus. The techniques for developing muscular endurance and self-testing items are discussed in Chapter 4.

Muscular Strength

Muscular strength is the ability of a muscle or group of muscles to exert maximum force during one contraction through a full range of motion. Strong muscles are important in all kinds of work and physical activities. Strong muscles offer protection of body joints, help keep the skeleton in proper alignment, and provide greater endurance, power, and resistance to fatigue. In many cases, a primary cause of low back pain is the lack of abdominal strength. Weak abdominal muscles allow the pelvis to tip forward, causing an abnormal arch in the lower back resulting in low back pain. Muscular strength is important in body composition. The greater the lean body mass the higher rate of metabolism and faster energy use. Maintaining muscular strength is essential for healthy aging. Strength training helps maintain muscle mass and function as you grow older. As with endurance, muscular strength is present in most sports. Sports such as football, field events in track, wrestling, and basketball require a high level of strength. Those of us who are nonathletes require strength as well (e.g., moving furniture, lifting children, or picking up heavy book packs). The principles of

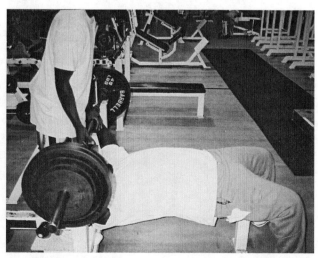

developing muscular strength and self-testing items are discussed in Chapter 4.

Flexibility

Flexibility is the ability to move a joint through its full range of motion. Flexibility is improved through stretching exercises and is not the same thing as stretching. Stretching is the primary mode used to improve flexibility. Stretching exercises can help ensure a normal range of motion for the joints. Inactivity (hypokinetic disease) can cause the tendons in the joints to shorten and stiffen, which can restrict the range of motion around the joints. Flexibility is important for maintaining good posture and for performance in most sports. Some athletes, gymnasts for instance, need a great deal of flexibility while the average person needs less to perform activities of daily living. As we grow older we become less flexible and need to perform exercises that improve the range of motion in the joints. Flexibility has also been shown to be useful in reducing back pain. Flexibility helps prevent injury, aids in motor tasks,

and is the most neglected of the five components. Remember that flexibility is one of the health-related components and alone it will not make a person physically fit (Edlin, Golanty, & McCormack-Brown, 2002). A fit person can move the joints through their full range of motion. Flexibility techniques are discussed further in Chapter 5.

Body Composition

Body composition refers to the ratio of fat tissue to lean muscle mass. Healthy body composition involves having more lean muscle mass (muscle, bone, and water) and an acceptable lower percentage of body fat. An excess of body fat is unhealthy and requires more energy for movement. A person with a high percentage of body fat is more likely to experience a variety of health problems. It is believed that obesity contributes to heart disease, high blood pressure, diabetes, and atherosclerosis. A balance between caloric intake and caloric output is necessary to maintain adequate body fat. Exercise and diet are effective in maintaining this balance. A fit person has a low but not too low percentage of body fat. Body composition is discussed in detail in Chapter 6.

Why Is Fitness Important for College Students?

Physical fitness needs for college students are similar to the fitness needs for other adults. Maintaining fitness is a process that continues

Table 1.3 Components of Health-Related Physical Fitness

Cardiorespiratory endurance—The ability of the body to perform prolonged physical activity that requires the ability of the heart and lungs to deliver oxygen and blood to the working muscles.

Muscular endurance—The ability of a muscle or a group of muscles to continue exerting force during contraction for long periods without undue fatigue.

Muscular strength—The ability of a muscle or group of muscles to exert maximum force during one contraction through a full range of motion.

Flexibility—Ability to move a joint through its full range of motion.

Body composition—The ratio of fat tissue to lean muscle mass.

from birth to death. The age period between 18 and 40 is the best time to develop physical fitness. The body is reaching its peak of maturity and physiological functioning. During these years it is vital to learn and develop one's fitness needs in order to make lifestyle behavior changes.

The time to lay the foundation of physical fitness for a lifetime is during the college years. Students have a great demand on their time and during the college years problems such as weight gain develop. Students become preoccupied with studies, dating, and extracurricular activities and as a result they forget about their fitness needs. The college years should be the time to develop lifelong fitness habits that will guarantee a healthy life.

★ Physical activity improves quality of life.

★ Physical activity extends longevity and protects against CHD, stroke, obesity, hypertension, and other health-risk disease.

★ Physical activity is related to improved health in the following ways:

  ★ A reduced oxygen demand at any level of physical activity

  ★ A reduced tendency for blood to clot

  ★ An increased elasticity in the arteries

★ Men and women of all ages benefit from a moderate amount of daily physical activity.

Where to Begin?

If you are leading a sedentary life, you should consider a physical fitness program. There are many reasons for poor fitness, such as being overweight, having a poor diet, or leading an unhealthy lifestyle. A fitness program could address the cause or causes. If the cause is diet, unhealthy lifestyle, or lack of physical activity consult a physical education instructor at your college for advice. You are never too old or too sedentary to begin a fitness program. The following are some basic ideas to follow when starting a program:

★ Get a physical checkup.

★ Decide why you want to become fit (motivation).

★ Determine your present level of fitness (assessment).

★ Develop goals and objectives.

★ Choose the appropriate fitness program (what you like to do).

★ Develop a plan.

★ Stick with your program (fun, success).

★ Dress properly.

★ Progress slowly.

The laboratory activities at the end of each chapter will help you evaluate/assess the various components of physical fitness. The chapters will provide information that will allow you to develop a lifelong physical fitness program.

In order to see fitness results you must put effort into the program. All of the fitness gimmicks, machines, saunas, or fad diets do not help you become fit. You cannot look for shortcuts to achieve fitness, as there are none. It takes at least 8 weeks of consistent exercising to achieve physical fitness. The following chapters in the text will provide you with knowledge and understanding about the health-related components of fitness. The chapters will provide an explanation of how to assess, develop, and maintain an adequate physical fitness level. You will learn, also, how to plan, develop, and implement your own individualized fitness program.

Most people participate in physical activity for the following reasons:

★ Feel better physically and psychologically

★ Feel enjoyment and personal accomplishment

Table 1.4 Elements of Moderate Amounts of Activity

Washing and waxing a car for 45-60 minutes
Washing windows or floors for 45-60 minutes
Playing volleyball for 45 minutes
Playing touch football for 30-45 minutes
Gardening for 30-45 minutes
Wheeling self in wheelchair for 30-40 minutes
Walking 1¾ miles in 35 minutes (20 min/mile)
Basketball (shooting baskets) for 30 minutes
Bicycling 5 miles in 30 minutes
Dancing fast (social) for 30 minutes
Pushing a stroller 1½ miles in 30 minutes
Raking leaves for 30 minutes
Walking 2 miles in 30 minutes (15 min/mile)
Water aerobics for 30 minutes
Swimming laps for 20 minutes
Wheelchair basketball for 20 minutes
Basketball (playing a game) for 15-20 minutes
Bicycling 4 miles in 15 minutes
Jumping rope for 15 minutes
Running 1½ miles in 15 minutes (10 min/mile)
Shoveling snow for 15 minutes
Stairwalking for 15 minutes

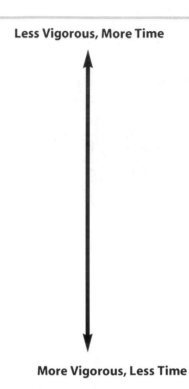

Less Vigorous, More Time

More Vigorous, Less Time

*A moderate amount of physical activity is roughly equivalent to physical activity that uses approximately 150 Calories (kcal) of energy per day, or 1,000 Calories per week.

† Some activities can be performed at various intensities; the suggested durations correspond to expected intensity of effort.

U.S. Department of Health and Human Services. (1996). *Physical Activity and Health: A Report of the Surgeon General.* Atlanta, GA: U.S. Department of Health and Human Services, Centers for Disease Control and Prevention, National Center for Chronic Disease Prevention and Health Promotion.

★ Shed pounds

★ Look good in clothes (appearance)

Make physical activity a regular part of your day. Choose activities that you enjoy and can do on a regular basis. Fitting activity into a daily routine can be easy. Keep it interesting and try something different on alternate days. It is important to be active most days of the week and make it a part of your daily routine.

How often do you exercise during the week? Do you think you get enough exercise to stay fit? Take a look at the Physical Activity Pyramid to find out if you're exercising enough to stay fit.

The Physical Activity Pyramid promotes physical activity based on a healthy dose of physical activity, 3–5 times a week. Each health-related component is placed on a level of the pyramid depending on the degree of physical activity involved: level 1 includes general activities; level 2 is cardiorespiratory activities; level 3 includes muscular fitness activities (strength, endurance, and flexibility); and level 4 is sedentary activities. The Pyramid follows the FITT guidelines.

The American College of Sports Medicine (ACSM) and the U.S. Centers for Disease Control and Prevention (CDC) recommend the following concerning physical activity:

★ Engage in 30 minutes or more of moderate-intensity physical activity each day of the week.

★ Incorporate more physical activity into your daily routine.

PHYSICAL ACTIVITY PYRAMID

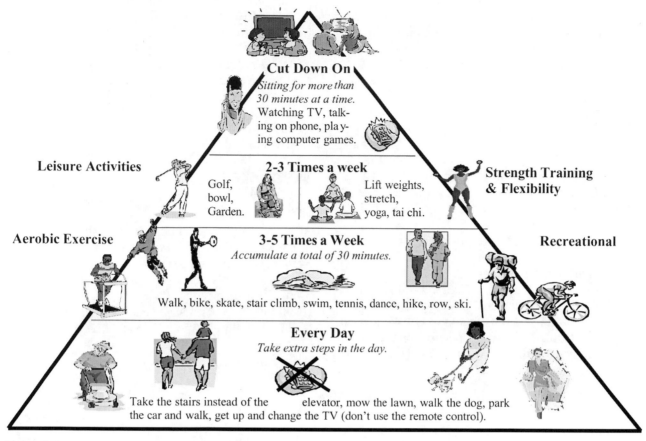

Cut Down On
Sitting for more than 30 minutes at a time. Watching TV, talking on phone, playing computer games.

Leisure Activities

2-3 Times a week
Golf, bowl, Garden.

Lift weights, stretch, yoga, tai chi.

Strength Training & Flexibility

Aerobic Exercise

3-5 Times a Week
Accumulate a total of 30 minutes.

Recreational

Walk, bike, skate, stair climb, swim, tennis, dance, hike, row, ski.

Every Day
Take extra steps in the day.

Take the stairs instead of the elevator, mow the lawn, walk the dog, park the car and walk, get up and change the TV (don't use the remote control).

Figure 1.1

★ Daily activities include walking stairs, dancing, mall walking while shopping, and parking in the farthest parking spot.

★ 30 minutes of physical activity may come from recreation, athletics, or planned exercise.

References

American College of Sports Medicine. (2006). *Resource manual for guidelines for exercise testing and prescription*, 6th ed. Hagerstown, MD: Lippincott, Williams & Wilkins.

Anspaugh, D. J., Hamrick, M. H., & Rosato, F. D. (2000). *Wellness: Concepts and applications*, 4th ed. Boston: McGraw-Hill.

Bishop, J. G. & Aldana, S. G. (1999). *Step up to wellness*. Boston: Allyn & Bacon.

Corbin, C. B., Welk, G. J., Corbin, W. R., & Welk, K. A. (2006). *Fundamental concepts of fitness and wellness*, 2nd ed. Boston: McGraw-Hill.

Douglas, K. A., Collins, J. L., Warren, C., Kann, L., Gold, R., Clayton, S., Ross, J. G., & Kolbe, L. J. (1997). Results from the 1995 national college health risk behavior survey. *Journal of American College Health, 46,* 55–66.

Edlin, G., Golanty, E. & McCormack-Brown, K. (2002). *Health & Wellness*. Boston: Jones & Bartlett Publishers.

Howley, E. T. & Franks, B. D. (2003). *Health fitness instructor's handbook.* Champaign, IL: Human Kinetics.

Jenkins, F. C. (2001). *Dynamics of fitness and health,* 8th ed. Dubuque, IA: Kendall/Hunt Publishing Company.

McArdle, W. D., Katch, F. L., & Katch, V. L. (1996). *Exercise physiology.* Baltimore: Williams & Wilkins.

PennState. (1995). Stretching, the truth. *Sportsmedicine newsletter, 4,* 4–5.

Politano, V., McCormick, M. R., & Jeffreys, A. (1995). *Lifetime physical fitness.* Dubuque, IA: Kendall/Hunt Publishing Company.

Seiger, L., Kanipe, D., Vanderpool, K., & Barnes, D. (1998). *Fitness and wellness strategies,* 2nd ed. Boston: WCB/McGraw-Hill.

Swanson, J. R. (2005). Promoting lifelong fitness and health within an athletic population. *Strength and Conditioning Journal, 27,* 50–55.

Thygerson, A. L. & Larson, K. L. (2006). *Fit to be well.* Sudbury, MA: Jones & Bartlett Publishing.

University of California at Berkeley. (1994). Stretching, the truth. *Newsletter of Nutrition, Report of the Surgeon General.* Atlanta, GA: U.S. Department of Health and Human Services.

U.S. Department of Health & Human Services. (1996). *Physical Activity and Health: A Report of the Surgeon General.* Atlanta, GA: U.S. Department of Health & Human Services.

U.S. Department of Health and Human Services. (2000). *Healthy people 2010 objectives: National health promotion and disease.* Washington, D.C.: U.S. Government Printing Office.

U.S. Department of Health and Human Services. (1996). *Healthy people 2000: Midcourse review and 1995 revisions.* Washington, D.C.: U.S. Government Printing Office.

Web Sites

ACSM's Fit Society Page *www.acsm.org/health+fitness/fit_society*

ACSM'S Health and Fitness Journal *www.acsm.org/publications/health_fitness_journal*

American Council on Exercise *www.acefitness.org*

CDC Physical Activity Information www.cdc.gov/nccdphp/physactiv

Healthy People 2010 *www.health.gov/healthypeople*

National Wellness Institute *www.nationalwellness.org*

Name: _____ Section: _____ Date: _____

Lab Activity 1.0
Importance of Physical Fitness

Purpose: To determine the importance of physical fitness to you and if it is important for you to engage in physical fitness activities.

Procedure: Check the appropriate rating for each item. Total your responses, multiply by 1 through 5 and add together.

	RATING				
FACTOR	**Extremely Important 5**	**Very Important 4**	**Important 3**	**Not So Important 2**	**Of Little Concern 1**
Lose weight	❑	❑	❑	❑	❑
Feel better	❑	❑	❑	❑	❑
Lessen the risk of heart attack	❑	❑	❑	❑	❑
Have a better self-image	❑	❑	❑	❑	❑
Be more successful in sports	❑	❑	❑	❑	❑
Have more strength	❑	❑	❑	❑	❑
Relieve stress	❑	❑	❑	❑	❑
Increase efficiency for study, work, and other responsibilities	❑	❑	❑	❑	❑
Help my sleep pattern	❑	❑	❑	❑	❑
Reduce tension	❑	❑	❑	❑	❑
Increase energy	❑	❑	❑	❑	❑
Have a better-looking figure	❑	❑	❑	❑	❑
Contribute to my health	❑	❑	❑	❑	❑
Have greater resistance to illness and disease	❑	❑	❑	❑	❑
Improve cardiorespiratory function	❑	❑	❑	❑	❑
Increase flexibility	❑	❑	❑	❑	❑
Improve my posture and appearance	❑	❑	❑	❑	❑
Improve my outlook on life	❑	❑	❑	❑	❑
Increase my social outlets	❑	❑	❑	❑	❑
Outlet for frustration/anger	❑	❑	❑	❑	❑
Total	_____	_____	_____	_____	_____

Source: Prentice, W. E. (1999). *Fitness and Wellness for Life,* 6th ed. Dubuque, IA: WCB/McGraw-Hill. Page 31.

After considering each item, analyze your basic motivation for becoming involved in some fitness activity.

"Extremely important"	____	×	5	=	
	Total		Factor		____
"Very important"	____	×	4	=	
	Total		Factor		____
"Important"	____	×	3	=	
	Total		Factor		____
"Not so important"	____	×	2	=	
	Total		Factor		____
"Of little concern"	____	×	1	=	
	Total		Factor		____
			Sum Total	____	

Interpretation

Total Score

85-100   Physical fitness has extreme importance to you.

70-84   You believe being physically fit is very important.

50-69   Physical fitness is important but not a very high priority.

35-49   You do not believe physical fitness has as much importance in your life as it does for others.

20-34   You are not concerned about being physically fit.

Based on this assessment, to what extent do you believe physical fitness is important?

Name: _____ Section: _____ Date: _____

Lab Activity 1.1
Attitude and Behavior Scale

Purpose: To assess attitude and behavior toward physical fitness.

Attitude Scale
Procedure:
- Read each statement carefully

- Select the response that best describes the way you **FEEL** about the statement

- Place an X over the appropriate circle using the choices stated below:

> A = Strongly agree
> B = Agree
> C = Undecided
> D = Disagree
> E = Strongly disagree

Statement	A	B	C	D	E
1. Exercise can help me control my weight.	O	O	O	O	O
2. Regular exercise can help me stay healthy.	O	O	O	O	O
3. I feel better about myself when I exercise.	O	O	O	O	O
4. Exercise can help me live longer.	O	O	O	O	O
5. I have more energy when I exercise on a regular basis.	O	O	O	O	O
6. I seldom think about my eating habits.	O	O	O	O	O
7. The information on a nutrition label is important.	O	O	O	O	O
8. As long as my weight remains constant, I do *Not* need to worry about my diet.	O	O	O	O	O
9. It is important to keep up with the latest nutrition information.	O	O	O	O	O
10. I do *Not* need to be concerned about my diet if I supplement it with vitamins.	O	O	O	O	O
11. When under pressure one should try to remain calm.	O	O	O	O	O
12. A person should make time to relax every day.	O	O	O	O	O
13. Exercise can help me reduce my stress level.	O	O	O	O	O
14. Relaxation exercises are a waste of time.	O	O	O	O	O

Attitude Scoring

Numerical values of 1 through 5 will be assigned to the responses. For items 1-5, 7, 9, and 11-13, a *strongly agree* response is worth 5 points and a *strongly disagree* response is worth 1 point. The remaining four attitude items should be reverse scored from those stated previously. Each response to the 14 attitude items should be summed. The higher the total score, the more positive an individual's attitude. The maximum score possible is 70 points.

Behavior

Procedure: Read each statement carefully. Select the response that best describes your behavior relative to the statement. Fill in the corresponding circle on your answer sheet, using the choices stated below:

A = Always
B = Most of the time
C = Some of the time
D = Not very often
E = Never

Statement	A	B	C	D	E
1. I exercise aerobically for at least 20 minutes, three times per week.	○	○	○	○	○
2. I do some form of stretching exercises at least three times per week.	○	○	○	○	○
3. I engage in some sort of physical activity every weekend.	○	○	○	○	○
4. I engage in some sort of physical activity every day.	○	○	○	○	○
5. I engage in exercises to enhance my muscular strength and/ or muscular endurance (for example, weight lifting or calisthenics) at least two times per week.	○	○	○	○	○
6. I choose foods based on how they may affect my future health.	○	○	○	○	○
7. I choose foods based on how they taste.	○	○	○	○	○
8. I minimize my intake of fats.	○	○	○	○	○
9. I read the nutritional labels of the foods I eat.	○	○	○	○	○
10. I eat fast foods.	○	○	○	○	○
11. I eat vegetables.	○	○	○	○	○
12. I eat fruit.	○	○	○	○	○
13. I make time to relax daily.	○	○	○	○	○
14. I skip meals in order to complete my work and other responsibilities.	○	○	○	○	○
15. Whenever possible I try to do two things at once, such as eating and driving.	○	○	○	○	○
16. I cram for exams.	○	○	○	○	○
17. I procrastinate.	○	○	○	○	○

Attitude Scoring

Numerical values of 1 to 5 are assigned to the responses of the 17 Behavior Scale items. Responses to Items 1-6, 8, 9 and 12-13 should be scored as follows: *Always* equals 5 points and *Never* equals 1 point. The remaining 6 behavior items should be reverse scored (never *equals* 5 and *always* equals 1) opposite from those mentioned. The responses are to be summed to obtain a total score. Higher scores indicate that the individual engages in more positive and healthy behaviors. The maximum score for this scale is 85 points.

1. What is your Attitude score? How can you improve the score?

2. What is your Behavior score? How can you change your behavior?

Name: _____ Section: _____ Date: _____

Lab Activity 1.2
Time Management Awareness Check

Directions: Place an "X" in the appropriate box and check your responses with the answer key.

	Yes	No
1. Do you make a calendar and plan your coursework for the entire semester?	☐	☐
2. Do you follow a weekly time schedule?	☐	☐
3. Do you use a daily calendar or notebook to keep you aware of high priority items to do now?	☐	☐
4. When you take a course, do you know the criteria for assigning grades?	☐	☐
5. Are there times when you have difficulty starting to study?	☐	☐
6. Is it sometimes necessary for you to cram for a test?	☐	☐
7. Do you have trouble getting to class on time?	☐	☐
8. Do you have difficulty concentrating on an assignment?	☐	☐
9. Is it sometimes hard for you to finish term papers, reports, and projects on time?	☐	☐
10. Are you easily distracted when studying?	☐	☐
11. Do you become bored with the subject when studying?	☐	☐
12. Do you reward yourself when you have studied effectively?	☐	☐
13. Do you schedule large blocks of time for study?	☐	☐
14. Do you have a comfortable place where you study regularly?	☐	☐
15. Do you put off starting on a big assignment because you think it is too hard?	☐	☐
16. Do you use short periods of free time for studying effectively?	☐	☐
17. Do you plan time for rest periods when studying?	☐	☐
18. Do you plan time for recreation and relaxation?	☐	☐
19. Do you panic or become anxious in test situations?	☐	☐
20. Do you study your hardest subjects when you are more alert?	☐	☐
21. When you have a high priority assignment, do you work at smaller, routine jobs instead of the important one?	☐	☐

From *Keys to Excellence, Fourth Edition* by Cooper et al. Copyright © 1997 by Kendall/Hunt Publishing. Reprinted by permission.

Model Answer Key

1. Yes	8. No	15. No
2. Yes	9. No	16. Yes
3. Yes	10. No	17. Yes
4. Yes	11. No	18. Yes
5. No	12. Yes	19. No
6. No	13. Yes	20. Yes
7. No	14. Yes	21. No

Author Unknown

Few people achieve all these ideal answers. Examine your "wrong" responses to see if you can find a better system than you have at present.

Name: _____   Section: _____   Date: _____

Lab Activity 1.3
Monitor Summary

(Indicate Hours Spent in Each Area)

Activity	Monday	Tuesday	Wednesday	Thursday	Friday	Saturday	Sunday	Total
Classes								
Work								
Studying								
Travel								
Recreation								
Exercise								
Eating								
Family								
Personal								
Sleep								
Other (explain)								
	24	24	24	24	24	24	24	168

From *Keys to Excellence, Fourth Edition* by Cooper et al. Copyright © 1997 by Kendall/Hunt Publishing. Reprinted by permission.

Getting Ready for Physical Activity

Objectives

After completing this chapter, you will be able to do the following:

★ Discuss the basic principles of exercise.

★ Identify the basic elements of an exercise program.

★ Discuss the benefits of a warm-up session.

★ Identify the steps in designing an exercise program.

There are many different physical fitness programs and you can incorporate one of these exercise programs into your life and enjoy the benefits of being physically fit. It is a personal responsibility to be fit and healthy. In order to lead a healthy and fit lifestyle, you must be committed and motivated to make the effort. This is your job as no one else can do it for you. If you make the effort, you will see and feel the results.

This chapter provides an overview of physical fitness and sets forth the basic principles of training for those who wish to become physically fit. The principles defined in this chapter will be followed and developed in subsequent chapters. The chapter explains the essential elements of a well-rounded exercise program, each of which will be developed with each health-related component of physical fitness (Chapters 3–7). There is a correct amount of physical activity for promoting health benefits and developing physical fitness. There are several principles of physical activity that help determine the correct amount of physical activity.

Goal-Setting

Manage your time. Plan your life. *In case you have not caught on yet, you are talking about managing yourself. You are talking about getting rid of habits that tend to interfere with what you need to do.* You need to set goals and priorities around your commitment to obtain a college education and a profession. Managing your time will help you successfully achieve these commitments. If you are having problems on the job, evaluate the situation, set goals and give yourself a specified period of time to complete them.

Time management calls for planning. You cannot plan without making decisions about what you want to do and where you want to go. *Effective time management requires you to be a decision-maker.* When you make the decisions about what you want and where you want to go, you have established GOALS. *Goals are important because they allow you to put your values into action. Goals are no more than your aims in life and they give you purpose and direction in which to focus your energies.*

To develop a goal is the first step in time management. *The next step is to write your goal down in explicit and concrete terms. Until it is written, it is just an idea. A goal should have the following characteristics:*

REACHABLE—Set it up in small increments so you don't bite off more than you can chew at one time. If you do, you will only become frustrated. Set only moderate goals you know you can reach.

REALISTIC—*Know your limitations and capabilities. Don't ask more of yourself than you know you are capable of doing.* Set a realistic time-frame to achieve it.

MEASURABLE—*State your goal in such a way that you as well as others will know when it has been achieved.* Be very specific and concrete about what you want to do.

For each goal, always write out a step-by-step plan as to what you are going to do to achieve it. Be concrete and specific. Each goal should always have a time-frame. Some people would put-off and put-off and never carry out the plan.

Goals are described as short-term and long-term. Long-term goals usually take a while to

---

Long-Term Goal

I want to get my associate in arts degree in business in _____ (year).

Short-Term Goal

I want to pass English and Social Environment with a grade of "C" or above this semester.

Daily To-Do List

August 31, _____ (year).

Rank

Ordering

4 Visit with Mark and Gary

___ See "Star Trek" movie

3 Practice essay writing

___ Watch television

1 Go to work 8:00 a.m. to 12:00 noon

2 Study chapters 1 and 2 of Social Environment

---

accomplish while short-term goals help you achieve the long-term goal. They are activities you carry out on a daily, weekly, or monthly schedule.

Now that you have your goal, you must develop a "TO-DO LIST" which may be daily, weekly, or monthly. Then PRIORITIZE. As a student, you should develop a "daily to-do list." Look at an example of how goals and priorities can be utilized.

According to the example above, the number one priority on August 31, ____ is to go to work. The second priority is to study, and the third is to practice essay writing. This is good prioritizing since this student's short-term goal is to pass English and social environment.

Remember, you must set your goals and then begin to organize your time by using "to-do" lists which you prioritize. Most students tend to function better if they divide their goal-setting into three levels:

DAILY—WEEKLY—SEMESTER

Goal-setting should be established at the beginning of each term. This includes analysis of information on course selection, what grades you want to receive in each course, how you plan to go about it, and the evaluation of your first class sessions. Put all of this information together before setting time schedules. Remember, a goal is no good unless it is explicit and concrete. For example, to say you want to do well would be too general and vague. "I plan to make an 'A' in Psychology" is better.

Planning Your Time?

If you have not purchased your academic calendar planner for the year, you should rush right out and do it now. It should be large enough so you can write in your assignments. The ideal one would also have space for your daily "to-do" list. However, do not worry about that space since all you have to do is buy a pack of 3" × 5" cards and on a nightly basis before going to bed, write out all the tasks you are planning for the next day. Don't forget to prioritize. Before writing in your planner, use these tips when planning your time.

Tip 1

Balance your time.
Balance your work, travel, sleep, domestic chores, class, study, personal, and recreational times. All work and no play truly do make Jack a dull boy. You will no doubt become frustrated if you spend too much time in some areas and your goals are not being met in other areas.

Tip 2

Plan for the semester.
Plan your school work for an entire semester based on the school's calendar. This refers to due dates for papers, hours for study time, dates for major exams, etc.

Tip 3

Set goals for each study session.
Always set a goal for each study session and be definite in your schedule about what you plan to study. Be definite about what you plan to do in each session.

Tip 4

Know how long your study session should be.
Study in short sessions. The idea is to avoid marathon sessions where you remember little of what you tried to learn. Plan to take at least a ten-minute break during every hour. During the break, try exercising or doing something else that will refresh your mind/body. This will help you maintain your concentration.

Tip 5

Study in the right place.
Select a quiet and not-too-comfortable place to study. It should allow you to concentrate on the task at hand. Make sure it has proper lighting, ventilation, and a comfortable temperature.

Tip 6

Let others in on your plans.
Let your friends and significant others know your study schedule so they will not disturb you. You are the person who must control someone else's use of your time. If you have children, plan activities for them while you study.

Tip 7

Plan to see your professor.
Make sure you understand your notes and/or assignment before trying to study. If you are not clear on what you have to study, make an appointment to visit your professor for clarification. Don't flounder. Record your appointment to see the professor if it is necessary in your appointment book.

Tip 8

Know how much time you should study for each class.
Plan two hours of study for every hour you are in class.

Tip 9

Prioritize subjects to study.
Study the subject you like least first since it will no doubt require more of your time and energy. Once you have completed this task, reward yourself by doing something you like.

Tip 10

Know when to review notes.
Review, study, and/or rewrite your lecture notes within 24 hours to help with memory and effective note taking. Forty-eight hours should be the maximum amount of time you allow to lapse before reviewing.

Tip 11

Know purpose of studying.
Study to pass tests. When reading and/or reviewing notes, always practice asking and

answering questions. Study as though at the end of your study session, you will be required to pass a test.

Tip 12

Know how to begin reading text material.
Survey required chapters (material) before you begin to read.

Tip 13

Develop questions you should ask as you study.
Ask questions about what you must learn during the study period. Turn all headings into questions and then answer them.

Tip 14

Always read with a purpose.
Read the assigned chapters and/or material. Look for answers to questions posed in order to complete the assignment. Read with the purpose of finding the answers.

Tip 15

Memorize.
Go over the content which you want to remember. If necessary, orally recite and make notes to help you remember.

Tip 16

Review.
Review the material and ask questions.

Tip 17

Decide when you should study.
Determine your best time of day and schedule your study time then. In addition, a brief review before class and immediately after class is strongly suggested.

Tip 18

Use your time productively.
Don't waste time. If you are waiting, use that time for review. If you have recorded your notes and you are driving, listen to the tape. If you are riding with someone else, read your notes.

Basic Principles of Training

The body is adaptable to the stress placed upon it. The greater the demands, the more it adjusts to meet the demands. As the breathing

and heart rate increase during exercise the heart will pump more blood to the working muscles with each beat. Once an individual is physically trained to exercise, the heart does not have to beat as often to meet the body's demand for oxygen and blood. Regardless of the type of exercise program you participate in, there are certain principles that you should incorporate into your program. In order to have an effective program, you should incorporate these training principles into your program. The general principles of physical fitness are the same for everyone. The principles discussed in this chapter will help develop an effective yet safe physical fitness program.

Fun and Enjoyment

One of the most critical factors of any successful physical fitness program is that the individual must enjoy the activity and want to stick with the program. The activity chosen must be one that you will stick with over a lifetime and will meet your needs. A successful program will be considered fun rather than work. If you like swimming and have fun at it, you are more likely to continue it. Enjoying your exercise is one of the most important strategies you can employ.

Overload

The basis for improved fitness is the concept of **overloading** muscle groups and body systems beyond their accustomed levels. Overload is the most basic principle and is necessary to achieve fitness benefits of physical activity. For the muscles to become stronger, they must be

overloaded or taken beyond their normal limit. In order to improve your fitness level you must work your system harder than it is accustomed to working. The muscle or system must experience additional stress over a period of time so that it will improve to a point at which it can accommodate additional work.

The **SAID** principle (Specific Adaptation to Imposed Demands) (Prentice, 1997) states that when the body is subjected to higher workloads, the body will adapt and overcome the demands of the higher workload. Too much overload or stress can produce damage or injury. Gradual overloading is essential to becoming physically fit. **Overload** is a gradual increase in frequency, intensity, time, and type **(FITT)** of exercise. Overload is one of the most critical factors in any activity program.

If you are swimming to improve cardiorespiratory endurance, and you swim a mile in 30 minutes, the cardiorespiratory system will be able to accommodate this distance and intensity. After a few weeks, you will need to swim

farther or reduce the time for the mile in order to force the cardiorespiratory system to work more efficiently and harder.

In order for physical activity to be effective it must include frequency, intensity, time (duration), and type (FITT).

★ **Frequency:** (How Often) If exercise is to be effective it must be performed on a regular basis. The American College of Sportsmedicine (ACSM 2000) recommends that a person exercise 3–5 times a week.

★ **Intensity:** (How Hard) The person must exercise more vigorously than normal (overload). To develop cardiorespiratory endurance, you must raise your heart rate above normal; muscular strength development requires lifting heavier weights; flexibility involves stretching the muscles beyond normal. Moderate activity is enough to produce cardiorespiratory fitness.

★ **Time:** (How Long) Exercise sessions should last long enough for any benefit to occur. A

duration of 20–30 minutes is recommended by the American College of Sports Medicine.

★ **Type:** (What Kind) The exercise session should include aerobic activities, flexibility, and muscular strength and endurance exercises. The type of exercise you perform is as important as different components of fitness and promotes different wellness benefits.

The FITT formula includes the threshold of training and the target heart zone. The **threshold of training** is the minimum amount of activity necessary to produce training benefits. This is the beginning of activity and intensity that will produce a training effect for you. The **target zone** is the area in which you should exercise to get the optimal benefits of training. The target zone starts at the threshold of training and goes to the point where physical activity becomes counterproductive. The target zone keeps you progressing but you should not go beyond the target zone as it could become counterproductive.

Progression

In order to produce the training effect of the body, you must start gradually and increase a little each day to continuously overload the body. You add a little each day in terms of repetitions, time, distance, or load and the body will adapt to the demands of the exercise. The rate of progression should be within the body's ability to adapt.

Progression and overload are closely related. When the amount of exercise (load) is increased, fitness continues to improve. Progression should occur when the muscles have adapted to an increased overload. Interest level in the activity will remain high as long as you continue to see improvement in your physical fitness. Progressing too slowly will result in limited physical fitness. Even minimal increases are important in maintaining interest and motivation.

Once you have reached a certain level of fitness, it becomes more important to maintain your fitness level. At this point it is important to be consistent.

Consistency

"I don't have time to exercise" is often the excuse most often given for not following an exercise program. One of the most difficult problems when beginning an exercise program is finding time to exercise. Most individuals have a busy schedule; however, it is important to schedule a specific time of day for exercising and to stick with the schedule. The individual needs to look at his or her daily schedule and work an exercise program into the day.

When is the best time of the day to exercise? The answer to this question depends on the person exercising. The best time of the day is whenever you have time and have the motivation to exercise. The important thing is to set a time and make exercising a part of your daily routine. Some people like to exercise early in the morning, some during lunch or early afternoon, and still others work out in the evening. The least desirable times would be after a meal, when you are full and uncomfortable, or before bedtime, when the activity may keep you awake. It is recommended by ACSM that you engage in at least 20–30 minutes of activity per day and 3 days per week.

Reversibility

The benefits of an exercise program will stay with you as long as you continue to exercise. The principle of reversibility is overload in reverse. Long intervals between sessions of exercise can result in a loss of fitness benefits. This sums up the old adage "If you don't use it you will lose it." Physiological changes begin to reverse if a person is inactive for 48 hours or longer. Fifty percent of fitness improvements are lost within 2 months if you stop exercising. It is important to remain active and maintain the exercise frequency, intensity, and time (duration) and continue with specific exercises. If you do not continue to exercise, the benefit obtained will be lost.

Specificity

The principle of **specificity** states that exercise must be specific for those muscles involved in the activity. If your program is cardiorespiratory, the gain will be primarily in this area; strength oriented programs will produce strength gains. If you wish to improve the cardiorespiratory system, you must choose activities such as jogging, brisk walking, swimming, and other aerobic activities that are specific to that system. You cannot expect your arms to become trained after an aerobic program.

Individuality

When planning your exercise program it is important to meet your training needs. The program should meet the needs, goals, motivation, and state of physical fitness of the individual. The exercise must be adapted to the individual's needs, interests, and abilities.

Recuperation

The principle of **recuperation** requires adequate rest periods between bouts of training. The body has time to adapt to the exercise stress during the recovery periods by either increasing endurance or becoming stronger (Powers & Dodd, 2003). It is essential that the body get this period of rest in order to receive maximal benefit from exercise. How do we know how much rest is required? For most individuals, 24 to 48 hours is adequate. If one does not get enough rest overtraining may occur. Overtraining is a fatigue syndrome and this may lead to chronic fatigue and injuries (Powers & Dodd, 2003).

The Physical Activity Pyramid will help you select the different types of activities you can use to develop health, wellness, and physical fitness. The activity pyramid provides clear and consistent recommendations for physical activity.

There are four levels to the pyramid and these include lifetime physical activity, aerobic activity and active sports and recreation, flexibility and muscular strength and endurance, and rest or inactivity. Each of the four levels are important as the individual can choose the level at which he or she wants to start to participate. Each of the four levels are based on the health benefits that are associated with regular physical activity. Lifestyle *(level one)* activities can help the individual with modest fitness gains, and if the person is sedentary, lifestyle activities are encouraged. Everyday activities such as walking, working in the yard, or climbing the stairs are considered lifestyle activities. The Surgeon General's Report on Physical Activity and Health (1996) suggests 30 minutes of physical activity (a brisk walk) on most, if not all, days of the week (See Figure 2.1, level 1.) Lifestyle activity can be viewed as the minimal physical activity that should be performed. Even the lifestyle activities can yield healthy benefits. *Level 2* includes aerobic and active sports. These activities have a higher intensity than lifestyle activities and can be performed for long periods of time with elevated heart rates. The benefits from activities at this level can be accomplished in 3 days a week and are basically good for cardiorespiratory fitness and controlling body fat. Active sports and active recreation include basketball, tennis, hiking, and rock climbing. Even though these activities have short and intense bursts of activity followed by intermittent rest, they can provide benefits similar to aerobic activities. It is likely that if you are active at this level, you will be fit enough to continue moderate activities as you grow older. *Level three* includes exercises for flexibility and muscular strength and endurance. These activities are necessary for total fitness and they are included in the lower level activities

PHYSICAL ACTIVITY PYRAMID

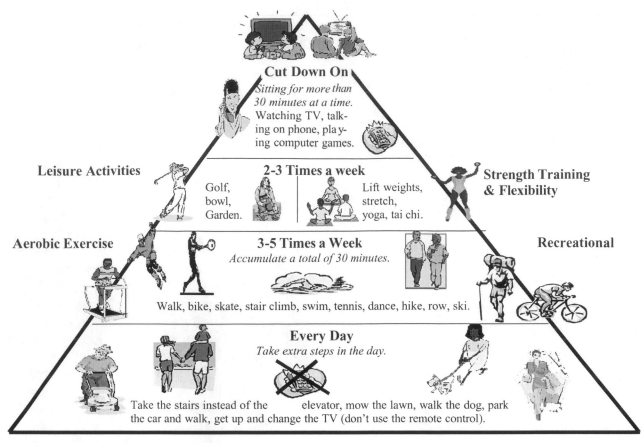

Figure 2.1 Physical Activity Pyramid

because activities in the lower levels of the pyramid do not contribute to flexibility development. Activities in this level are designed to increase the range of motion and to develop strength and muscular endurance. *The final level* is rest or inactivity. It is important to have time for rest or a period of inactivity after an exercise bout; however, long periods of inactivity are discouraged. The body needs to recuperate after a vigorous bout of aerobic activities or weight training. Eight hours of uninterrupted sleep are necessary to allow for recuperation. Sedentary living (hypokinetic) disease results in low fitness. However, too many adults are at this level and it results in poor fitness and health. This level of activities should be done sparingly compared with other types of activity in the pyramid.

The American College of Sports Medicine (2006) states that physical activity cannot be rigid and recommendations presented in the activity pyramid should be used in accordance to the goal of the individual. No single type of activity will improve all five components of the health-related components. Therefore, one should cross train which means performing activities from all levels of the pyramid.

Basic Elements of an Exercise Session

The basic elements of any physical fitness session are mode of exercise, warm-up, actual workout, and cool-down.

Mode of Exercise

When designing an exercise prescription, it must include a mode of exercise—a specific type of exercise to be performed. If one expects to improve cardiorespiratory fitness, one must select from a wide variety of aerobic activities such as swimming, jogging, walking, bicycling, water aerobics, or aerobic dance. Flexibility can be improved by doing stretching exercises. The factors to consider when choosing a type of exercise are fun, availability, cost, and risk of injury.

Warm-Up

The warm-up exercises should take place before the actual workout. The warm-up phase prepares the body for the workout by increasing the body temperature, prepares the muscles for the workout, and increases flexibility. Warm-ups are important in preventing injury and muscle soreness. They can do this by elevating the body's core temperature and increasing the heart rate. The warm-up tells the body that you are getting ready to exercise and prepares the body physiologically for the upcoming physical work.

The benefits of a warm-up include:

★ Gradual increase of body temperature
★ Gradual increase in heart rate
★ Gradual increase in blood pressure
★ Increase in muscle temperature
★ Increase in blood flow to the muscles
★ Increase in circulatory and respiratory function
★ Prevents injuries and soreness
★ Improves performance

The warm-up should be gradual as vigorous stretching of cold muscles can result in muscle injury.

The type of warm-up recommended is to move the body slowly for 3–5 minutes by light jogging, brisk walking, or stationary cycling to warm the muscles before stretching. The warm-up period should last 8–10 minutes. A good warm-up should begin with 2–5 minutes of light jogging, then 3–5 minutes of stretching followed by the actual workout. The warm-up should prepare you physically and mentally for your vigorous workout. An adequate warm-up for most people is to a point of very light perspiration. The cardiorespiratory warm-up prepares the heart and circulatory system for physical activity. A warm-up allows the blood to flow to the heart and muscles. It is suggested that 2–5 minutes of walking or light jogging be used as warm-up activities. The skeletal muscles need to be warmed up as well. This part of

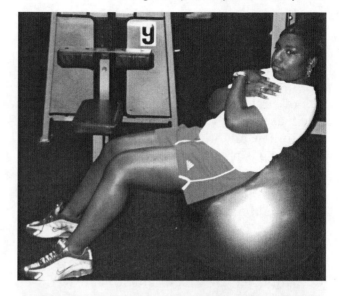

Figure 2.2 Sample warm-up and cool-down exercises.

the warm-up phase also includes stretching exercises. There are two views on stretching as part of the warm-up workout. Some experts suggest that stretching makes the muscle more elastic, which helps to prevent injury and enhance performance. Recent evidence places doubt on the benefit of stretching to prevent injury. Some suggest that stretching prior to weight lifting activities may cause poorer performance. There is a lack of research supporting the performance or injury-preventing benefits of stretching during warm-ups. In activities such as diving and gymnastics, where static flexibility beyond normal range is needed, stretching is recommended.

Workout Bout

This is the conditioning phase of the exercise program. The actual workout is the basic component of a daily workout. All fitness experts agree that a warm-up should precede the workout, followed by a cool-down. The warm-up prepares the body for activity and the cool-down allows the body to return to rest. The cool-down allows the blood to return from the working muscles and keeps the blood from pooling in the extremities. The chosen mode of exercise should be a vigorous, continuous workout for 20 minutes or more. The **FITT** principle makes up the workout phase—frequency, intensity, and time (duration). Each workout should have these components regardless of the type (mode) of exercise. More information will be said about **FITT** in later chapters. A workout might consist of the following:

1. 5–10 minutes of warm-up
2. 8 minutes of stretching
3. 20–45 minutes of conditioning exercises
4. 5 minutes of cool-down

Cool-Down

The cool-down is an essential but often neglected aspect of the workout and is done immediately after exercise. The purpose of the cool-down is to let the body return to its normal physiological functioning. This part of the training helps the blood to circulate and prevents pooling of the blood in the extremities. The cool-down has a stretching and cardiorespiratory component. As in the warm-up phase, static muscle stretching is important, and some believe it more important to stretch the muscles after a vigorous workout than before a workout. Stretching during this period may be effective for lengthening the muscles. The cardiorespiratory portion of the cool-down is as important as the stretching portion. The best

way to prevent blood pooling is to taper off or slow down gradually. The cool-down should include 2–5 minutes of walking or other non-vigorous activity that uses the muscles used in the workout. For example, after completing a run, you should continue to walk or do a light jog. Stretching should be done during the cool-down phase.

Designing Your Own Program

You have been given the basic principles and elements for beginning a physical fitness program. The key to any program is designing one that you will enjoy and will meet your needs. If you are sedentary or over 35 you should have a medical examination before beginning an exercise program. The steps to use when designing your own program are discussed next. You will be given more detail in designing your program in Chapter 9.

Assessment

The first step in designing a program is to assess your current level of fitness for each of the health-related fitness components. The results will help you plan your specific goals and know what component needs the most work. Assessment tests in Chapters 3, 4, 5, and 6 will help you determine your fitness level.

Setting Goals

Select realistic goals that result in a lifetime of wellness. Think carefully about your goals and your reasons for exercising. Whatever the goals, they should be important enough to keep you motivated. You should be exercising for you and not for others. When setting goals the SMART guideline should be followed. All fitness goals should be Specific, Measurable, Attainable, Realistic, and Timely.

Choosing Activities

Fitness training is easier if you enjoy the activities. You should include activities from each of the health-related fitness components when selecting the activities for your program. Cardiorespiratory endurance is developed by activities that involve continuous movement of large muscle groups such as walking, jogging, cycling, and aerobic dance. Muscular strength and endurance can be developed through weight training and calisthenics. Stretching the major muscle groups with proper technique develops flexibility. Body fat can be reduced through a sensible diet and exercise. No single type of exercise will improve all five of the health-related components. Therefore, one should cross train, which means combining two or more different fitness activities.

References

American College of Sports Medicine. (1998). The recommended quantity and quality of exercise for developing and maintaining cardiorespiratory and muscular fitness and flexibility in healthy adults. *Medicine and Science in Sports & Exercise, 30,* 975–990.

American College of Sports Medicine. (2000). *Guidelines for exercise testing and prescription.* Philadelphia: Lea & Febiger.

American College of Sports Medicine. (2000). *Resource manual for guidelines for exercise testing and prescription,* 4th ed. Hagerstown, MD: Lippincott, Williams & Wilkins.

American College of Sports Medicine. (2006). *Resource manual for guidelines for exercise testing and prescription.* 6th ed. Hagerstown, MD: Lippincott, Williams & Wilkins.

Axen, K. & Vermitsky-Axen, K. (2001). *Illustrated principles of exercise physiology.* Upper Saddle, NJ: Prentice Hall.

Corbin, C. B., Welk, G. J., Corbin, W. R., & Welk, K. A. (2006). *Concepts of fitness and wellness,* 6th ed. Boston: McGraw-Hill.

Fahey, T. D., Insel, P. M., & Roth, W. T. (1997). *Fit and well.* Mountain View, CA: Mayfield Publishers Company.

Hoeger, W. W. K. & Hoeger, S. A. (2006). *Principles and labs for physical fitness,* 5th ed. United States: Thompson–Wadsworth.

Howley, E. T. & Franks, B. (2003). *Health fitness instructor's handbook.* Champaign, IL: Human Kinetics.

Jenkins, F. C. (2001). *Dynamics of fitness and health.* Dubuque, IA: Kendall/Hunt Publishing Company.

McArdle, W. D., Katch, F. L., & Katch, V. L. (1996). *Exercise physiology.* Baltimore: Williams & Wilkins.

Politano, V., McCormick, M. R., & Jeffreys, A. (1996). *Lifetime physical fitness.* Dubuque, IA: Kendall/Hunt Publishing Company.

Powers, S. K. & Dodd, S. L. (2003). *Total fitness and wellness: Brief edition.* Boston: Benjamin Cummins.

Prentice, W. (1997). *Fitness for College and Life.* St. Louis, MO: Mosby-Year Book.

U.S. Department of Health & Human Services (1996). *Physical activity and health: A report of the Surgeon General.* Atlanta, GA: U.S. Dept. of Health & Human Services.

Web Sites

ACSM's Fit Society Page *www.acsm.org/health+ fitness/fit_society*

ACSM's Health and Fitness Journal *www.acsm.org/ publications/health_fitness_journal*

American Council on Exercise *www.acefitness.org*

MedlinePlus: Exercise & Physical Fitness *www.nlm .nih.gov/medlineplus/exercisephysicalfitness*

Lab Activity 2.0
Making a Commitment

Purpose: To determine whether you have decided to adopt a healthier lifestyle in the area of exercise and/or fitness.

My long term goals in exercise and fitness are as follows:

1.

2.

3.

4.

5.

I will accomplish these goals by: (date)

Trying to do everything at once can be overwhelming, and I may injure myself or get discouraged. So I am going to take small steps in the right direction each week.

Step 1 (tomorrow):

Step 2 (after one week):

Step 3 (after 4 weeks):

My support and encouragement group will consist of:

In other areas of my life I have demonstrated the ability to get things done and overcome challenges to make things happen. I can use those same skills to improve my personal fitness.

Challenges   Solutions

I will reward myself for staying with the exercise/fitness program and achieving my goal by:

I have the power to choose a healthier lifestyle. I am committed to make a difference in my health and developing a healthier lifestyle that works for me.

Signed _____ Date _____

Instructor _____ Date _____

Lab Activity 2.1

Planning for a Physical Fitness Program

Purpose: To plan your own exercise fitness program.

Procedure: Answer each of the following questions.

1. Based upon the information gained from Chapters 1 and 2, list the goals you want to accomplish in your fitness program.

2. Estimate your level of fitness related to the five health-related fitness components. Although you have not been tested in each of the components and you do not know your precise level of fitness, you have a good idea of your level. If you are inactive, you will be in the low fitness levels.

Components	Level of Fitness		
Cardiorespiratory Endurance	Low	Medium	High
Strength (Lower Body)	Low	Medium	High
(Upper Body)	Low	Medium	High
Muscular Endurance (Upper Body)	Low	Medium	High
(Lower Body)	Low	Medium	High
Flexibility	Low	Medium	High
Body Composition	Low	Medium	High

3. Based upon your score, choose activities that will help you meet your goals.

A. Cardiorespiratory

   Types of Activities _____

   Time dedicated to the workout _____

   Number of workouts per week _____

B. Strength

   Types of Activities _____

   Time dedicated to the workout _____

   Number of workouts per week _____

C. Muscular Endurance

   Types of Activities _____

   Time dedicated to the workout _____

   Number of workouts per week _____

D. Flexibility

   Types of Activities _____

   Time dedicated to the workout _____

   Number of workouts per week _____

E. Body Composition (reduction)

Types of Activities _____

4. Plan a weekly program.

Monday		Tuesday		Wednesday	
Activities	Times	Activities	Times	Activities	Times

Name: _____ Section: _____ Date: _____

Lab Activity 2.2

Warm-Up and Cool-Down

The exercises shown here can be used before a moderate workout as a warm-up or after a workout as a cool-down. Perform these exercises slowly, preferably after completing a cardiovascular warm-up. Do not bounce or jerk against the muscle. Hold each stretch for at least 15–30 seconds. Perform each exercise at least once and up to three times. Other stretching exercises are presented in the concept on flexibility and they can be used in a warm-up or cool-down.

Cardiovascular Exercise
Before you perform a vigorous workout, walk or job slowly for two minutes or more. After exercises, do the same. Do this portion of the warm-up prior to muscle stretching.

Leg Hug
This exercise stretches the hip and back extensor muscles. Lie on your back. Bend one leg and grasp your thigh under the knee. Hug it to your chest. Keep the other leg straight and on the floor. Hold. Repeat with the opposite leg.

Calf Stretcher
This exercise stretches the calf muscles (gastrocnemius and soleus). Face a wall with your feet 2 or 3 feet away. Step forward on left foot to allow both hands to touch the wall. Keep the heel of your right foot on the ground, toe turned in slightly, knee straight, and buttocks tucked in. Lean forward by bending your front knee and arms and allowing your head to move nearer the wall. Hold. Repeat with the other leg.

Seated Side Stretch
This exercise stretches the muscles of the trunk. Begin in a seated position with the legs crossed. Stretch the left arm over the head to the right. Bend at the waist (to right), reaching as far as possible to the left with the right arm. Hold. Do not let the trunk rotate. Repeat to the opposite side. For less stretch the overhead arm may be bent. This exercise can be done in the standing position but is less effective.

Hamstring Stretcher
This exercise stretches the muscles of the back of the upper leg (hamstrings) as well as those of the hip, knee, and ankle. Lie on your back. Bring the right knee to your chest and grasp the toes with the right hand. Place the left hand on the back of the right thigh. Pull the knee toward the chest, push the heel toward the ceiling, and pull the toes toward the shin. Attempt to straighten the knee. Stretch and hold. Repeat with the other leg.

Zipper
This exercise stretches the muscle on the back of the arm (triceps) and the lower chest muscles (pecs). Lift right arm and reach behind head and down the spine (as if pulling up a zipper). With the left hand, push down on right elbow and hold. Reverse arm position and repeat.

Lab Activity 2.3
Wellness Lifestyle Assessment

Directions: Using the following scale, answer each statement by placing the number that most closely corresponds to your lifestyle and feelings in the space preceding each statement.

KEY: 1 = "no/never" or "don't know"
  2 = "rarely" or "1–6 times a year"
  3 = "occasionally" or "1–4 times a month"
  4 = "often, frequently" or "2–5 times a week"
  5 = "yes/always" or "almost daily"

A. Physical Assessment

_____1. I perform aerobic exercises for twenty minutes or more per session.

_____2. When participating in physical activities, I include stretching and flexibility exercises.

_____3. My body fat composition is appropriate for my gender. (Men: 10–18 percent; Women: 16–25 percent)

_____4. I have appropriate medical checkups regularly and keep records of test results.

_____5. I practice safer sex or abstinence. I never have sex when intoxicated.

B. Nutritional Assessment

_____1. I eat at least 3 to 5 servings of vegetables and 2 to 4 servings of fruits daily.

_____2. I eat at least 6 to 11 servings daily of foods from the bread, cereal, rice, and pasta group.

_____3. I choose or prepare foods that tend to be lower in cholesterol and saturated fat.

_____4. When purchasing foods, I read the "Nutrition Facts" labels.

_____5. I avoid adding salt to my food.

C. Alcohol and Drugs Assessment

_____1. I avoid smoking and using smokeless tobacco products.

_____2. I avoid drinking alcohol or limit my daily alcohol intake to two drinks or less.

_____3. I do not drive after drinking alcohol or after taking medications that make me sleepy.

_____4. I follow directions when taking both prescription and over-the-counter medications.

_____5. I keep a record of drugs to which I am allergic in my wallet or purse.

D. Emotional Wellness Assessment

_____1. I feel positive about myself and my life. I set realistic goals for myself.

_____2. I can effectively cope with life's ups and downs in a healthy manner.

_____3. I do not tend to be nervous, impatient, or under a high amount of stress.

_____4. I can express my feelings of anger.

_____5. When working under pressure, I stay calm and am not easily distracted.

E. Intellectual Wellness Assessment

_____1. I seek advice when I am uncertain or uncomfortable with a recommended treatment.

_____2. I ask about the risks, benefits, and medical necessity of all medical tests and procedures.

_____3. I keep informed of the latest trends and information concerning health matters.

_____4. I feel comfortable about talking to my doctor.

_____5. I know the guidelines for practicing good preventive medicine and self-care.

F. Social and Spiritual Wellness Assessment

_____1. I am able to develop close, intimate relationships.

_____2. I am involved in school and/or community activities.

_____3. I have recreational hobbies and do something fun just for myself at least once a week.

_____4. I know what my values and beliefs are and I am tolerant of the beliefs of others.

_____5. My life has meaning and direction. I have life goals. Personal reflection is important.

Cardiorespiratory Fitness

Objectives

After completing this chapter, you will be able to do the following:

- List the risk factors for cardiovascular disease.
- Explain the effect of cardiorespiratory fitness on risk factors.
- Explain the metabolic, cardiorespiratory, and respiratory response to aerobic exercise.
- Identify methods for assessment of cardiorespiratory endurance.
- Identify the principles of training.
- Explain FITT and its relationship to the principles of training.

Many experts in health and fitness consider cardiorespiratory endurance as the single most important component of health fitness because of its importance to good health and optimal performance. Individuals who have a reasonable level of fitness have a decreased incidence of heart attack, high blood pressure, stroke, and an improved quality of life. By definition cardiorespiratory fitness is the ability to sustain cardiac, pulmonary, and musculosketal exertion over time. Several other terms in the literature that refer to this ability are aerobic fitness, cardiorespiratory fitness (ability to deliver and utilize oxygen), and cardiorespiratory endurance (ability to persist in physical activity for long periods of time without undue fatigue). Aerobic capacity is considered the best indicator of cardiorespiratory fitness. Improved cardiorespiratory efficiency lowers several modifiable risk factors for cardiovascular disease (CVDs), and research has shown that people who participate in moderate continuous exercise are less likely to develop colon cancer, non-insulin-dependent diabetes mellitus, osteoarthritis, osteoporosis, and symptoms of depression and anxiety (U.S. Department of Health and Human Services, 1996).

Risk Factors for Cardiovascular Disease

A risk factor is "a single characteristic statistically associated with, although not necessarily causally related to, an increased risk of morbidity or mortality" (Dirckx, 1997, p. 771). The risk factors for cardiovascular disease are high blood pressure, smoking, high total cholesterol, low cardiorespiratory fitness, diabetes mellitus, obesity, older age, family history, gender, race, high fat diet, and excessive psychological stress. These characteristics are of two types and can be categorized into groups. The modifiable and controllable risk factors are in the first group and those over which the individual has no control are in the second group.

The modifiable and controllable risk factors include high blood pressure, smoking, high total cholesterol, low cardiorespiratory fitness, high fat diet, obesity, and non-insulin-dependent diabetes mellitus. The risk factors that cannot be controlled or modified are age, family history, gender, and race. While race is listed as a risk factor here, some authorities believe that ". . . although African Americans and Hispanics are at greater risk for CVDs than Anglo-Americans, the risk factor may be related more to lifestyle patterns" (Floyd, Mims, & Yelding-Howard, 1995, p. 214). Cardiorespiratory fitness is associated with a reduced risk of heart disease and reduced risk for early death. Research has shown that the risk factors are highest for individuals with a low level of fitness. Cardiorespiratory fitness can reduce the health benefits of most persons, even those who smoke or are overweight. It is a known fact that poor cardiorespiratory fitness increases the risk for both lean and overfat people.

Effect of Cardiorespiratory Fitness on Risk Factors

A program of cardiorespiratory fitness training can readily modify low cardiorespiratory fitness. Moreover, by improving cardiorespiratory fitness, a significant reduction in the risk of developing high blood pressure can be achieved (Blair, Piserchia, Wilbur, & Crowder, 1986). Improved cardiorespiratory fitness also lowers total cholesterol. There are a number of **lipids** (fats) in the bloodstream. Cholesterol is probably the most well known. Blood lipids contribute to the development of deposits on the walls of the artery. Among these are **high-density lipoprotein (HDL),** and the **low-density lipoprotein (LDL).** Low-density lipoprotein is a major reason for atherosclerotic deposits. **LDL** (often called "bad" cholesterol) is cholesterol surrounded by protein and another substance and this makes it water soluble. Regular exercise can help reduce blood lipids. To decrease the risk of elevated LDL, we need to decrease the intake of saturated fat and *trans* fats as well as decrease the dietary intake of cholesterol. Another type of blood lipid is **triglycerides.** Research has shown that elevated triglycerides are positively related to heart disease. Triglycerides are blood fats associated with increased risk for heart disease. **High-density lipoprotein (HDL)** ("good cholesterol") picks up cholesterol and helps to eliminate it from the body. Because it is the "good cholesterol" high levels are considered desirable. In addition to lowering total cholesterol, cardiorespiratory training will lower LDLs and increase HDLs. HDLs are considered to be the "good cholesterol" because they ". . . are known to transport cholesterol away from the peripheral tissues and to the liver" (Guyton, 1981, p. 851). This action retards deposit of cholesterol in the blood vessels. Since cardiorespiratory fitness is associated with reducing total cholesterol and increasing HDLs, cardiorespiratory fitness training improves the ratio of total cholesterol to the high-density cholesterol. Cardiorespiratory fitness training also increases the rate and number of kilocalories used. Thus, cardiorespiratory fitness training when coupled with diet management will reduce obesity. Onset of non-insulin-dependent diabetes mellitus (NIDDM) can be delayed or avoided by maintaining cardiorespiratory fitness. NIDDM starts gradually and is usually found in obese individuals over age 35 (Dirckx, 1997). However, recent studies show that teens are developing the disease.

Metabolic, Cardiorespiratory, and Respiratory Response to Aerobic Exercise

Aerobic exercise is any physical activity that elevates the heart rate and respiration significantly above resting levels while the body maintains aerobic respiration. Aerobic respiration is the consumption of molecular oxygen and production of carbon dioxide and water by the body (Dirckx, 1997). The body is thought to be maintaining aerobic respiration when the exercise is rhythmical and can be maintained for an extended period of time (30 or more minutes).

Maximal oxygen consumption (VO_2 max) or aerobic capacity is considered the most accurate measure of cardiorespiratory fitness. Aerobic capacity is defined as how much oxygen a person can use during maximal exercise. When the body is subjected to aerobic activity regularly, physiological changes occur that enable the body to sustain aerobic exercise in the future. Among these changes are a decreased resting heart rate and a lower exercise heart rate at a given work level. This change is the result of an increase in the amount of blood the heart pumps with each beat (stroke volume) and results in improved cardiac output.

One's ability to ventilate the lungs is improved. The exchange of oxygen and carbon dioxide between the lungs and blood becomes more efficient. The exchange of oxygen and carbon dioxide between the red blood calls and exercising muscle tissue is also improved. Other physiological changes include an increase in the blood plasma volume, number and concentrations of mitochondria (the cellular organelle responsible for producing ATP with oxygen), muscle capillaries, and enzymes that facilitate aerobic metabolism.

The overall benefit of the physiological changes produced during cardiorespiratory training is threefold. First, there is the lower risk of certain diseases for the long term. Second, the body's energy stores are increased and, third, the body recovers from physical activity quickly. The increased energy stores and ability to recover from physical activity quickly are immediate benefits that can help individuals reach their personal goals.

Cardiorespiratory Endurance and Personal Goals Achievement

Everyone has personal goals and is highly motivated to reach them. Our personal goals, more often than not, are rooted in one of three desires. These are the desire to meet the basic survival needs of life, the desire to live a high-quality life, and the desire for a long life. A number of factors influence the career goals of young adults, but these factors can usually be linked to the desire to meet life's basic survival needs and the desire to live a high-quality life. No matter what career goals you set, thought should be given to the role of physical fitness and performance in reaching a given career goal (Howley & Franks, 2003). For example, health problems can lead to absence from classes or work. Such absences without question adversely affect the attainment of career goals. Therefore, physical fitness goals designed to reduce the risk of developing health problems and improve one's quality of life are important to enabling one to achieve his or her career goals.

Performance goals can also contribute significantly to the achievement of personal career goals. There are activities that must be completed each day. Examples are walking to class, carrying books, sitting at attention, preparing clothes for the next day, and sometimes preparation of meals. These activities require strength, flexibility, and endurance. Recreation is an extremely important part of a quality life. Quality recreation requires strength, flexibility, and endurance in order to achieve quality results. Achievement of personal goals requires that each individual have personal physical fitness goals and performance goals. Moreover, it is important that behavior common to the achievement of personal, fitness, and performance goals be identified and performed. Eating a healthy diet, getting proper rest, abstaining from smoking and drug abuse, and engaging in regular aerobic exercise are four of the more important behaviors.

Techniques of Assessing Cardiorespiratory Endurance

The importance of aerobic exercise in our daily lives is clear. Therefore, everyone should have a plan for including cardiorespiratory fitness training in his or her daily activities. It is always good to start planning and goal setting with an assessment of present status. There are many tests of cardiorespiratory fitness. They are categorized as either laboratory tests or field tests. Laboratory tests can be either maximal or submaximal. The maximal cardiorespiratory fitness tests require individuals to exercise until they reach their predicted maximum heart rate or until physiological responses reach criterion for terminating the test. Both the maximal and submaximal laboratory tests of cardiorespiratory fitness require specialized equipment and are not practical to the average person interested in assessing his or her own cardiorespiratory fitness.

Researchers have developed several field tests that allow individuals to evaluate their own cardiorespiratory endurance. Four of the most commonly used cardiorespiratory endurance field tests are the **Rockport One-Mile Walk Test** (Jenkins, 2001), the **Cooper One and One/Half Mile Run Test** (Cooper, 1982), the **Cooper Twelve Minute Run/Walk Test** (Cooper, 1982), and the **Three Minute Step Test** (YMCA, 1982). Instructions and scoring scales for these tests are included in the laboratories at the end of the chapter. Two cardiorespiratory fitness tests designed to meet the needs of persons over the age of 50 are the **Post 50 Walk Test** and the **Post 50 Step Test** (Adams, 1990). Both these tests require a shorter duration of exercise than those previously mentioned. Instructions and scoring scales for these tests are also in the laboratories at the end of the chapter.

Scoring scales for all cardiorespiratory endurance tests in this chapter will provide a predicted maximal oxygen consumption and/or a cardiorespiratory fitness category rating such as Excellent, Good, Fair, or Poor. These ratings are important in designing a personal cardiorespiratory training program. Procedures for their use will be discussed later in the chapter.

Principles of Training

The health benefits derived from cardiorespiratory training programs come most readily when the training principles of **Overload, Progression, Specificity, Recuperation,** and **Reversibility** are understood and applied. Three of these principles, Overload, Progression, and Specificity are commonly used in the fitness literature (Howley & Franks, 2003; Jenkins, 2001). Some other authors include Reversibility or Detraining (McArdle et al., 1991; Powers & Howley, 1994). Though not presented as a principle, most authors of cardiorespiratory fitness discuss the importance of Recuperation or recovery periods between sessions. Politano, McCormick, and Jeffreys (1995) present recuperation as a principle of training.

Overload Principle

This principle says that the body is stimulated to make cardiorespiratory fitness adaptations only when the amount of aerobic work during cardiorespiratory training is greater than the body's customary aerobic workload. Adaptations in the cardiorespiratory system are gradual and require approximately 6 weeks before significant performance improvements can be measured. Adaptations will continue as long as there is a gradually increasing overload. There is, however, a point at which the cardiorespiratory system is no longer capable of adapting. Care must be taken to control the overload. Overtraining occurs when the overload is so great that the body cannot adjust. When cardiorespiratory training results in decreased aerobic exercise performance, overtraining is likely to have occurred. Overload is controlled by manipulating the frequency, intensity, and time duration of cardiorespiratory exercise. Learning to control the overload-training stimulus is important to planning a personal cardiorespiratory fitness program and will be discussed later.

Principle of Progression

The cardiorespiratory adaptation stimulus is most safely and effectively elicited when the initial cardiorespiratory training workload is at a comfortable level and increases gradually. There should be a progressive increase in the training workload once the body can handle the existing training workload fairly easily. Cardiorespiratory adaptations cease when no further increase in the workload is made. Knowledge of your present cardiorespiratory fitness level is essential to setting the initial workload intensity and adhering to the principle of progression.

Principle of Specificity

This principle refers to the fact that adaptations in the body's systems are specific to the type of exercise overload. A cardiorespiratory training overload is necessary to produce cardiorespiratory fitness whereas a strength training overload is necessary to elicit increased strength. Specificity also refers to the fact that development of cardiorespiratory fitness for swimming, bicycling, running, or rowing is best achieved by aerobic exercises, which use the large muscle groups that will be active in the anticipated performance. Specificity in training is the reason that health-related fitness programs are designed to include cardiorespiratory, muscular strength, muscular flexibility, and muscular endurance exercises. All adaptations in body systems that produce health benefits will not occur when weight training is the only type of exercise stress placed upon the body.

Principle of Recuperation

Recuperation relates to overload and overtraining. It says that the period of time available for rest and recovery between training bouts should be sufficient for the body to recuperate from the exercise stress. When recuperation time is insufficient adaptations will not occur. In fact, there is likely to be a decline in performance. Overtraining can result in injuries to muscle and bone tissue. Such injuries are sometimes referred to as overuse injuries. An alternate day workout plan is often used to accommodate this principle. It will be discussed later in the chapter.

Principle of Reversibility

This principle says that the physiological adaptations resulting from a cardiorespiratory overload reverse when the overload ceases. Detraining and reversibility are used interchangeably. Detraining starts immediately and after just 1–2 weeks of inactivity, a significant reduction in physical working capacity can be measured (McArdle et al., 1991). Optimal cardiorespiratory fitness can be maintained by holding the training workload constant once the desired fitness level has been reached. Training programs that continue with the same level of work long after the body has adapted to it are often called maintenance programs. This

PHYSICAL ACTIVITY PYRAMID

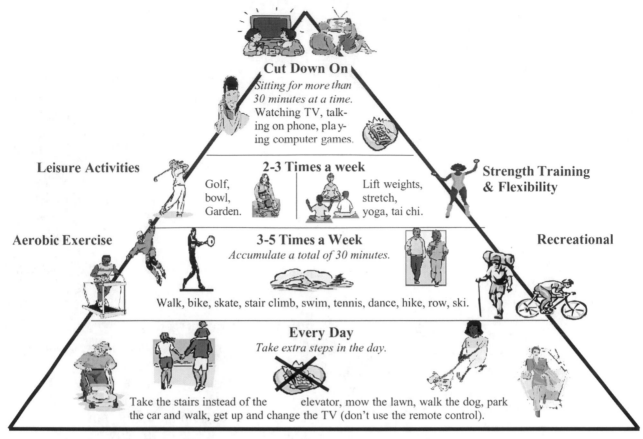

Figure 3.0   Physical Activity Pyramid—Select Activities from Level 2

principle makes it clear that only those persons who make a lifetime commitment to an active lifestyle, which includes an ongoing exercise overload, will enjoy the health benefits associated with cardiorespiratory fitness.

Using FITT to Adhere to the Principles of Training

The principles of training are important guides for developing a personal training program. Adherence to these principles is made easy when you understand how to control frequency and intensity of cardiorespiratory training. An appreciation for selecting a type of exercise appropriate for your fitness goals and selecting an exercise time duration that will stimulate physiological adaptations are also important. The Physical Activity Pyramid follows the FITT guidelines.

The acronym **FITT** uses the first letters of the phrases **F**requency of exercise, **I**ntensity of exer-

cise, **T**ype of exercise, and **T**ime duration of exercise. This is a convenient way to remember the variables that must be manipulated in order to control a cardiorespiratory work overload. The **FITT** recommendations that follow describe the frequency, intensity, type, and time duration of exercise necessary to stimulate physiological adaptations that will lead to improved cardiorespiratory fitness and the health benefits previously mentioned. These adaptations are commonly referred to as the training effect.

The U.S. Center for Disease Prevention and Control (CDC) and the American College of Sports Medicine (ACSM) make the following recommendation about the frequency, intensity, and time duration of cardiorespiratory exercise for minimum health benefits: "All people over the age of 2 years should accumulate at least 30 minutes of endurance type physical activity, of at least moderate intensity, on most—preferably all—days of the week" (U.S. Department of Health and Human Services, 1996, p. 28). This

Table 3.0 Classification of Physical Activity Intensity, Based on Physical Activity Lasting up to 60 Minutes

	Endurance-type activity								Strength-type exercise
	Relative intensity			Absolute intensity (METs) in healthy adults (age in years)					Relative intensity*
Intensity	VO$_2$ max (%) heart rate reserve %	Maximal heart rate (%)	RPE[†]	Young (20–39)	Middle-aged (40–64)	Old (65–79)	Very old (80+)	RPE	Maximal voluntary contraction (%)
Very light	<25	<30	<9	<3.0	<2.5	<2.0	≥1.25	<10	<30
Light	25–44	30–49	9–10	3.0–4.7	2.5–4.4	2.0–3.5	1.26–2.2	10–11	30–49
Moderate	45–59	50–69	11–12	4.8–7.1	4.5–5.9	3.6–4.7	2.3–2.95	12–13	50–69
Hard	60–84	70–89	13–16	7.2–10.1	6.0–8.4	4.8–6.7	3.0–4.25	14–16	70–84
Very hard	≥85	≥90	>16	≥10.2	≥8.5	≥6.8	≥4.25	17–19	>85
Maximal[‡]	100	100	20	12.0	10.0	8.0	5.0	20	100

*Based on 8–12 repetitions for persons under age 50 years and 10–15 repetitions for persons aged 50 years and older.

[†]Borg rating of Relative Perceived Exertion 6–20 scale (Borg 1982).

[‡]Maximal values are mean values achieved during maximal exercise by healthy adults. Absolute intensity (METs) values are approximate mean values for men. Mean values for women are approximately 1–2 METs lower than those for men.

recommendation recognizes that the quality and quantity of exercise necessary for some health benefits differ from what is necessary to improve cardiorespiratory fitness (maximal oxygen consumption). In order to meet personal fitness goals, it may be necessary to exercise at intensities, frequencies, and durations greater than recommended in the ACSM and CDC statement.

Frequency—Frequency of exercise is measured in the number of days per week training takes place. The recommended frequency for cardiorespiratory exercise is each day when the exercise intensity is moderate. Persons training for cardiorespiratory fitness levels necessary to meet specific fitness goals should use frequencies between 3 and 5 times per week. The sedentary person (poor fitness rating on a cardiorespiratory fitness test) should start with 3 days per week and progress to 5. The alternate day arrangement with 2 days off will allow time for recuperation.

Intensity—Endurance type physical activity can be measured in several ways. These are:

(1) percentage of maximal oxygen consumption, (2) percentage of the heart rate reserve, (3) percentage of maximal heart rate, (4) rating of perceived exertion (RPE), and (5) metabolic equivalent (METs). Each of these will be discussed in the following paragraphs.

A measure of **maximal oxygen consumption** requires specialized laboratory equipment. Although it can be estimated from some field tests, monitoring cardiorespiratory exercise intensity by this method is not practical in a personal fitness program for apparently healthy individuals. **Percentage of heart rate reserve (HRR)** is a practical means of monitoring cardiorespiratory exercise intensity and easily can be estimated by means of the Karvonen method. The percentages representing the various intensities of endurance type activity are identical for the maximum oxygen consumption and the heart rate reserve methods of monitoring intensity. By using the percentage in Table 3.0, you can maintain your exercise intensity. This method is considered accurate because it

Table 3.1 Heart Rate Reserve Calculations

220 – age Maximal Heart   220 – 19 = 201
Minus the Resting Heart Rate   (55) 201 – 55 = 146
Times Intensity (.65)   164 × .65 = 94.9 rounded to 95
Plus Resting Heart Rate (55)   95 + 44 = 150
Target Heart Rate is 150

New Formula for Calculating Maximal Heart Rate
MaxHR   208 – .7 × 19 (age)   .7 × 19 = 13.3
208 – 13.3 = 194.7 (rounded up to 195)

Maximal Heart Rate	195
Minus Resting Heart Rate	– 55
Heart Rate Reserve (HRR)	140

Calculate Threshold Heart Rate (Lower Limit Heart Rate)

Threshold Heart Rate	140 bpm
× 50%	× .50
Equals	70 bpm
+ RHR	+ 55 bpm
Equals Threshold Rate	125 bpm

Calculate Upper Limit Heart Rate

HHR	140 bpm
× 85%	× .85
Equals	119 bpm
+ RHR	+ 55 bpm
Upper Limit	174 bpm

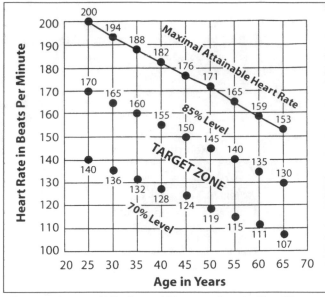

Zonman, Lenore, M.D., *Beyond Diet . . . Exercise Your Way to Fitness and Heart Health.* CPC International, Inc., 1974.

Figure 3.1   Maximal attainable heart rate and target zone.

takes into account the individual's resting heart rate (RHR) when calculating the percentage of the HRR. The RHR is determined by counting the pulse for 15 seconds and multiplying by 4. The pulse may be taken at a variety of body locations (see Figure 3.4). HRR is calculated by subtracting the RHR from the maximal heart rate (220 – age). The formula for calculating the heart rate reserve and an example for a 19-year-old with a resting heart rate of 61 beats per minute is shown in Table 3.1.

In order to calculate your thresholds and target zones (Figure 3.1) you must have an estimate of your maximal heart rate (maxHR). This is the highest heart rate level attained in maximum exercise. The formula of 220 – age = maxHR was used until recently. After extensive research a new formula is now recommended. This method is said to be more beneficial to both young and old adults because the previous formula overpredicted the maxHR for the young people and underpredicted the maxHR for

adults over 40. Instead of 220 – age, the new formula is maxHR = 208 – (.7 × age) (Corbin et al., 2006, p. 112). Table 3.1 illustrates the maxHR for a 19-year-old. The lower limit of the heart rate is achieved by calculating 55% of the working heart rate and adding the resting heart rate. The upper limit is calculated by determining 85% of the working heart rate and adding the resting heart rate.

The fourth method that could be used to monitor cardiorespiratory exercise intensity is **Borg's Rating of Perceived Exertion (RPE).** Borg (1982) developed a scale for rating cardiorespiratory exercise intensity in terms of one's feelings to determine if a person is exercising in the target zone (Figure 3.2). These feeling statements are related to physiologic stress and are reliable for the purpose of monitoring exercise intensity. The scale gives points between 6 and 20 for feeling statements of very, very light at 7 to very, very hard at 19. Ratings of perceived exertion correlate well with VO_2 and HRR. The RPE can be used to estimate exercise intensity. The RPE keeps the individual from counting heart rates during exercise. A rating of 12 is equal to the Lower Heart Limit and 17 to the Upper Heart Rate Level. After practice most people will be able to accurately use the RPE.

0	Nothing at all
1	Very, very weak
2	Very weak
3	Weak
4	Moderate
5	Something strong
6	Strong
7	
8	Very Strong
9	
10	Very, very strong
	Maximal

Figure 3.2 Borg's Rating of Perceived Exertion

The fifth and final method of monitoring exercise intensity requires selecting specific activities that represent a given **metabolic equivalent (MET)**. The MET is a measure of the oxygen cost of energy expenditure at supine rest (1 MET = 3.5 O_2 per kg of body weight per minute). Researchers have used multiples of MET to estimate the oxygen cost of activity. Specific exercise intensities in METs can be identified from Table 3.0. For example, Table 3.0 shows that a moderate exercise intensity is between 4.5 and 5.9 METs for a 55-year-old. Walking 4.5 mph on a level firm surface, very briskly, is equal to 4.5 METs. Doing this every day for 30 minutes will meet the moderate physical activity recommendation. Very light activities such as typing, driving, and daily care activities are equal to 2–2.5 METS. Moderate activity (4.7–7 METS) includes brisk walking, social dancing, and shoveling. Level jogging, cycling, and skiing represent hard activities and require 7–10 METS. Very hard (10–12 METS) activities are running and full-court competitive basketball. The maximum level (12+ METS) would be running a 6-minute mile.

Type of Activity. The type of activity will not only influence the type of fitness developed (principle of specificity), but it could influence willingness to continue in an exercise program. Any rhythmic large muscle activity that can be sustained for a prolonged period will improve cardiorespiratory fitness. Some examples are bicycling, cross-country skiing, running, brisk walking, aerobic dance, rowing, lap swimming, and stair climbing. Brisk walking is probably the most available aerobic activity for most people. The important thing to keep in mind is that any activity is better than no activity.

Time Duration of Activity. The most recent recommendation is to accumulate 30 minutes or more per day of moderate physical activity. This means that bouts of physical activity that last 5 minutes or more can be added together over the course of one's day to obtain the 30-minute daily requirement. Moreover, one might choose to accumulate minutes with different physical activities—some work, some recreational, and some exercise. Remember! This recommendation is for minimum health benefits. To develop the higher levels of cardiorespiratory endurance that will be necessary to reach your physical fitness and performance goals, a single bout of aerobic exercise in the target training zone for 20–30 minutes is more appropriate.

A word about progression will illustrate the use of **FITT** to adhere to the principles of training. The ACSM (2006) recommends that progression be considered in three stages. During the **initial conditioning stage** *intensity* should be conservative (1 MET below the intensity indicated by an initial fitness test). The recommended *frequency* is three training bouts per week of the cardiorespiratory exercise *type* for time *duration* of 10–15 minutes. This stage should last between 4 and 6 weeks. An **improvement conditioning stage** should have an intensity in the target training zone and be increased every 2–3 weeks. After the first 6 months the **maintenance conditioning stage** starts. In this stage realistic goals are set for maintaining fitness.

Optimal Cardiorespiratory Exercise Dose

How much cardiorespiratory exercise is enough? While research has demonstrated clearly that physical activity or fitness is associated with a reduction of risk of cardiovascular disease, an optimal exercise intensity or level of fitness has remained elusive. Williams (2002) conducted a research synthesis of 23 studies of sex specific physical cohorts and concluded that the weighted average of the relative risks decreased drastically for individuals whose fitness level was at or just above the 25th percentile. An earlier study (Blair et al., 1989)

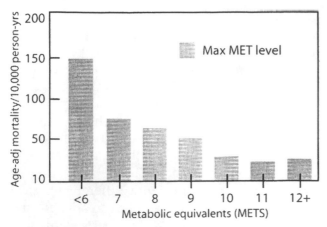

Reprinted by permission, from Blair et al., 1989, "Physical fitness and all-cause mortality," *Journal of American Medical Association* 262:2395–2401.

Figure 3.3 Age-adjusted, all-cause mortality rates per 10,000 person-years of follow-up by physical fitness levels.

seems to suggest that there is a great drop in all-cause mortality when maximum aerobic capacity increases from 6 METs to 7 METs. These studies suggest that the optimal cardiorespiratory exercise dose be at 7 METs. Table 3.0 shows this intensity to be vigorous rather than moderate for ages 20–64. This intensity is achieved when one works at 70–89% of the maximal heart rate. Of course, greater benefits are derived as the dose of cardiorespiratory exercise increases. Figure 3.3 shows that the age-adjusted mortality per 10,000 person-years decreases and the cardiorespiratory exercise dose in METs increases. While age-adjusted mortality per person-years continues to decrease with increasing MET physical working capacities, such decreases are small in comparison to the age-adjusted mortality decrease when physical-working capacity increases from 6 to 7 METs.

Phases of an Aerobic Workout

The aerobic workout should be done in three distinct phases. These are warm-up, aerobic conditioning, and cool-down phases. During the **warm-up phase** total body exercises such as walking, jogging, cycling, or swimming slowly should be used. Warm-up prepares the body for exercise by gradually increasing heart rate and blood flow to the muscles. It also improves muscle function by increasing muscle core temperature. This type of warm-up is referred to as general warm-up and should always be used before stretching or engaging in vigorous aerobic exercise. Individuals training or preparing for a specific sport should do specific warm-ups in addition to general warm-ups. Specific warm-ups involve performing specific sport activities less vigorously. Specific warm-ups not only prepare the body for more vigorous activity but also prepare the individual mentally to perform activities that require skill and coordination. The time devoted to warm-up should be increased as the temperature decreases. Warm-up duration should also increase when an extremely hard workout is anticipated. The recommended duration for warm-up is 5–10 minutes.

The **aerobic conditioning phase** is the period in which a progressive, aerobic overload is placed upon the body. Exercise intensity and duration should be controlled so as to produce improved functional capacity. Initially, this phase should consist of moderate duration (20–30 minutes) and moderate intensity (60–70% of functional capacity, reserve heart rate or maximum heart rate) aerobic exercise. Duration can be increased from 20–45 minutes after the first 2 weeks of conditioning provided the conditioning response is normal. It is important to note that undue fatigue 1 hour after your workout is a sign that the intensity and duration of the conditioning phase are set too high.

It is important to end each exercise bout with a **cool-down period** of 5–10 minutes. The cool-down consists of continuing aerobic exercise at a gradually decreasing intensity until exercise heart rate is approximately 110 beats per minute and stretching exercises. By slowly reducing exercise intensity, heart rate is allowed to return to the resting level gradually. In addition, blood pooling in the extremities is not likely to occur because the skeletal muscles of the extremities continue to promote venous return.

Monitoring Exercise Heart Rate During the Cardiorespiratory Training Period

We have discussed the techniques of monitoring exercise intensity by percentage of the MHR and by percentage of HRR. In order to make sure that you are exercising at a safe but effective intensity of exercise, you should calculate ULHR and LLHR after determining the

THR. As previously illustrated the **resting heart rate (RHR)** is used in calculating the Heart Rate Reserve (HRR). The RHR used to calculate HRR and the different exercise heart rates (Target Heart Rate (THR), Lower Level Heart Rate (LLHR), and Upper Level Heart Rate (ULHR)) should be taken in the early morning immediately after waking or after resting quietly for 30 minutes.

Heart rate and pulse rates are identical. Consequently, both resting heart rate and exercise heart rates may be taken by placing the index and second finger over the pulse point. The brachial artery on the anterior, thumb side of the wrist is most often used. The carotid artery at the neck is sometimes used, but may yield an inaccurate reading due to the pressure reflex. Should you choose to use the carotid pulse point, make sure that you apply only light pressure. Additional pulse points are shown in Figure 3.4.

Resting heart rate in beats per minute (bpm) is the number of beats in 60 seconds. To obtain RHR place the fingers over the pulse, watch the second hand or second digital readout of a watch, count zero on the first beat of a 60-second period, and continue counting pro-

Figure 3.5 Heart rate monitor.

gressively until the end of the 60 seconds. The final number is HRR in bpm. Three alternative methods of taking the resting pulse are:

1. Count the pulse for 30 seconds and multiply by 2 to obtain beats per minute.

2. Count the pulse for 15 seconds and multiply by 4 to obtain beats per minute.

3. Count the pulse for 10 seconds and multiply by 6 to obtain beats per minute.

Exercise heart rate must be taken immediately after exercise because the heart rate starts to drop rapidly upon stopping. For this reason it is important that the pulse count be taken for only 10 seconds and multiplied by 6 to obtain beats per minute. Counting the pulse for 6 seconds and multiplying by 10 simplifies the multiplication; however, 6 seconds is such a short period of time so getting the correct count may be difficult. A heart rate monitor like the one in Figure 3.5 could also be used to monitor heart rate.

Types of Aerobic Exercise and Sample Programs

Aerobic Walking

Walking is one of the simplest forms of aerobic activity. It is learned early in life and used often. However, there are some techniques that will make fitness walking more efficient and enjoyable. You should attempt to perfect the posture and alignment, arm swing, heel strike, push off, and breathing techniques as you walk for fitness.

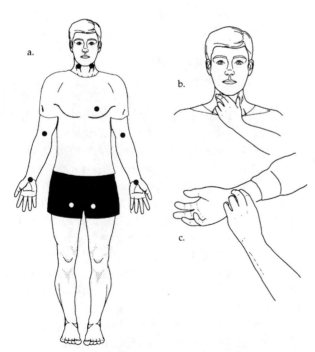

Figure 3.4 Palpitation of the heart rate. The pulse may be taken at a variety of body locations (a), but the two most common locations are (b) the neck (carotid artery) and (c) the wrist (radical artery). Source: Politano, et. al (1995) Lifetime Physical Fitness. Kendall/Hunt, page 40.

Posture should be erect, head up, shoulders back and relaxed, chest up, and abdominal muscles contracted. Good body **alignment** requires that you stand tall and keep the body's weight balanced side to side.

The **arm swing** during warm-up and cooldown should be straight forward and backward with elbow joints extended and hands relaxed. During the aerobic training period or as the speed of walking increases, the arms should continue to swing forward and backward, but the elbow joints should flex to approximately 90 degrees and the arms should pump more vigorously. The hands should remain relaxed and may be either open or slightly closed.

Foot contact with the walking surface should be with a **heel strike** during which the ankle joint is dorsi flexed. Toeing out slightly is normal. Contacting the walking surface with a flat foot should be avoided. As weight is transferred from the back foot, a smooth roll from the outside heel, along the outside sole, to the ball of the foot should occur.

Push off occurs at the end of the foot roll from heel to ball of the foot. Increasing the force of push will help increase walking speed. The major characteristic that distinguishes walking from running is the period of time when the body's weight is supported by both feet. This dual support phase is the major reason that walking does not produce the ankle, knee, and hip joint compression associated with running.

Breathing comes natural and most people do not consider it a technique. However, during fitness walking or any other type of cardiovascular exercise, proficiency can be improved by establishing an optimum rate and depth of breathing. The appropriate rate and depth is unique to the individual; therefore, experimentation is necessary. Experiment by making sure that you breathe from the diaphragm (deep) and not shallow in the chest. An attempt should be made to inhale and exhale over similar periods of time. One way to do this is to inhale over 2–4 steps and exhale over the same number. Nasal breathing is best and it should be maintained as long as possible. Most individuals seem to start oral breathing when they feel the exercise is strenuous.

Sample Walking Program There are many examples of walking programs in the literature. A good example is shown in Table 3.2.

You could develop your own walking program by starting with a comfortable speed, duration, and gradually increasing the duration by 5-minute intervals. Speed increases can be made as you see fit as long as you remain in your training heart rate zone. Brisk walking (4 miles per hour) should be a goal. Four miles per hour is 1 mile in 15 minutes. You can determine your rate of walking or running by timing a mile and using rate equals distance in miles, divided by time in fraction of an hour. For example, if your time for 2 miles is 30 minutes your average rate is:

Rate in mph = 2 miles / .5 hrs.

Rate in mph = 4 mph

Jogging/Running Jogging and running are excellent types of aerobic exercise. Jogging/running has been a consistently popular activity for both men and women. At least 15 to 20 million Americans profess to jog/run regularly. The major advantage of jog/run over other aerobic activities is that it is relatively inexpensive. All that is needed is a good pair of shoes and inexpensive clothing. The primary difference between jog/run technique and walking technique is that there is no double support in jogging or running. In other words, both feet are never in contact with the ground at the same time. In addition, the period of time that the foot is in contact with the ground is shorter. Jog/run technique will be considered under the headings of foot contact, heel to toe roll, stride, upper body movement, and arm swing. The aerobic demand for outdoor running at 5m/s is 5–7% higher than that for treadmill running.

Table 3.2   Walking Program

Rules
1. Start at a level that is comfortable to you.
2. Be aware of new aches or pains.
3. Don't progress to the next level if you are not comfortable.
4. Monitor your heart rate and record it.
5. It would be healthful to walk at least every other day.

Stage	Duration	Heart rate	Comments
1	15 min	_____	_____
2	20 min	_____	_____
3	25 min	_____	_____
4	30 min	_____	_____
5	30 min	_____	_____
6	30 min	_____	_____
7	35 min	_____	_____
8	40 min	_____	_____
9	45 min	_____	_____
10	45 min	_____	_____
11	45 min	_____	_____
12	50 min	_____	_____
13	55 min	_____	_____
14	60 min	_____	_____
15	60 min	_____	_____
16	60 min	_____	_____
17	60 min	_____	_____
18	60 min	_____	_____
19	60 min	_____	_____
20	60 min	_____	_____

Reprinted by permission from B. D. Franks and E. Howley, 1998, *Health Fitness Leader's Handbook,* 2nd edition (Champaign, IL: Human Kinetics).

Foot Contact. Foot contact should be made with the heel or lateral border of the foot. The heel strikes before the rest of the foot; then you rock forward and push off on the ball of the foot. You should not jog on your toes. The foot should stay under your knees; do not swing the feet out to the side. While sprinters may contact the ground on the ball of the foot, distance runners use a heel strike. The heel strike is thought to absorb shock better and reduce the incidence of shinsplints and other musculoskeletal injuries. The lollygag principle states that long distance runners who heel strike tend to waste a lot of time and energy. The most efficient runners will have minimal ground contact which means running on your mid to forefoot. This is done by shortening your running stride and increasing your stride frequency.

Heel to Toe Roll. Once the heel has made contact with the running surface, body weight is transferred along the lateral border of the foot to the ball of the foot then to the toes where push occurs. This action is called **heel to toe roll.** The designers of running shoes take this action into account and design their shoes with a great deal of cushioning material in the heel area and the outside border of the shoe.

Stride. Push off is the first phase of the **stride.** Immediately after push off, the knee flexes and the hip extends. Flexion of the hip and extension of the knee follow this movement. It is important that the leg muscles contract and relax at the appropriate time in order to avoid muscle pulls. Good flexibility in the hamstrings and proper warm-up are extremely important to facilitate proper muscle functioning during running. Stride length and stride frequency determine the speed of running just as they do in walking. The best stride length and stride frequency are unique to the individual and must be identified by experimentation. As you jog/run you should have a relatively comfortable stride and it should be several inches longer than your walking stride. Stride length and frequency determine the speed of running. The stride length and frequency are unique to the individual and must be determined through experimentation.

Trunk Position. The **upper body** should be erect with a slightly forward incline, with the head and chest up. Do not lean forward. The head should be up with the eyes focused on the running surface several yards ahead.

Arm Movement. The hands may be either open or partially closed. It is important to keep both the hands and arms as relaxed as possible. The arms should be flexed to approximately 90 degrees and swing freely from the front to the back in the direction you are moving. This type of arm movement eliminates excessive upper body rotation on the vertical axis and conserves energy. Swinging the arms from side to side is not efficient and uses excessive energy. Breathing techniques like the ones discussed under walking should be used with jogging or running.

Sample Jog/Run Programs. There are many examples of jog/run programs in the literature. A good example is found in Table 3.3.

You could develop your own interval jogging program, starting with a comfortable speed of running for a comfortable duration then walking a duration that will allow you to repeat the run. Gradually increase the duration by 5-minute intervals. Speed increases can be made as fitness improves as long as you remain in your training heart rate zone. Walking speeds in excess of 5 miles per hour are not as economical as jogging at the same rate. Therefore, thought should be given to jogging, once the walking program's rate has reached 4.5 mph or more.

Fitness Swimming

Swimming is an excellent cardiovascular activity and has the advantage of being able to produce the training effect without stressing the joints. Persons with orthopedic problems could benefit from this activity. However, good swimming ability is required before fitness swimming can be used as a cardiovascular fitness activity. Beginning swimming instruction is beyond the scope of this text; consequently, you should take a beginning swimming course if you cannot swim and think that you might want to use fitness swimming as a cardiovascular fitness activity.

Table 3.3 Jogging Program

Rules
1. Complete the Walking Program before starting this program.
2. Begin each session with walking and stretching.
3. Be aware of new aches and pains.
4. Don't progress to the next level if you are not comfortable.
5. Stay at the low end of your THR zone; record your heart rate for each session.
6. Do the program on a work-a-day, rest-a-day basis.

Stage 1 Jog 10 steps, walk 10 steps. Repeat five times and take your heart rate. Stay within THR zone by increasing or decreasing walking phase. Do 20 to 30 min of activity.

Stage 2 Jog 20 steps, walk 10 steps. Repeat five times and take your heart rate. Stay within THR zone by increasing or decreasing walking phase. Do 20 to 30 min of activity.

Stage 3 Jog 30 steps, walk 10 steps. Repeat five times and take your heart rate. Stay within THR zone by increasing or decreasing walking phase. Do 20 to 30 min of activity.

Stage 4 Jog 1 min, walk 10 steps. Repeat three times and take your heart rate. Stay within THR zone by increasing or decreasing walking phase. Do 20 to 30 min of activity.

Stage 5 Jog 2 min, walk 10 steps. Repeat two times and take your heart rate. Stay within THR zone by increasing or decreasing walking phase. Do 30 min of activity.

Stage 6 Jog 1 lap (400 m, or 440 yd) and check heart rate. Adjust pace during run to stay within the THR zone. If heart rate is still too high, go back to the Stage 5 schedule. Do 6 laps with a brief walk between each.

Stage 7 Jog 2 laps and check heart rate. Adjust pace during run to stay within the THR zone. If heart rate is still too high, go back to Stage 6 activity. Do 6 laps with a brief walk between each.

Stage 8 Jog 1 mi and check heart rate. Adjust pace during the run to stay within THR zone. Do 2 mi.

Stage 9 Jog 2 to 3 mi continuously. Check heart rate at the end to ensure that you were within THR zone.

Reprinted by permission from B. D. Franks and E. Howley, 1998, *Health Fitness Leader's Handbook*, 2nd edition (Champaign, IL: Human Kinetics).

Fitness swimming is often referred to as **lap swimming** because swimmers lap the pool time after time using an individual stroke or a combination of strokes. Aquatic facilities have specific times set aside for this activity because it requires that lane lines be in the pool and there be no diving or playing of games during this period. The times are usually posted in the facility or you should ask management for the times.

During lap swimming, lane lines are used to divide the pool and disperse the wake of the swimmers in other lanes. The lanes are usually marked according to swimming speed or skill level. Examples are slow, medium, fast or beginner, intermediate, and advanced. It is important that you get into the lane that best fits your swimming speed or skill. Circle swimming is recommended when there is more than one swimmer using the lane. This requires that you stay to the right of the pool bottom lane marker and pass slower swimmers on the wall.

It is important that you stay out of the way of turning swimmers when resting and move to a more appropriate lane if you find that you misjudged your speed or ability.

Just as with walking and running, the swimming workout should contain the three phases of warm-up, conditioning phase, and cool-down. The term **main set** is often used for the conditioning phase of swimming workouts and **swim down** is sometimes used for the cool-down phase. However, the same general principles apply **except that when monitoring exercise intensity by heart rate, 10–13 beats per minute should be subtracted from the predicted maximum heart rate before calculating the target heart rate zone.** Research suggests that this difference is the result of the smaller muscle mass that is used in exercises that primarily use the arms. In swimming, the horizontal body position and the cooling effect of the water also contribute to the lower maximum heart rate (McArdle, Katch, & Katch, 1991).

Lap swimmers often train by using kickboards during kick drills and pull buoys while swimming with the arms only. These should be returned to the appropriate storage location when you finish using them. Finally, it is extremely important that you learn and obey the pool's safety rules.

Sample Beginning Swimming Workout. A sample swimming workout follows. It uses interval training for the main set and continuous swimming for warm-up and cool-down. Interval training refers to a type of training that breaks vigorous work periods with short rest periods. It has been found that training in this way accelerates improved aerobic capacity.

Warm-Up

Swim relaxed crawl stroke	1 × 100 yards	Rest 2 minutes
Kick	1 × 50 yards	Rest 1 minute
Pull	1 × 50 yards	Rest 1 minute
Swim	1 × 50 yards	Rest 2 minutes

Main Set

Swim crawl stroke	10 × 50 yards	Rest 1 minute between each 50

Swim Down

Swim continuous crawl stroke 1 × 100 yards; check pulse if greater than 110 bpm; then walk in the water until the heart rate is less than 110 bpm.

Water Aerobics

Water exercises are good cardiovascular activities and they provide some of the benefits of resistance training. Water aerobics are especially good for people who have musculoskeletal problems or arthritis and for individuals

who are overfat. Many injured athletes use water exercise for rehabilitation. They enable a nonswimmer to benefit from exercising with reduced stress on the joints. Many of the movements are similar or identical to exercise performed on dry land. These exercises include walking or jogging in shallow water, jumping jacks, and hopping. Many variations of these movements are put together in a single workout. The exercise intensity varies; therefore, individuals should work at their own pace. These exercises may also be done to music. When music is used, the warm-up and cool-down tempo should be between 100 and 120 beats per minute. The conditioning phase should be between 130 and 140 beats per minute.

Water aerobic exercises are organized according to the body parts exercised. The body part categories usually used are Total Body, Lower Body, Middle Body, and Upper Body. Following are some exercises in each category.

Walking or jogging with an erect stance in chest-deep water is an excellent *total body* water aerobic exercise. There are several variations that will increase the workload on the heart. In *one variation* a kickboard is placed in the water at arms length and vertical to the surface of the water. This produces a frontal resistant against which you must push when walking or jogging. A *second variation* requires that you run in place lifting the knees as high as possible without bouncing and a *third variation* requires you to walk with the knees straight by lifting the leg to the front, placing the heel down first and rolling the body's weight over the foot. Water jumping jacks are also total body exercises. They are performed by starting from a standing position in chest-deep water with your arms at your sides. The knees bend slightly to create a forceful jump during which the legs are straddled and the arms lifted to waist height. The jump is then repeated and the legs are brought together and the arms are returned to the sides.

Hopping is a good *lower body* water aerobic exercise. As with walking and running, you start in an erect position in chest-deep water. With the knees together and slightly bent, balance on the ball of one foot and hop forward. The arms should remain under water. Sculling can be used to help maintain balance. *One variation* requires that you lift one knee toward the chest to a 90-degree hip and a 90-degree knee position, support it with the hands, fingers laced together, at the underside of the thigh and then hop forward. A *second variation* requires that two hops be taken alternately on each leg while the nonsupport leg is abducted to an approximate 45 degree angle and held in that position. To maintain balance, the hands should scull under water with the elbow flexed at 90 degrees.

Upper body exercises tone the muscles in the chest and arms and when used in an aerobic routine, they contribute to cardiovascular endurance. One popular exercise in this category is pulling and pushing at the wall in chest-deep water. You start by taking a standing position facing the pool wall with the arms extended to the wall in chest-deep water. The exercise action is to pull the body to the wall then push it away. The water resistance created by the broad surface of the front and rear of the body places a workload on the arm muscles. Another upper body exercise requires that you stand erect in chest-deep water with the elbows close to the side of the body and bent to 90 degrees. The palm of the hand should face up. In the exercise action you use the palm of the hand to push up toward the surface of the water and the back of the hand to push down. A good variation of this exercise is to start with the palms facing down, then push up with the back of the hand and press down with the palm.

Many *middle body* exercises can be done while holding the pool wall. One popular exercise for the abdominal muscles is to stand with the back to the wall, arms abducted from sides and resting either in the pool gutter or on the edge of the deck. In the exercise action the upper body is supported by the pool gutter or deck and the legs, knees together, are drawn to the chest then extended straight out. A good variation from the same position is to extend the legs and perform a large flutter kick covering the area from just below the surface to near the bottom of chest-deep water. This exercise conditions the abdominals and the quadriceps.

Sample Water Aerobic Workout. Water aerobic workouts should start with a warm-up and end with a cool-down. A 15- to 30-minute conditioning period is between them. A simple program could be developed from the exercises

aerobic dances are available for different levels. Aerobic dance is typed according to the shock produced at the joints of the legs.

Low impact was developed to reduce the risk of injury or soreness. With low impact aerobics, one foot stays on the floor at all times. Low impact is recommended for beginners and older exercisers.

High impact aerobic dance produces a higher level of shock to the joints than *low impact* aerobic dance. In high impact both feet are off the floor for a large part of the routine. High impact aerobics is recommended for advanced exercisers. Advanced exercisers are still at an increased risk of injuries while doing high impact aerobics.

High–low combines routines from low and high impact aerobics to provide a more balanced routine. By changing routines, the risk of injuries is less.

described in the previous section. They should be put together as follows:

Warm-Up Phase (5 minutes)

Do 20, four count, aqua jumping jacks, then walk in chest-deep water for the remainder of the 5 minutes. Adjust the walking speed to your fitness level and remember to keep your heart rate below the training zone heart rate.

Conditioning Phase (20 minutes)

Hop on the right leg one width of the pool, then hop on the left leg one width. Rest 30 seconds and repeat sequence 3 times. Do alternating leg every two hops with the nonsupport leg abducted to approximately 45 degrees. Repeat 3 times. Check the pulse and adjust hopping speed up or down to attain or maintain target heart rate. Remember that 10 to 13 beats per minute should be subtracted from the predicted maximum heart rate before calculating the target heart rate zone for exercising in the water. Alternately jog one width of the pool, then walk, rest 30 seconds, and repeat 6 times.

Cool-Down (5 minutes)

Walk slowly in chest-deep water for 5 minutes. Allow the heart rate to return to approximately 100 beats per minute.

Aerobic Dance

Dance aerobics is a series of choreographed exercises done to music. A variety of forms of

15-minute phase that is designed to tone and strengthen is attached to the aerobic dance session. Typically, the warm-up and cool-down phases are from 5 to 10 minutes and the aerobic segment (same as conditioning phase) is 20 to 50 minutes depending upon individual fitness levels. Warm-up routines will include total body movements such as marching in place and step-touches. Common exercises such as knee lifts, light jogging, leg kicks, lunges, jumping jacks, and/or various dance movements make up the aerobic segment. Step aerobics developed out of straight bench stepping which proved to be both a predictor of aerobic capacity and a conditioner for aerobic ability.

Cycling

Cycling is a great way to get an aerobic workout. It does require a properly fitted bicycle and safety equipment. Because of the mechanical efficiency of the bike, cycling is more efficient than running. However, if you are cycling on the level at 5 mph it is less intense than running. The typical cycling workout would require that you cycle at a pace that will keep your heart rate in the target zone for 20–50 minutes. A warm-up and cool-down should be done by cycling at a slower pace. There is variety in the ways that cycling can be done. *Mountain biking* usually takes the cyclist onto wooded, hilly trails. *Leisure cycling* on neighborhood streets with a partner on two bikes or with a partner on a tandem bike is a good way to get an aerobic workout and enjoy comradery. *Stationary cycling* can be done

Step aerobics uses a small 3- to 4-foot bench with adjustable heights off the floor and is an adaptation of dance aerobics. The performer steps up and down on the bench while performing different routines. These routines can also be either high or low impact. Most routines are low impact but there are high impact routines for advanced steppers. Step aerobics can be done with or without music. Step aerobics is popular for beginners, professional athletic teams, and advanced exercisers to promote cardiorespiratory fitness. Both dance and step aerobics are suited for either group or individual training sessions. In getting started it is beneficial to participate in a class or group with an experienced leader.

Both aerobic dance and step aerobic routines include the three traditional phases of an aerobic workout. Often an additional 10- to

alone or as a group. *Spinning,* a group cycling class, is performed on stationary cycles. An instructor takes the group through a variety of intervals, adjusting the pace, resistance, paddling style, and cadence to use. Spinning involves routines with intermittent bursts of high-intensity intervals, followed by spinning at a lower-intensity level. The group leader helps the riders to simulate hill climbing, speed sprints, and competitive cycling. Cycling appeals to many because, like swimming, it is a no-impact activity.

Stair climbing is an excellent way to obtain the training effect while going about one's daily activities or during a special training period set aside specifically for that purpose. It can be done indoors, out-of-doors, while traveling, or in the gym on a stair climbing machine. A good workout would require that you warm up by walking or climbing at a fairly slow rate for 5–10 minutes. The same thing could be done for a cool-down. The conditioning period would consist of 20–50 minutes climbing at a steady but brisk pace to elevate the heart rate to between 60 and 85% of the maximum heart rate. Remember! You should adjust the duration of climbing and percentage of maximum heart rate to your fitness level. Individuals with poor fitness will need to climb for a shorter duration and at a lower percentage of the maximum heart rate.

Skating and **cross-country skiing** are excellent aerobic fitness activities. Workouts with these activities can be patterned after jogging and walking workouts. Speed play suits these activities very well. In speed play, or fartlek training as it is also known, the rate or exercise is continuous but varied between slow, moderate, and fast in either a systematic or not so

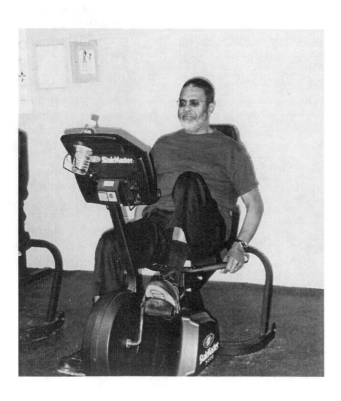

systematic pattern. An example would be to skate or ski slowly for 5 minutes then build from slow to moderate to fast over the next 6 minutes, spending 2 minutes on each of the three rates. The pattern could then be repeated or some other pattern adopted.

References

Adams, G. M. (1990). *Exercise physiology laboratory manual.* New York: W. C. Brown Publishers.

American College of Sports Medicine. (2006). *ACSM's resource manual for guidelines for exercise testing and prescription.* 6th ed. Philadelphia: Lea & Febiger.

American Red Cross. (1992). *Swimming and diving.* St. Louis: Mosby Lifeline.

Blair, S. N., Kohl, H. W., III, Paffenbarger, R. S., Clark, D. G., Cooper, K. H., & Gibbons, L. W. (1989). Physical fitness and all-cause mortality: A prospective study of healthy men and women. *Journal of the American Medical Association, 262,* 2395–2401.

Blair, S. N., Piserchia, P. V., Wilbur, C. S., & Crowder, J. H. (1986). A public health intervention model for worksite health promotion: Impact on exercise and physical fitness in a health promotion plan after 24 months. *Journal of the American Medical Association, 262,* 2395–2401.

Borg, G. (1982). Psychological bases of perceived exertion. *Medicine and Science in Sports and Exercise, 14,* 377.

British Columbia Ministry of Health. (1978). *Par-Q validation report.* British Columbia: Cani.

Cooper, K. H. (1982). *The aerobics program for total well-being.* New York: Bantam Books.

Corbin, C. B., Welk, G. J., Corbin, W. R., & Welk, K. A. (2006). *Concepts of physical fitness: Active lifestyles for wellness,* 13th ed. Boston: McGraw-Hill.

Dirckx, J. H. (Ed.). (1997). *Stedman's concise medical dictionary for the health professions.* Baltimore: Williams & Wilkins.

Floyd, P. A., Mims, S. E., & Yelding-Howard, C. (1995). *Personal health: A multicultural approach.* Englewood, CO: Morton Publishing Company.

Friel, J. (1998). *The triathlete's bible.* Boulder, CO: VeloPress.

Girandola, R. N. (1988). *Running for lifelong fitness.* Englewood Cliffs, NJ: Prentice Hall.

Guyton, A. C. (1981). *Textbook of medical physiology.* Philadelphia: W. B. Saunders Company.

Howley, E. T. & Franks, B. D. (2003). *Health fitness instructor's handbook.* Champaign, IL: Human Kinetics.

Jenkins, F. C. (2001). *Dynamics of fitness and health.* Dubuque, IA: Kendall/Hunt Publishing Company.

Jones, A. M. & Doust, J. H. A. (1996). 1% treadmill grade most accurately reflects the energetic cost of outdoor running. *Journal of Sports Science, 14,* 321–327.

Katz, J. (1996). *The aquatic handbook for lifetime fitness.* Boston: Allyn & Bacon.

McArdle, W. D., Katch, R. I., & Katch, V. L. (1991). *Exercise physiology: Energy, nutrition, and human performance.* Philadelphia: Lea & Febiger.

Politano, V., McCormick, M. R., & Jeffreys, A. (1995). *Lifetime physical fitness: Concepts, assessments and prescription.* Dubuque, IA: Kendall/Hunt Publishing Company.

Powers, S. K. & Howley, E. T. (1994). *Exercise physiology: Exercise, performance and clinical applications.* St. Louis: Mosby Year Book.

U.S. Department of Health and Human Services. (1996). *Physical activity and health: A report of the Surgeon General.* Atlanta, GA: U.S. Department of Health and Human Services, Centers for Disease Control and Prevention, National Center for Chronic Disease Prevention and Health Promotion.

Williams, P. T. (2002). Physical fitness and activity as separate heart disease risk factors: A meta-analysis. *Medicine and Science in Sports, 33,* 74–81.

YMCA. (1982). *Y's way to fitness.* The YMCA of USA.

Web Sites

www.acsm.org American College of Sports Medicine

www.cooperinst.org The Cooper Institute

www.sportQuest.com

www.fitness.gov

www.sportfit.com

www.acefitness.org

www.americanheart.org American Heart Association

www.acsm.org/health+fitness/fit_society ACSM's Fit Society Page

www.shapeup.org/fitness

Name: _____ Section: _____ Date: _____

Lab Activity 3.0
The Physical Activity Readiness
Questionnaire (PAR-Q) and You

Purpose: To identify adults for whom physical activity might be inappropriate or for those who should have medical advice concerning the type of activity most suitable for them.

Procedure: Read the questions carefully and answer each one honestly.

PAR-Q &You

Regular physical activity is fun and healthy, and increasingly more people are starting to become more active every day. Being more active is very safe for most people. However, some people should check with their doctor before they start becoming much more physically active.

If you are planning to become much more physically active than you are now, start by answering the seven questions in the box below. If you are between the ages of 15 and 69, the PAR-Q will tell you if you should check with your doctor before you start. If you are over 69 years of age, and you are not used to being very active, check with your doctor.

Common sense is your best guide when you answer these questions. Please read the questions carefully and answer each one honestly: check YES or NO.

YES	NO	
❏	❏	1. Has your doctor ever said that you have a heart condition and that you should only do physical activity recommended by a doctor?
❏	❏	2. Do you feel pain in your chest when you do physical activity?
❏	❏	3. In the past month, have you had chest pain when you were not doing physical activity?
❏	❏	4. Do you lose your balance because of dizziness or do you ever lose consciousness?
❏	❏	5. Do you have a bone or joint problem that could be made worse by a change in your physical activity?
❏	❏	6. Is your doctor currently prescribing drugs (for example, water pills) for you blood pressure or heart condition?
❏	❏	7. Do you know of <u>any other reason</u> why you should not do physical activity?

IF YOU ANSWERED

YES TO ONE OR MORE QUESTIONS

Talk with your doctor by phone or in person BEFORE you start becoming much more physically active or BEFORE you have a fitness appraisal. Tell your doctor about the PAR-Q and which questions you answered YES.

- You may be able to do any activity you want—as long as you start slowly and build up gradually. Or, you may need to restrict your activities to those which are safe for you. Talk with your doctor about the kinds of activities you wish to participate in and follow his/her advice.
- Find out which community programs are safe and helpful for you.

NO TO ALL QUESTIONS ⇨

If you answered NO honestly to <u>all</u> PAR-Q questions, you can be reasonably sure that you can:

- start becoming much more physically active—begin slowly and build up gradually. This is the safest and easiest way to go.
- take part in a fitness appraisal—this is an excellent way to determine your basic fitness so that you can plan the best way for you to live actively.

DELAY BECOMING MUCH MORE ACTIVE:

- if you are not feeling well because of a temporary illness such as a cold or a fever—wait until you feel better; or
- if you are or may be pregnant—talk to your doctor before you start becoming more active.

Please note: If your health changes so that you then answer YES to any of the above questions, tell your fitness or health professional. Ask whether you should change your physical activity plan.

Lab Activity 3.1
1.5-Mile Timed Run Test

Purpose: To determine the level of cardiorespiratory endurance by completing and recording the time required to complete the 1.5 miles.

Procedure:

1. Warm-up and stretch.
2. On signal, run/walk, jog the 1.5 mile distance. Complete the distance as quickly as possible.
3. Record the time required to cover the distance.
4. Consult the chart below to find your fitness rating.

1.5 Mile Run Test. Time (minutes)
Age (years)

Fitness Category		13–19	20–29	30–39	40–49	50–60	60+
Very poor	(men)	> 15:31	> 16:01	> 16:31	> 17:31	> 19:01	> 20:01
	(women)	> 18:31	> 19:01	> 19:31	> 20:01	> 20:31	> 21:01
Poor	(men)	12:11–15:30	14:01–16:00	14:44–16:30	15:36–17:30	17:01–19:00	19:01–20:00
	(women)	16:55–18:30	18:31–19:00	19:01–19:30	19:31–20:00	20:01–20:30	21:00–21:31
Fair	(men)	10:49–12:10	12:01–14:00	12:31–14:45	13:01–15:35	14:31–17:00	16:16–19:00
	(women)	14:31–16:54	15:55–18:30	16:31–19:00	17:31–19:30	19:01–20:00	19:31–20:30
Good	(men)	9:41–10:48	10:46–12:00	11:01–12:30	11:31–13:00	12:31–14:30	14:00–16:15
	(women)	12:30–14:30	13:31–15:54	14:31–16:30	15:56–17:30	16:31–19:00	17:31–19:30
Excellent	(men)	8:37–9:40	9:45–10:45	10:00–11:00	10:30–11:30	11:00–12:30	11:15–13:59
	(women)	11:50–12:29	12:30–13:30	13:00–14:30	13:45–15:55	14:30–16:30	16:30–17:30
Superior	(men)	< 8:37	< 9:45	< 10:00	< 10:30	< 11:00	< 11:15
	(women)	< 11:50	< 12:30	< 13:00	< 13:45	< 14:30	< 16:30

< Means "less than"; > means "more than."

"Tests," from *The Aerobics Program for Total Well-Being* by Kenneth H. Cooper, M.D., M.P.H. Copyright 1982 by Kenneth H. Cooper. Used by permission of Bantam Books, a division of Bantam Doubleday Dell Publishing Group, Inc.

1. Record the time required to complete the 1.5-mile run _____
2. Record your age   _____
3. Record your sex   _____
4. Record your fitness category as indicated on the chart _____

Name: _____ Section: _____ Date: _____

Lab Activity 3.2
Cooper's 12-Minute Walking/Running Test

Purpose: To determine your level of cardiorespiratory endurance using the 12-minute run/walk activity.

Procedure:

1. Warm-up with light jogging and stretching.
2. Run/walk as far as possible in 12 minutes (timed by a stopwatch).
3. Record the distance you covered to the nearest ⅛ mile.
4. Consult the chart below to determine your fitness level.
5. Cool-down with light jogging and stretching.

Distance (miles) Covered in 12 Minutes
Age (years)

Fitness Category		13–19	20–29	30–39	40–49	50–60	60 +
Very poor	(men)	> 1:30	> 1.22	> 1.8	> 1.14	> 1.03	> .87
	(women)	> 1.0	> .96	> .94	> .88	> .84	> .78
Poor	(men)	1.30–1.37	1.22–1.31	1.18–1.30	1.14–1.24	1.03–1.16	.87–1.02
	(women)	1.00–1.18	.96–1.11	.95–1.05	.88–.98	.84–.93	.78–.86
Fair	(men)	1.38–1.56	1.32–1.49	1.31–1.45	1.25–1.39	1.17–1.30	1.03–1.20
	(women)	1.19–1.29	1.12–1.22	1.06–1.18	.99–1.11	.94–1.05	.87–.98
Good	(men)	1.57–1.72	1.50–1.64	1.46–1.56	1.40–1.53	1.31–1.44	1.21–1.32
	(women)	1.30–1.43	1.23–1.34	1.19–1.29	1.12–1.24	1.06–1.18	.99–1.09
Excellent	(men)	1.73–1.86	1.65–1.76	1.57–1.69	1.54–1.65	1.45–1.58	1.33–1.55
	(women)	1.44–1.51	1.35–1.45	1.30–1.39	1.25–1.34	1.19–1.30	1.10–1.18
Superior	(men)	> 1.87	> 1.77	> 1.70	> 1.66	> 1.59	> 1.56
	(women)	> 1.52	> 1.46	> 1.40	> 1.35	> 1.31	> 1.19

< Means "less than"; > means "more than."

"Tests," from *The Aerobics Program for Total Well-Being* by Kenneth H. Cooper, M.D., M.P.H. Copyright 1982 by Kenneth H. Cooper. Used by permission of Bantam Books, a division of Bantam Doubleday Dell Publishing Group, Inc.

1. Measure distance covered, and round off to nearest ⅛ mile _____

2. Record age _____

3. Record sex _____

4. Determine fitness level _____

Lab Activity 3.3
Three-Minute Step Test

Purpose: To evaluate your level of cardiorespiratory endurance using the 3-minute step test.

Procedure:

1. Warm-up before testing and cool-down after testing.

2. For 3 minutes, continuously step up and down on a 12-inch bench at a rate of 24 steps per minute for 3 minutes. One complete cycle consists of "up with the left foot, up with the right foot, down with the left foot, down with the right foot."

3. Immediately after the 3 minutes of stepping, sit down. Within 5 seconds of sitting, count the heart rate for 1 full minute.

4. Record the 1-minute recovery rate and the fitness classification.

YMCA 3-Minute Step Test Postexercise 1-Minute Heart Rate (beats/min)

Age (yr)	18–25		26–35		36–45		46–55		56–65		> 65	
Gender	M	F	M	F	M	F	M	F	M	F	M	F
Excellent	50–76	52–81	51–76	58–80	49–76	51–84	56–82	63–91	60–77	60–92	59–81	70–92
Good	79–84	85–93	79–85	85–92	80–88	89–96	87–93	95–101	86–94	97–103	87–92	96–101
Above average	88–93	96–102	88–94	95–101	92–98	100–104	95–101	104–110	97–100	106–111	94–102	104–111
Average	95–100	104–110	96–102	104–110	100–105	107–112	103–111	113–118	103–109	113–118	104–110	116–121
Below average	102–107	113–120	104–110	113–119	108–113	115–120	113–119	120–124	111–117	119–127	114–118	123–126
Poor	111–119	122–131	114–121	122–129	116–124	124–132	121–126	126–132	119–128	129–135	121–126	128–133
Very poor	124–157	135–169	126–161	134–171	130–163	137–169	131–159	137–171	131–154	141–174	130–151	135–155

Note: Pulse is to be counted for 1 full minute following 3 minutes of stepping at 24 steps/minute on a 12-inch bench.

Source: YMCA. *Y'S Way to Fitness,* 4th ed., 1998. Reprinted with permission from the YMCA of the USA.

1. Record the 1-minute recovery rate _____

2. Record your age   _____

3. Record your sex   _____

4. Record your fitness category   _____

Lab Activity 3.4
Post-50 Walk Test

Purpose: To determine the aerobic fitness category by a simple walk test.

Procedure:

1. Establish a 400-m distance on a level terrain.
2. Start timing the walk on the first movement.
3. Proceed walking at a pace within the personal comfort zone.
4. Record the time in minutes needed to cover the 400-m.
5. Use the chart below to find your aerobic fitness.

	MEN					WOMEN		
Ages		**Time (mins) for 400-m Walk**						
50–64	> 5:09	5:08–4:12	4:11–3:46	< 3:45	> 5:06	5:05–4:15	4:14–3:56	< 3:55
65–74	> 5:09	5:08–4:15	4:14–3:46	< 3:45	> 5:43	5:42–4:37	4:36–4:17	< 4:16
75–84	> 5:40	5:39–4:31	4:30–3:55	< 3:54	> 7:01	7:00–5:30	5:29–4:57	< 4:56
> 84	> 8:50	8:49–5:55	5:54–4:48	< 4:47	> 8:51	8:50–6:20	6:19–5:10	< 5:09
FITNESS	**LOW**	**FAIR**	**GOOD**	**HIGH**	**LOW**	**FAIR**	**GOOD**	**HIGH**

Bell, R. D, et. al. (1984) *The post-50 "3-S" physical performance test.* Durkin and Assoc., Ltd.

1. Record the time in minutes to cover 400-m _____
2. Record your age   _____
3. Record your sex   _____
4. Record your aerobic fitness level   _____

Lab Activity 3.5
Post-50 Step Test

Purpose: To estimate the aerobic capacity by stepping in place.

Procedure:

1. Start in the standing position with or without a hand support (back of a chair or person).
2. Begin the time as soon as the person lifts the right foot.
3. Each step should raise the knee parallel to hip level (close to 90 degree angle).
4. The stepping intensity should be within a personal comfort zone.
5. Count the number of times the left foot touches the floor within a 2-minute period.
6. Use the chart below to estimate the aerobic fitness category.

Aerobic Fitness Category as Determined by Number of Steps in 2 Min.

	MEN					WOMEN		
Age (y)			Number of steps in 2 min					
50–64	0–67	68–85	86–100	> 100	0–60	51–75	76–96	> 96
65–74	0–57	58–78	79–96	> 97	0–55	56–68	69–90	> 91
75–84	0–50	51–75	76–92	> 93	0–33	34–57	58–79	> 80
> 85	0–50	51–70	71–87	> 88	0–31	32–53	54–66	> 67
FITNESS	LOW	FAIR	GOOD	HIGH	LOW	FAIR	GOOD	HIGH

Bell, et al., (1984). *The post 50 "3-S" physical performance test.* Durkin and Associates, Ltd.

1. Record the number of steps in 2 minutes _____
2. Record your age _____
3. Record your sex _____
4. Record your fitness level _____

Lab Activity 3.6

The Rockport Fitness Walking Test

Purpose: To determine aerobic fitness.

Procedure: The Rockport Fitness Walking Test estimates aerobic capacity. The guidelines for taking the test are as follows:

1. Set up a walking course, preferably a 440-yard track.
2. Warm up for 5 to 10 minutes.
3. Wear good walking shoes and loose-fitting clothes.
4. Walk 1 mile as fast as possible.
5. Record your heart rate immediately after the test (end of one mile). Count your pulse for 15 seconds and multiply by 4, record this number. Mark this rate on the chart on the following pages that is appropriate for your age and gender.
6. Find your time in minutes and your heart rate per minute. Follow these lines until they meet, and mark this point on the chart. This point lets you know how you compare to other individuals of your same age and sex.
7. Cool down. Repeat the stretching exercises you used in the warm-up.

Age 20–29

Males Females

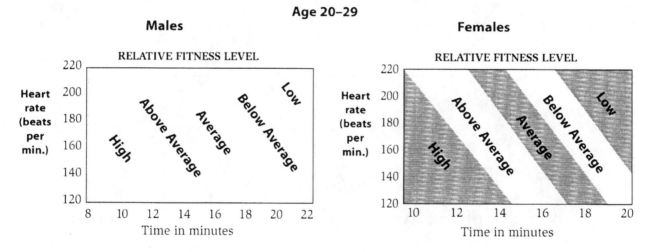

Age 30–39

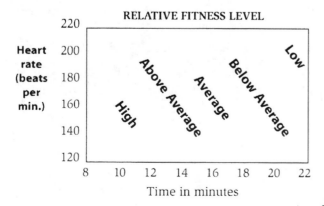

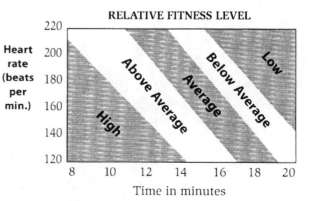

Males   **Females**

Age 40–49

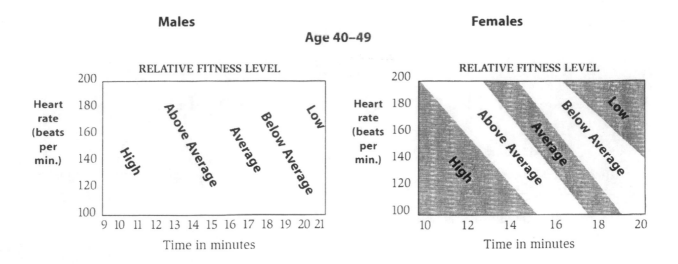

Age 50–59

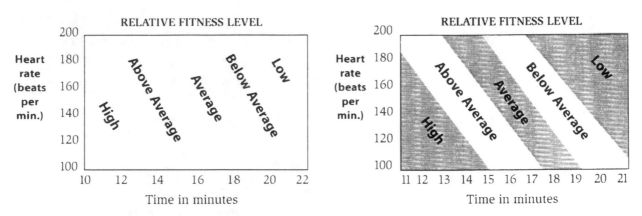

Age 60–69

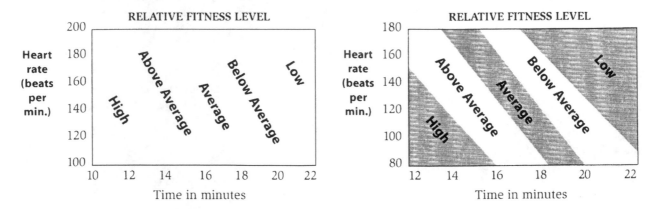

80

% of Maximum Heart Rate Chart (10-second Count)

Age	60%	70%	80%
20–29	19–20	22–23	25–27
30–39	18–19	21–22	24–25
40–49	17–18	20–21	23–24
50–59	16–17	19–20	21–23
60 +	14–16	16–18	19–21

Resting Heart Rate _____

Heart Rate at the end of the mile _____

Time to walk the mile _____

Name: _____ Section: _____ Date: _____

Lab Activity 3.7
Cardiorespiratory Progress

Purpose: To track your cardiorespiratory endurance ratings

Procedures:

1. Choose one or more of the test listed in the lab activities in this chapter to evaluate your cardiorespiratory endurance.
2. Record your scores on the following charts.

Test 1 Date_____

Test	Scores	Fitness Rating
1.5-Mile Timed Run Test	Time:	
12-Minute Walking/ Running Test	Time:	
3-Minute Step Test	Pulse Rate:	
Rockport Fitness Walking Test	Time: Pulse Rate:	

Test 2 Date_____

Test	Scores	Fitness Rating
1.5-Mile Timed Run Test	Time:	
12-Minute Walking/ Running Test	Time:	
3-Minute Step Test	Pulse Rate:	
Rockport Fitness Walking Test	Time: Pulse Rate:	

Lab Activity 3.8
Measuring Your Heart Rate

Purpose: To measure your heart rate in several locations

Procedures:

1. Use your fingertips to measure your pulse at the radial artery (wrist). Do not use your thumb to measure the pulse.
2. Count the beats for 15 seconds
3. Multiply by 4 to get the beats per minute
4. Using the fingertips measure the pulse in the carotid artery in the neck.
   a. count the beats for 10 seconds and multiply by 6
   b. count the beats for 30 seconds and multiply by 2

15 seconds × 4 = _____

10 seconds × 6 = _____

30 seconds × 2 = _____

Which method was the easiest to complete? _____

Which method was the most accurate? _____

Which method do you prefer? _____ Why? _____

_____

_____

Muscle Strength and Muscle Endurance

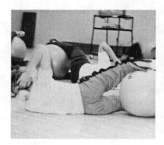  

Objectives

After completing this chapter, you will be able to do the following:

★ Define muscular strength and muscular endurance.

★ Identify benefits of resistance training.

★ Discuss the anatomy and physiology of skeletal muscles.

★ Identify weight training principles, exercise techniques, and the composition of program design.

★ List and explain weight training components such as amount of weight, frequency of training, number of sets and repetitions to use, and know the features of exercise safety.

★ Evaluate your strength and muscular endurance.

★ Discuss various ways to motivate yourself and keep your training habits consistent.

★ *Muscle strength and muscle endurance development is absolutely essential if you are trying to reach your full fitness potential. Whether you are an athlete or someone who leads a sedentary lifestyle, weight training can help you attain your fitness goals. Weight training is one of the most widely practiced forms of exercise, yielding many positive results. Men, women, children, older adults, people in rehabilitation, athletes, nonathletes, fitness enthusiasts, individuals with disabilities, and couch potatoes can all benefit from weight training.*

It would be impossible to list all of the benefits one can derive from a well-planned weight training program. And no, weight training will not transform you from a weak, unfit body into a bodybuilding or strength champion overnight. It takes dedication and a positive attitude.

Whether you think you can or think you can't, you're right.

—Henry Ford

Weight training imparts benefits physically, mentally, emotionally, socially, and even spiritually. In other words, weight training can have a positive impact on total personal development. A listing of the benefits of exercise can be found elsewhere in this book. Some research has even shown that weight training may improve all of the five components of health-related fitness better than any other single type of exercise. Think about the five fitness components: muscle strength, muscle endurance, flexibility, body composition, and cardiorespiratory endurance. Weight training, if performed according to sound principles, can improve all five of these fitness components. How many other single forms of exercise can make this statement? Very few, if any.

Besides all of the obvious physiological benefits, one of the greatest benefits of regular weight training is not the improved stamina, stronger muscles, and sculpted body, but the fact that you just simply feel better. When you feel good about yourself, you tend to exercise harder. When you exercise harder, you start looking better. When you start enjoying your new look, you tend to become more sociable. When you become more sociable, you make new friends, which in turn helps your emotional state, which in turn helps you mentally, which in turn enables you to learn more about exercise, which in turn . . . well, I think you get the idea.

Weight training can help us attain our goals and to feel good about ourselves. Maybe one day soon we can echo the words of Thoreau:

I inhabit my body with inexpressible satisfaction.

Muscle Strength

Muscle strength can be defined as the amount of force that can be exerted by a muscle or muscle group in one repetition. Muscle strength may be referred to as one repetition maximum, or **1 RM.** Maintenance of a certain level of muscle strength is essential for normal living. In general, the most efficient way to attain muscular strength is to lift heavy weights with low repetitions. This will be discussed in more detail later in this chapter.

Power is associated with muscle strength, in that power is the product of strength and speed, generating a large amount of force quickly. For

purposes of this chapter, we will concentrate on development of muscle strength and muscle endurance.

Muscle Endurance

Muscle endurance is the ability to perform repetitions against resistance for an extended period of time. For example, performing 15 push-up exercises would be an example of muscle endurance. Again, as with muscle strength, a certain level of muscle endurance is essential for normal, everyday functioning. In fact, for most people, developing muscle endurance is more important than developing muscle strength, as far as carrying out activities that we all need to do in our day-to-day life. Muscle endurance can be attained through weight training of lighter resistance and higher repetitions.

Muscle Physiology

Your body has over 600 muscles. All human movement, from the blinking of an eye to lifting weights depends on muscle contraction.

There are three types of muscle tissue—*smooth, cardiac,* and *skeletal*—and each has different structures and functions. **Smooth muscle tissue,** also called involuntary muscle, consists of long, spindle-shaped fibers with each fiber containing only one nucleus. The smooth muscle tissue is located in the walls of the esophagus, stomach, and intestines, where they move food and waste products through the digestive tract. **Cardiac muscle** is found in the heart, and it too is not under our conscious control. The heart muscle contracts at a slow, steady rate while resting but increases the rate while exercising. For purposes of this chapter, we are more concerned with the **skeletal muscle.** We can consciously control skeletal muscle, also called voluntary muscles. These muscles provide the force needed to move the skeleton, so we need to look at how to exercise these muscles to enhance muscle strength and muscle endurance.

Skeletal muscles have four characteristics:

- *Extensibility*—ability of the muscle to stretch, or change length
- *Elasticity*—ability of the muscle to return to normal resting length after being stretched
- *Contractility*—ability of the muscle to contract, or shorten, in response to a stimulus
- *Excitability*—ability of the muscle to receive a stimulus from the nervous system

Connective tissue attaches a muscle to a bone. This juncture is called a tendon. Any contraction of the muscle pulls on the tendon, which in turn pulls the bone, causing movement. As you can see, muscles can only pull, they do not push to cause movement. In some exercises you push an object away from your body, such as a weight training exercise called a bench press. This is accomplished by muscles pulling on the bones, not by muscle tissue pushing the bone.

A muscle contracts in response to stimulation by the central nervous system. A single motor neuron controls a group of muscle fibers. A motor neuron and the muscle fibers it controls are called a motor unit. For a muscle to contract, an electrical impulse is sent from the central nervous system to the connection between a motor nerve and a muscle fiber. This is where communication between the nervous and muscular systems occurs. Also, when stimulated by the central nervous system, a muscle fiber contracts fully, to 100% of its potential, or it does not contract at all. This is referred to as the all-or-none principle, and it applies to all muscles in the body.

Two small protein filaments are primarily responsible for muscle contraction: *actin* and *myosin*. **Actin** filaments are thinner than myosin filaments. Remember muscle fibers contract by shortening. How does this occur? Basically, the actin filaments in the muscle slide inward and past the myosin filaments. During this sliding (contraction) the actin filaments are brought closer to each other, thus shortening the muscle fiber. This process, explained here in its simplest form, is called the sliding filament theory of muscular contraction (Figure 4.0). Again, this all started by receiving a message from the central nervous system.

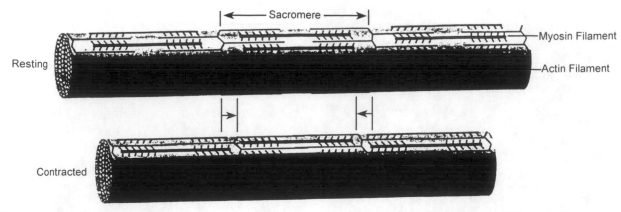

Resting

Sacromere

Myosin Filament

Actin Filament

Contracted

Figure 4.0 During muscle contraction, cross bridges from the myosin attach to actin filaments and pull the actin filaments toward the center of the sacromere.

Skeletal muscle consists of two types of fibers that respond to training. These are Type I (slow twitch) and Type II (fast twitch). Type I or slow twitch fibers generate less tension and have a greater capacity for aerobic work but are more resistant to fatigue. Endurance training activities use slow twitch fibers. Type II or fast twitch fibers are less resistant to fatigue but can produce greater tension. The individuals who possess a large number of Type II fibers have a capacity for anaerobic work. Each person is born with both types of fibers. Individuals who have a larger percent of fast twitch fibers will develop larger muscles and more strength. Slow twitch fibers allow an individual to develop muscular endurance.

Types of Muscle Actions

Skeletal muscle is capable of three different types of contractions: *an isometric contraction, a concentric contraction,* and *an eccentric contraction.* An **isometric** contraction occurs when a muscle generates force against a fixed or immovable resistance, but there is no change in length of the muscle. An example of an isometric contraction is if you were to pull against an object that was too heavy for you to move. Your muscles contract and generate force but do not shorten or lengthen. In an isotonic movement the muscle will undergo both a concentric and an eccentric contraction. A **concentric** contraction is when your muscles shorten to overcome resistance, such as lifting a barbell from your waist to your shoulders with a supinated grip.

In this exercise your biceps shorten or contract to lift the resistance. An **eccentric** contraction occurs when muscles lengthen, such as in the previous example of a bicep curl exercise. Your bicep shortens to lift the resistance, then lengthens as you lower the barbell. Both types of contractions will build the muscle. Delayed onset muscle soreness is more likely to be caused by eccentric contraction.

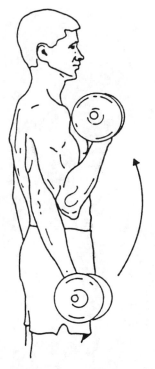

Figure 4.1 Concentric contraction by elbow flexors.

It is important to know what muscles you are strengthening as you perform different exercises. Knowing and understanding this list will help you to make the connection between your body and the exercises you choose for your individual program.

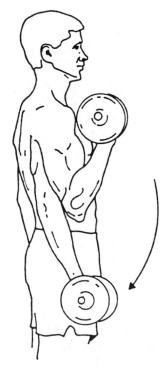

Figure 4.2 Eccentric contraction by elbow flexors.

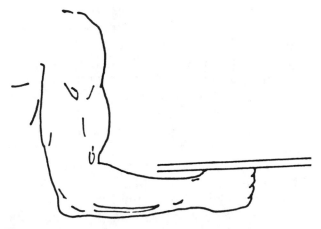

Figure 4.3 Isometric contraction by elbow flexors.

Type of Resistance Training

There are a number of different techniques of resistance training for you to use, and all can have a positive effect on muscle strength and endurance. The key is to determine what type of equipment is available to you, what works for you, and what you enjoy. **Isometric** exercise is when the muscle contracts against a fixed resistance but does not change length. We discussed an isometric muscle contraction earlier in this chapter. You can train isometrically with or without weights, such as barbells or exercise machines. Naturally, since your muscles are not changing length with isometric exercise, strength gains are limited to the general area of range of motion, approximately 20 degrees on either side of the joint angle trained. An example of this would be if you performed an isometric leg press at 90 degrees of flexion. You could expect strength gains to occur between

70 degrees and 110 degrees of flexion. An option would be to perform isometric leg presses at different degrees of flexion to attempt to illicit gains in strength throughout the entire range of motion. Isometric exercise is often used in rehabilitation settings when joint motion is contraindicated. There are other advantages of isometrics, such as working through *sticking points* in weight training. For example, there may be a point in the range when doing the bench press exercise that is very difficult to lift through. This is a *sticking point,* and performing an isometric contraction in this particular difficult range of motion may help to overcome this problem.

One drawback to isometric exercise may be that it could produce a rise in blood pressure, as pressure tends to increase within the chest cavity as you hold your breath while contracting against an immovable resistance. To avoid or minimize this, regulate your breathing patterns.

Another type of resistance training is **DCER—Dynamic Constant External Resistance.** In this type of training there is a fixed resistance that your muscles contract against while undergoing either concentric or eccentric muscle actions, or both. Examples of this type of resistance training are barbells, dumbbells, and certain weight machines.

Isokinetic exercise causes a muscle to change in length, but the contraction is performed at a constant velocity. An isokinetic machine will have a preset speed that helps to regulate speed of movement, which is important when resistance training. Some people tend to lift entirely too fast, and isokinetic machinery may be ideal in this situation.

Variable resistance machines adapt to the body's strength curves. These machines will change the resistance as you go through the range of motion. This can be useful as you tend to be stronger or weaker depending on the angle of pull in an exercise. For example, with the squat exercise, in which you are attempting to stand up from a squatting position, you are stronger in the top half of the range of motion, which is the last half of the movement before straightening the legs. This is called an **ascending strength curve.** On a variable resistance machine, the resistance will be more in that angle of pull in which you are stronger, and less in the angle of pull in which you are not as

strong. With some exercises you have a **descending curve** in which you are stronger in the bottom half of the lift, or first half. An example of this would be an upright row barbell exercise, in which you attempt to pull a bar from your waist toward your chin, than you would be from this halfway point up to your chin. When lifting dumbbells or barbells, you may have noticed that at some points in the range of motion, it is easier or more difficult for you, even though the resistance did not change. With variable resistance training, your muscle will contract closer to maximum at all times. Another strength curve is the **bell-shaped curve** where you tend to be stronger toward the mid-point of the exercise.

Plyometric training is another form of resistance exercise. This type of training attempts to take advantage of powerful concentric contractions. Plyometrics involve abrupt, explosive movements. The faster a muscle is stretched with rapid eccentric loading, the more powerful its concentric contraction potential becomes. Some examples of plyometric exercise are hops, bounds, depth jumping, and medicine ball throws. This type of training can be very intensive and should be used wisely and care-

Table 4.0 Advantages/Disadvantages of Isometric, Isotonic, & Isokinetic Contractions

Contraction	Advantages	Disadvantages
Isotonic	Improves strength through full range of motion Improves joint flexibility Motivating	Requires more equipment Higher risk of muscle soreness If not done correctly the benefits will diminish Risk of injury increases
Isometric	Requires little or no equipment Low risk of muscle soreness Can be done in small spaces Rapid strength improvement Used to rehabilitate joints	Not very motivating Difficult to devise a full-body workout Raises blood pressure Muscles do not change in length
Isokinetic	Moves muscles through full range of motion Maximum resistance applied at all angles Speed of muscle contraction is kept constant	Equipment is specialized and expensive

fully. Athletes use this type of training for power development. It is not recommended for those of us who are primarily interested in the health benefits of exercise. A drawback of this type of resistance exercise is that there is a higher risk for injuries.

Principles of Weight Training

There are many principles and/or key concepts to know and to put to use if you want to improve your levels of muscle strength and muscle endurance. Invest some quality time into learning what these principles mean, and then you can apply them to your exercise program in a wise and efficient manner.

Principles

- All-or-None Principle—A muscle fiber contracts completely or not at all.
- Muscle Atrophy—Muscles shrink in size.
- Muscle Hypertrophy—Muscles increase in size.
- Overload—Place a greater stress on the musculature than normal, progressively increasing the amount of work to be performed.
- Reversibility—If strength training is discontinued, the muscle will atrophy.

Consistency in training will help you maintain and further improve.

- Progression—Overload and progression go hand in hand. Progression is necessary to prevent muscle soreness. Instead of starting your weight training program at a high rate of intensity, it is wise to start slowly with light weights.
- Specificity—Use different types of resistance training programs depending on the specific muscle you want to develop.
- SAID—Specific Adaptation to Imposed Demand—The type of demand placed on the body dictates the type of adaptation or results that will occur. For example, a lot of distance running may improve your level of cardiovascular endurance, but will do little to improve your muscle strength. Train with a purpose in mind.
- Individuality Principle—Everyone responds to training differently, and each of us adapts to exercise at our own rate.
- Muscle Isolation—Do not contract muscles not directly involved in exercise.
- Muscle Balance—Exercise your entire body so you will develop muscles in proportion.
- Continuous Tension—Perform repetitions smoothly, no jerking.

PHYSICAL ACTIVITY PYRAMID

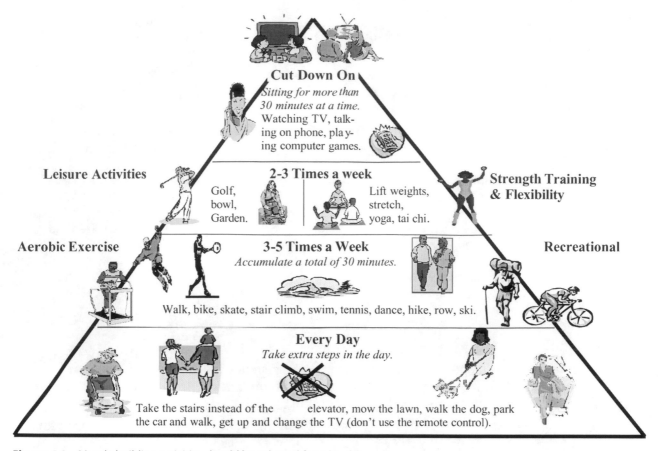

Figure 4.4   Muscle building activities should be selected from level 3.

- Priority Training—At times, it may be useful to train weaker areas of your body first in the workout.
- Cycle Training—Vary the intensity levels of your workouts.
- Cheating—Using extraneous body motion takes away from the effectiveness of the exercise.
- Concentration Principle—Feel the muscle being worked; do not worry so much about the amount of weight being lifted.
- Overtraining—Doing more than your body can adapt to can lead to regression of your goals.
- Diminishing Returns—Most health and fitness benefits are achieved in one set, not five sets. Research has shown that more than 50% of benefits may occur in the first set. Each additional set produces less benefit. ACSM recommends one-set programs for most people.

Program Design

The amount of resistance used when weight training is an aspect of your exercise program that needs careful analysis. Although you need to use an amount of weight that is most conducive for reaching your goals, do not fixate on how much you are lifting. Rather, concentrate on how the muscle or muscles that are performing the work feel. When using proper equipment, a muscle may contract more efficiently when moving a lighter weight, as opposed to moving a heavy weight with improper technique. At the same time, you need to be cognizant of how much resistance you are using, as you constantly need to be aware of trying to apply the overload principle, which means providing greater stress on the body than is normal.

One of the best methods of determining the amount of resistance to use when weight training is to use a percentage of the repetition max-

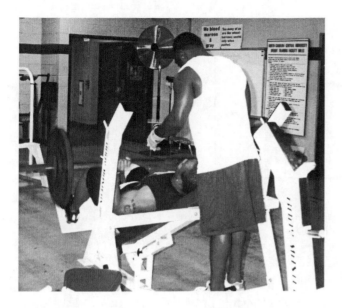

imum (RM). RM is the maximal number of repetitions that can be performed with a certain weight. For example, if an individual can perform five, but not six, repetitions on a certain exercise with 100 pounds, this individual has a 5 RM of 100 pounds. In general, strength and power are best developed from loads of 75 to 80% of 1 RM. Hypertrophy seems to develop best with loads between 60 and 75%, whereas muscle endurance is best developed with loads between 40 and 60%.

Another important consideration when developing a weight training program is how long you should rest between sets. Rest periods between sets can greatly influence the results you will get from your exercise program.

For strength gains, rest periods between sets should be approximately a 1:3 work-rest ratio. In other words, for every 1 minute of lifting, you should rest 3 minutes. Very heavy loads may require more rest time than this 1:3 work-rest ratio. This extended rest period allows the muscle to recover between sets. Exercises should be rotated so certain muscles are exercised on one day and others on the next day to allow adequate time for rest and recovery of muscle groups.

If your goal is muscle hypertrophy, muscle endurance, or both, your work-rest ratio should be approximately 1:1. You can even reduce your rest periods below this level, and good results should follow. Cutting back on your rest periods helps you to achieve the "muscle pump," which is the hard, tight feeling you

sometimes feel in a muscle when it is being exercised. Your muscles may feel this way after becoming engorged with blood.

When planning your rest periods, remember that they should be, for the most part, determined by the goals of the training program. Also be sure to allow for adequate rest between training sessions. A good general rule is to allow 48 hours rest between workouts for a particular muscle group. Of course, the amount of rest between training sessions depends on the recovery ability of the individual; this is an example of **Individuality Principle,** which we discussed earlier.

If your goal is to increase aerobic endurance through weight training, you may decrease your rest period between sets to 30 seconds or less. Circuit training, which is a workout with a series of exercises performed in sequence at various exercise stations, has shown to increase levels of muscle endurance and aerobic endurance.

How many training sessions should you perform on a weekly basis? Again, this would depend greatly on your training goals. When deciding how many days per week to train, always remember the general rule of allowing 48 hours rest time between workouts for a particular muscle group. There are exceptions to this guideline; some studies have even suggested that exercising 3 consecutive days and resting 3 consecutive days is superior to the alternating-day frequency. You have to adapt the training frequency to meet your individual response to training and your goals. For most individuals, it seems that two or more training sessions per week are necessary for strength gains, and once a week maintains the gains you have made. For optimal results, three to four training sessions per week may be advantageous for many people. When performing multiple-joint exercises, frequency should be lower than when performing single-joint exercises.

Training volume is the total amount of weight lifted in a workout. Volume can be determined by multiplying the number of sets times the number of repetitions times the amount of resistance lifted on each repetition. For example, if you perform 3 sets of 10 repetitions with 100 pounds in the bench press exercise, your training volume would be 3,000 pounds. Of course, as stated previously, training volume is

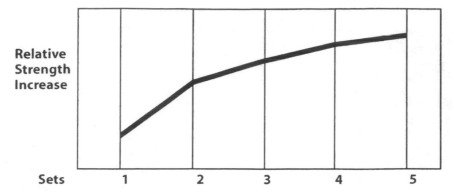

Figure 4.5 Relationship between the number of sets and increases in strength. Reprinted from *Getting Stronger* by Bill Pearl and Gary T. Moran. Copyright © 1986 Shelter Publications Inc., Bolinas, CA.

the total amount of weight lifted in a workout, so most volumes would be much higher than this example using the bench press.

How many sets are needed for optimum development of muscle strength and muscle endurance? This will vary with the individual and his or her goals. For beginners, a general guideline is to complete one to 3 sets for the major muscle groups. Three to five sets of exercise might produce the best gains in strength development for most people. Figure 4.5 illustrates this point.

When formulating your exercise plan, think about how many sets you will need to perform in order to reach your goals in a safe, efficient manner. Keep in mind that the volume of exercise for a beginner would be rather low but should increase as training adaptations occur. For most people, performing over 5 sets of a particular exercise may be detrimental, possibly

leading to overtraining. But again, the **Individuality Principle** prevails here, as some people respond positively to a low number of sets and others might need the stimulation of up to 5 or more sets. Incorporate what works for you, what is safe, and what your goals are.

Repetitions, which are how many times you lift the weight in each set, is another aspect of weight training to consider. As with most weight training guidelines, this aspect of your exercise program depends on many variables, one of which would be your training goals. For strength development, your repetitions should be relatively low, somewhere in the 1 to 8 range. For muscle hypertrophy, 8 to 12 repetitions will help you meet your objectives, and for muscle endurance, you should perform 12 to 20 repetitions.

Safety

Safety is a critical factor to consider when developing and implementing your program. ACSM (1998) suggests the program should:

- Be progressive
- Be individualized
- Use full range of motion
- Stimulate major muscle groups

Following are some guidelines to make your exercise session safe.

1. Warm up properly with light aerobic activities for 5–7 minutes.
2. Become thoroughly familiar with the technique of an exercise, especially before using heavy resistance.

3. Do not use a jerking, twisting body motion to lift the resistance; maintain your body in proper alignment. Use proper techniques to reduce risks for injury.

4. Use a spotter, especially if you are lifting heavy weights or are performing new exercises. Never lift alone.

5. Avoid unsafe exercises, such as full squats. Select exercises that involve all muscle groups.

6. A weight training belt may be useful if you are lifting heavy weights and/or performing exercise that stresses the lower back region.

7. Some people like to wear weight training gloves, while others prefer not to. You may want to experiment with this to see what feels comfortable to you.

8. Breathe normally while lifting and be sure not to hold your breath for long periods of time. Avoid holding your breath as it increases the pressure in your chest.

9. Be cognizant of other people in the weight room.

10. After using weight equipment, place it back where it should be. Do not leave weights on barbells or on the floor, where they can be a hazard.

11. Always remember that a weight training facility is to be used for working out, not as a play area.

12. Use collars on all free weight exercises, such as barbells and dumbbells.

13. Control your speed of movement when lifting.

14. Wear shoes that offer good support.

15. Keep up-to-date and accurate records.

16. Do not use anabolic steroids.

17. Customize your program to fit your specific needs and allow adequate recovery time between sets of exercise.

Testing and Evaluation

Before starting a weight training program, and at regular intervals once you have commenced your program, it will be useful for you to evaluate yourself. This testing will help you keep track of the progress you are making, and it can give you feedback on what kind of adjustments you need to make in your program. Two good evaluative procedures to use for testing of muscle endurance are the sit-up and push-up tests. For charting progress of muscle strength, the 1 RM (repetition maximum) bench press and the 1 RM seated leg press are good tools to use. Complete the lab activities at the end of the chapter.

Major Muscles of the Human Body

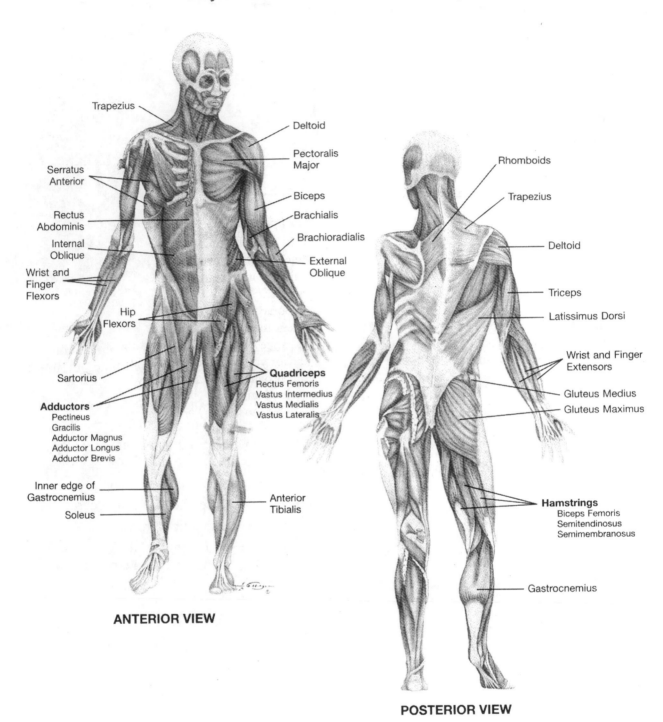

ANTERIOR VIEW

POSTERIOR VIEW

Figure 4.6 Major muscles of the human body.

Weight Training for Life

There are three keys to keep in mind when weight training. If you adhere to these basic guidelines, you will continue to progress with your exercise program. They are knowledge, consistency, and intensity. Educate yourself about weight training and learn all you can so you can incorporate what you learn into making your own individual exercise program. Use this knowledge when training and keep safety and efficiency in mind. Train consistently. Do not fall into the routine of training for a couple of weeks, taking a week off, then starting back, and so forth. This is not the way to go about exercising. Train on a regular basis.

Intensity does not mean you have to train with superhuman effort all the time, but you do need to exercise with the overload principle in mind. Be sure to progress slowly so your gains will not stagnate. Cycle your training, some days work out harder than other days, and listen to your body. If it tells you that you are doing damage, it would behoove you to listen.

Stay motivated and realize that exercise has a start line, but no finish line. Health is a never ending process. Think about the following quotations from time to time; they may help motivate you to keep on trying when you feel down. Remember there is *no doubt* weight training can help you attain your goals. It is up to **you** to make it work for **you.**

We all have a habit of inferiority to our full self.

William James

Exercise can narrow the gap between what we are and what we can be.

We do not decrease activity because we are old; we grow old because we decrease activity.

You only live once, but if you live right, once is enough.

Plato

Really think about this one!

The trained body gives us maximum available energy. Why place ourselves at a disadvantage? Are we going to get the most out of the person we are or aren't we?

Plato

References

American College of Sports Medicine. (2006). *ACSM's resource manual for guidelines for exercise testing and prescription*, 6th ed. Philadelphia: Lea & Febiger.

American College of Sports Medicine. (1998). The recommended quantity and quality of exercise for developing and maintaining cardiorespiratory and muscular fitness and flexibility in healthy adults. *Medicine & Science in Sports & Exercise, 30,* 975–991.

Anberg, E. (1996). *Bio-mechanically correct.* Dallas, TX: Realistic Individualized Professional Training Services.

Baechle, T.R. (1994). *National strength and conditioning association: Essentials of strength training and conditioning.* Champaign, IL: Human Kinetics.

Bailey, C. (1994). *Smart exercise.* Boston: Houghton Mifflin.

Edlin, I.G. (1996). *Health and wellness.* Sudbury, MA: Jones & Bartlett.

Fahey, T. (1997). *Fit and well.* Mountain View, CA: Mayfield Publishing.

Fleck, S. & Kraemer, W. (1997). *Designing resistance training programs.* Champaign, IL: Human Kinetics.

Hesson, J. (1998). *Weight training for life.* Englewood, CO: Morton Publishing.

Hoeger, W.W.K. & Hoeger, S.A. (2003). *Lifetime fitness and wellness,* 7th ed. United States: Thomson–Wadsworth.

Hoeger, W.W.K. & Hoeger, S.A. (2006). *Principles and labs for physical fitness,* 5th ed. United States: Thomson–Wadsworth.

Howley, E. & Franks, D. (1992). *Health fitness instructors handbook.* Campaign, IL: Human Kinetics.

McArdle, W.D., Katch, F.I., & Katch, V.L. (1991). *Exercise physiology: Energy, nutrition, and human performance.* Philadelphia: Lea & Febiger.

Moran, G. & McGlynn, G. (1990). *Dynamics of strength training.* Dubuque, IA: Wm. C. Brown Publishers.

Paffenbarger, R. (1996). *Lifefit.* Champaign, IL: Human Kinetics.

Prentice, W. (1997). *Fitness for college and life.* St. Louis, MO: Mosby-Year Book.

Web Sites

American College of Sports Medicine *www.acsm.org*

Exercise Prescription *www.exrx.net*

National Strength and Conditioning Association *www.ncsf.org*

Name: _____ Section: _____ Date: _____

Lab Activity 4.0
Push-Ups

Purpose: To evaluate muscular strength and endurance of the triceps and biceps.

Procedures:

1. Perform either the standard push-up or modified push-up. The Cooper Institute developed the ratings for men performing the push-ups and women performing the modified push-ups.

2. Push-ups: Start in the up position with your body supported by your hands and feet. Start the modified push-up position with the body supported by your hands and knees. Your arms and your back should be straight and your fingers pointed forward.

Figure 4.7a

Figure 4.7b

3. Lower your chest to the floor, keeping your back straight, then return to starting position. Have a partner place his or her fist directly under the chest. Lower yourself until your chest touches your partner's fist.

4. Perform as many push-ups or modified push-ups as you can without stopping.

5. Check the chart below to indicate your fitness level.

Ratings for the Push-Up and Modified Push-Up Tests

Number of Push-Ups

Men	Very Poor	Poor	Fair	Good	Excellent	Superior
Age: 18–29	Below 22	22–28	29–36	37–46	47–61	Above 61
30–39	Below 17	17–23	24–29	30–38	39–51	Above 51
40–49	Below 11	11–17	18–23	24–29	30–39	Above 39
50–59	Below 9	9–12	13–18	19–24	25–38	Above 38
60 and over	Below 6	6–9	10–17	18–22	23–27	Above 27

Number of Modified Push-Ups

Women	Very Poor	Poor	Fair	Good	Excellent	Superior
Age: 18–29	Below 17	17–22	23–29	30–35	36–44	Above 44
30–39	Below 11	11–18	19–23	24–30	31–38	Above 38
40–49	Below 6	6–12	13–17	18–23	24–32	Above 32
50–59	Below 6	6–11	12–16	17–20	21–27	Above 27
60 and over	Below 2	2–4	5–11	12–14	15–19	Above 19

Source: Based on norms from the Cooper Institute for Aerobics Research, Dallas, Texas.

1. Record the number of push-ups completed _____
2. Record your age _____
3. Record your sex _____
4. Record your fitness level _____

Lab Activity 4.1

Bent Knee Curl-Ups

Purpose: To assess abdominal muscle strength.

Procedure:

1. Lie flat on your back, knees bent with feet flat on the floor, and cross your arms across your chest, resting your hands on your shoulders. (Knees bent 90 degrees with feet flat and 18 inches from the buttocks).
2. Count the number of curl-ups you can do in 1 minute.
3. Arms must touch the thighs and back must touch the floor.
4. Check chart below to determine your fitness level.

Figure 4.8a

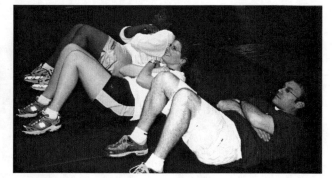

Figure 4.8b

Bent-Knee Curl-Ups Score

	Age (Years)	Superior	Excellent	Very Good	Good	Average	Poor	Very Poor
Males	17–29	55 +	51–55	48–50	42–47	36–41	17–35	0–17
	30–39*	48 +	44–48	39–43	33–38	27–32	13–26	0–13
	40–49	43 +	39–43	34–38	28–33	23–27	11–22	0–11
	50–59	38 +	34–38	29–33	22–28	17–21	8–16	0–8
	60–69	35 +	31–35	25–30	18–24	13–17	6–12	0–6
Females	17–29	47 +	43–47	36–42	33–35	29–32	14–28	0–14
	30–39*	45 +	41–45	35–40	29–34	23–28	11–22	0–11
	40–49	40 +	35–40	31–34	24–30	19–23	9–18	0–9
	50–59	35 +	31–35	25–30	18–24	13–17	6–12	0–6
	60–69	30 +	26–30	21–25	15–20	11–14	5–10	0–5

Fitness Level

*The number of curl-ups for ages over 30 is estimated.

Chart of scores from Prentice (1997). *Fitness for college and life.* 5th ed., St. Louis: Mosby

1. Record the number of curl-ups completed in 1 minute _____
2. Record your age   _____
3. Record your sex   _____
4. Record your fitness level   _____

Lab Activity 4.2

Assessing Muscle Strength: 1 RM

Purpose: To evaluate your muscle strength using 1RM.

Procedures: 1RM refers to the maximum amount of weight you can lift for a specific exercise. Try a few presses with a small amount of weight so you can practice your technique.

Leg Press

1. Use a resistance machine for the leg press. Estimate how much weight you can lift two to three times. It is better to set the machine for a weight that is lower than the amount you believe you can lift.

2. Adjust the seat so that your knees are bent at a 70-degree angle to start.

3. Grasp the side handlebars, and push with your legs until your knees are fully extended.

4. Rest for several minutes, then repeat the press with a higher weight setting. It will take several attempts to determine the maximum amount of weight you can press.

5. Rating your leg press results:

    a. Divide your 1RM value by your body weight.

      1 RM _____ lb   body weight _____ lb = _____

    b. Find this ratio on the table below to determine your leg press rating.

    c. Record your results

      Leg press strength rating _____

Bench Press

1. Use a resistance machine for the arm press. Estimate how much weight you can lift two to three times. It is better to set the machine for a weight that is lower than the amount you believe you can lift.

2. Lie on the bench with your feet firmly on the floor. Grasp the handles with palms away from you; the tops of the handles should be aligned with the tops of your armpits.

3. Push the handles until arms are fully extended. Exhale as you lift. Keep your feet firmly placed on the floor, don't arch your back, and push the weight evenly with both right and left arms.

4. Rest for several minutes, then repeat the lift with a heavier weight. It will take several attempts to determine the maximum amount of weight you can lift.

5. Rate your bench press results:

    a. Divide your 1 RM value by your body weight.

      1 RM _____ lb   body weight _____ lb = _____

    b. Find this ratio on the chart below to determine your bench press strength rating

      Bench press strength rating _____

Standard Values for Bench Press Strength in 1 RM lb/lb Body Weight*

Rating	Age (yrs)				
	20–29	30–39	40–49	50–59	60 +
Men					
Excellent	> 1.25	> 1.07	> 0.96	> 0.85	> 0.77
Good	1.17–1.25	1.01–1.07	0.91–0.96	0.81–0.85	0.74–0.77
Average	0.97–1.16	0.86–1.00	0.78–0.90	0.70–0.80	0.64–0.73
Fair	0.88–0.96	0.79–0.85	0.72–0.77	0.65–0.69	0.60–0.63
Poor	< 0.88	< 0.79	< 0.72	< 0.65	< 0.60
Women					
Excellent	> 0.77	> 0.65	> 0.60	> 0.53	> 0.54
Good	0.72–0.77	0.62–0.65	0.57–0.60	0.51–0.53	0.51–0.54
Average	0.59–0.71	0.53–0.61	0.48–0.56	0.43–0.50	0.41–0.50
Fair	0.53–0.58	0.49–0.52	0.44–0.47	0.40–0.42	0.37–0.40
Poor	< 0.53	< 0.49	< 0.44	< 0.40	< 0.37

*Adapted from The Institute for Aerobics Research. 1985 Physical Fitness Norms. [Unpublished Data.] Dallas, TX, 1985.

Standard Values for Upper Leg Press Strength in 1 RM lb/lb Body Weight*

Rating	Age (yrs)				
	20–29	30–39	40–49	50–59	60 +
Men					
Excellent	> 2.07	> 1.87	> 1.75	> 1.65	> 1.55
Good	2.00–2.07	1.80–1.87	1.70–1.75	1.60–1.65	1.50–1.55
Average	1.83–1.99	1.63–1.79	1.56–1.69	1.46–1.59	1.37–1.49
Fair	1.65–1.82	1.55–1.62	1.50–1.55	1.40–1.45	1.31–1.36
Poor	< 1.65	< 1.55	< 1.50	< 1.40	< 1.31
Women					
Excellent	> 1.62	> 1.41	> 1.31	> 1.25	> 1.14
Good	1.54–1.62	1.35–1.41	1.26–1.31	1.13–1.25	1.08–1.14
Average	1.35–1.53	1.20–1.34	1.12–1.25	0.99–1.12	0.92–1.07
Fair	1.26–1.34	1.13–1.19	1.06–1.11	0.86–0.98	0.85–0.91
Poor	< 1.26	< 1.13	< 1.06	< 0.86	< 0.85

*Adapted from The Institute for Aerobics Research. 1985 Physical Fitness Norms. [Unpublished Data.] Dallas, TX, 1985.

Flexibility

Objectives

After completing this chapter, you will be able to do the following:

★ Define flexibility and describe its importance as a health-related fitness component.

★ Determine the difference between the types of flexibility.

★ Describe why it is important to obtain flexibility.

★ Demonstrate basic flexibility exercises.

★ Know the critical elements of flexibility exercises.

★ Design a personal flexibility program based on your needs.

★ Demonstrate the ability to use one or more flexibility assessments.

★ Understand safety elements associated with muscular flexibility.

★ Know the ACSM guidelines on flexibility.

*An important component of physical fitness is flexibility. Most Americans suffer from too little flexibility or hypomobility. Hypermobility means that a person has an excessive amount of flexibility. **Flexibility** is* *the ability of the joint or a series of joints to move freely through its full range of motion (ROM). Flexibility is considered joint-specific. Stretching is the main technique used to improve flexibility. Flexibility programs can be planned exercises designed to increase the range of motion of the joint or series of joints. **Range of motion** in the joint or joints determines flexibility. The terms flexibility and ROM are often interchangeable. Flexibility and stretching are not the same. Consider extension of the knee joint at 180 degrees (straight leg). As one flexes the knee joint toward 90 degrees or beyond the joint goes through the range of motion. The range of motion of a joint or joints depends on structural limitations. The joint structures that limit flexibility are skin, bone, connective tissue, tendons, muscles, and ligaments of the joint capsules. With the exception of bone, these structures are elastic in nature. The major limiting factor of joints are bony structures (elbow and knee joints). Flexibility exercises enable us to increase the range of movement. Though often neglected, it is an important health-related component of fitness.*

All daily activities require some degree of flexibility. Bending to tie a shoe or reaching over your head for a glass on the top shelf requires you to be flexible. An elite volleyball athlete needs adequate shoulder flexibility, a postal employee needs adequate low back flexibility; therefore, flexibility is a critical component for daily activities. Age, gender, and sedentary lifestyles are major factors affecting flexibility. Women and children tend to be more flexible or have a greater range of movement about a joint. Men and the elderly, by nature, tend to be less flexible. Regardless of age or gender, flexibility is a component of a well-developed fitness program. Flexibility is needed by everyone in order to sustain daily activities. Specific basic flexibility exercises will enhance daily living for a lifetime and prevent aches and pains of the joints.

The American College of Sports Medicine (ACSM) recommends a general stretching routine using static or proprioreceptive neuromuscular facilitation (PNF) 2 to 3 times per week and stretching the muscle/tendons to a point of mild discomfort. ACSM also recommends holding the stretch for 10 to 30 seconds and doing each stretch 3 to 4 times. Understandably, these are just basic guidelines. Many instructors have students doing flexibility exercises before and after activity. Recent research suggests that stretching before activity is probably unnecessary. It is important to maintain good form while stretching and having adequate flexibility.

Historically, flexibility did not have an impact on fitness until after World War II. It has been popular in the last 40 years. The main types of stretching (PNF and static) exercises are still used today. Throughout this chapter you will engage in and contemplate the benefits, proper techniques, self-assessment, safety, and recent research to develop and prescribe the best flexibility program for yourself and your peers. Good Luck!

Factors Limiting Flexibility

The degree of the range of motion is an indicator of a person's flexibility. According to Corbin et al. (2006), joint range of motion is important to flexibility. The amount of flexibility needed is unknown. Too much flexibility can be as detrimental as too little. Joint flexibility is important because it allows the joint to move through its full range of motion. Joint inflexibility can inhibit activities of daily life. The joint structures that limit flexibility are skin, bone, connective tissue, tendons, muscle, and ligaments of the joint capsules. Factors that limit flexibility include: (1) the bony structures of the joints; (2) age and gender; (3) physical activity; and (4) body composition.

Muscle—Tendons—Bony Structures

The **bony structure** may restrict the endpoint in the range of motion. An injured joint may form an excess of calcium in the space joint that will cause a joint to lose its ability to reach its full range of motion (ROM). Long muscles and tendons allow for a greater ROM. In general, we rely on the bony structure to stop movement at its normal endpoints in the range. **Muscles** and their **tendons** are often responsible for limiting the ROM. The muscles and tendons are elastic in nature, and through stretching exercises it is possible to increase the elasticity. Elasticity is the ability of a muscle to return to normal resting length after being stretched. The major limiting factors are the joint capsules including connective tissue and muscle. However, flexibility can be maintained and increased through appropriate exercise.

Age and Gender

Flexibility increases until adolescence because of the rapid changes in growth and we become progressively less flexible. Flexibility peaks during the 20s. The decline of flexibility, as we age, is due to the loss of elasticity. Adults will lose 3 to 4 inches of flexibility in the lower back. Osteoarthritis can limit flexibility. When flexibility declines it interferes with our ability to function effectively during daily activities and in some cases live independently. The decline of flexibility as we age correlates to low back pain and muscle aches and pains. By incorporating flexibility exercises in their daily routines, including large muscle groups and particularly the regions of the low back and hamstrings, the elderly can enhance their flexibility. Regular stretching can help adults maintain good flexibility throughout the life span.

As a general rule, females are more flexible than males at a younger age but the differences are not as great during adulthood. The reason for this is not known; however, it could be due to anatomical (wider hips) differences in the joints and hormonal influences. Another reason could be that women spend more time on flexibility exercises than men do. It is important to maintain basic levels of flexibility as we age in order to enhance daily living activity. By incorporating flexibility exercises in our daily routines, including large muscle groups, lower back, and hamstrings, we will have less chance for low back pain. Regardless of age or gender, flexibility is a component of a well-developed fitness program for a lifetime. Therefore, men, women, and children of all ages should incorporate flexibility exercises after a brief warm-up session.

Genetic Factors

Hypomobility or loose joints can be passed down for generations. Individuals with hypomobility are more prone to joint dislocation. Hypermobility, excessive flexibility, may be a cause of athletic or dance injuries.

Physical Activity

People who are physically active and remain active tend to exhibit better flexibility than nonactive people. Inactivity is a major cause in the loss of flexibility. Planned programs of stretching can help to maintain flexibility as we age. Sedentary individuals are inflexible, while physically active individuals of all ages tend to maintain or even increase their flexibility. Sedentary living is a significant factor in limiting flexibility. Inaction causes the muscles to lose their elasticity and tendons and ligaments shorten and tighten. Increased adipose tissue goes hand in hand with inactivity and this further decreases the range of motion of the individual. You can maintain at least adequate levels of flexibility throughout your life by an appropriate stretching program. The secret to healthy, flexible joints is to use them—Move and Be Active.

PHYSICAL ACTIVITY PYRAMID

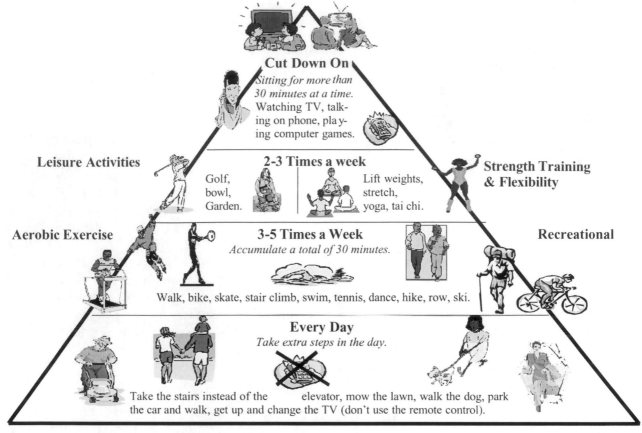

Cut Down On
Sitting for more than 30 minutes at a time. Watching TV, talking on phone, playing computer games.

Leisure Activities

2-3 Times a week

Golf, bowl, Garden.

Lift weights, stretch, yoga, tai chi.

Strength Training & Flexibility

Aerobic Exercise

3-5 Times a Week
Accumulate a total of 30 minutes.

Recreational

Walk, bike, skate, stair climb, swim, tennis, dance, hike, row, ski.

Every Day
Take extra steps in the day.

Take the stairs instead of the   elevator, mow the lawn, walk the dog, park the car and walk, get up and change the TV (don't use the remote control).

Figure 5.1 Flexibility exercises should be selected from level 3.

Body Composition

Fat may limit the ability of the joints through the range of motion. The amount of adipose tissue (fat) around the joint is another factor affecting flexibility. Excess adipose tissue restricts movement in the joints. Too much fat simply gets in the way of movement. The fat acts as a wedge between two lever arms, restricting movement. A person with bulging muscles may have a restricted range of motion if strength training is done improperly. If an individual weight trains properly, using good technique and proper range of motion, flexibility can be enhanced.

Types of Stretching

The goal of any stretching program would be to improve the range of motion at a given joint. In order to stretch, the muscles must contract. The contracting muscles are **agonist** and the lengthening muscle is **antagonist.** Whenever a muscle contracts (shortens) to produce a movement, a reciprocal lengthening must occur. For example, when the quadricep (agonist) muscle in the upper leg contracts, its opposite, the hamstring (antagonist) muscle must relax and lengthen. Exercises that overdevelop one muscle group while neglecting the opposing group can lead to a shortening of muscles and ligaments. Bodybuilders often overdevelop the biceps in comparison to the triceps and obtain a muscle-bound look. This restricts the range of motion at the elbow. Understanding the concepts of muscle contraction helps us to understand stretching techniques. Flexibility is the property of extensibility of muscles in a joint, and stretching techniques are divided into three common types. Three common types of stretching are static, ballistic, and proprioceptive neuromuscular facilitation (PNF). Each type of stretching facilitates flexibility in a different way.

several seconds. Decrease the stretch slowly after the hold. Static stretches are excellent for increasing range of motion at a joint and developing flexibility.

Static Stretching

Perform static stretching by slowly and gently stretching to a mild discomfort, hold for a period of several seconds (15–30 seconds), and then slowly release. A slow-sustained stretch causes the muscle to relax and achieve greater length. There is a low risk of injury and little pain involved in this type of stretching. Static stretching is the most frequently used and recommended type of stretching program. Static stretches are the preferred form of flexibility for minimizing soreness and safety. The probability of tearing the tissue is low. Static stretching can be done with **active assistance** or **passive assistance.**

When using active assistance, you contract the opposing muscle group to produce a relaxation in the muscles you are trying to stretch. This allows the muscle to stretch more easily. A partner aids you in passive assistance stretching. This type of stretching does not allow a muscle to be stretched completely. A combination of both types of stretching is recommended.

A good way to begin static stretching is to stretch until you feel the stretch, not pain, hold the position for a few seconds, then relax. A form of static stretching is the sitting hamstring stretch. With the legs together and straight, you extend your arms forward to touch your toes or stretch as far forward as you can or until you feel a mild discomfort. Hold this position for

Ballistic Stretching

Ballistic stretching uses momentum to produce the stretch. Ballistic stretches are performed with bouncing movements where you put the muscles in and out of a stretch by bouncing. Ballistic stretching can be either **active** or **passive.** The muscle can be actively forced through a bouncing movement or passively assisted by another person or gravity.

Ballistic stretching usually stretches the muscle beyond the normal range of motion and there is a potential for injury. The ballistic action may cause muscle soreness and injury from small tears to the muscle tissues. According to Hoeger and Hoeger (2006) ballistic stretching is effective if it is slow, gentle, and controlled. Static stretching is the preferred method of stretching for beginners. Ballistic stretching is not recommended for the general population. Sport specific ballistic stretches are appropriate for most athletes since most sport activities are ballistic in nature. Even among athletes, static stretching is the most preferred method of stretching. Always use static stretching before using ballistic stretching.

Proprioceptive Neuromuscular Facilitation (PNF) Stretching

Proprioceptive neuromuscular facilitation stretching involves alternating contraction and relaxation of opposing muscles (agonist and

the muscle, the muscle is slowly stretched. How do PNF techniques compare to static stretching? PNF has been proven to be safer and more effective than ballistic stretching and is equal to or in some cases superior to static stretching. A disadvantage is that it requires a partner and longer sessions.

PNF stretching was first used as a rehabilitation tool and has been popular since the 1960s. PNF is considered the most effective form of stretching but it requires a partner, time, and could result in soreness. Static stretching is almost as effective and is easier to perform. PNF combines slow, passive movements and requires a partner to assist the movement. There are a number of ways PNF can be performed. The most common ones are **contract-relax-antagonist-contract (CRAC)**, **contract-relax (CR)**, and **slow-reversal-hold-relax (SRHR)**. The most popular one is the CRAC. See Table 5.0 for a description of each of the stretches.

antagonist). A form of PNF stretch includes a partner assisting the performer. The subject stretching the hamstring is performing an isometric action while the partner is giving resistance. You are stretching the muscles to the limit with the assistance of a partner. The muscle to be stretched is contracted then, after relaxing

Benefits of a Stretching Program

If you stretch on a regular basis you will receive several benefits. Good flexibility allows you to have more efficient and effective movements. One of the main benefits of stretching is an increase in flexibility. The benefits of a stretching program are found in Table 5.1

Table 5.0   Proprioceptive Neuromuscular Facilitation (PNF)

Contract-Relax-Antagonist Contract (CRAC)	Contract-Relax (CR)	Slow-Reversal-Hold-Relax
Contract: Place the targeted muscle (example: calf muscle) in a lengthened position, contract muscle isometrically (agonist) against a partner, rope, another body part or towel.	*Contract:* Place targeted muscle (calf muscle) in a lengthened position, contract muscle isometrically against a resistance.	**(SRHR)** *Slow:* Perform a passive stretch for 10–15 seconds.
Relax: Release all tension in calf muscle and contract (shin muscles) in active stretch for 2–5 seconds.	*Relax:* Hold muscle in a passive stretch for 10–15 seconds.	*Reversal:* Perform a 6 second maximal isometric contraction of the target muscle against a resistance.
Contract: Perform active contraction with passive assist for 10–15 seconds.		*Hold:* Perform an active stretch of the target muscle (antagonist muscle).
		Relax: Perform a 10–15 passive stretch using resistance.

Table 5.1 Benefits of a Stretching Program

★ Prevention of low back pain
★ Muscle relaxation
★ Facilitation of strength development
★ Reduction of stress and fatigue
★ Reduction of muscle soreness
★ Improved fitness, posture, and body position for sports
★ Prevention of injury
★ Increased range of motion
★ May reduce muscle strain

Designing Your Flexibility Program

Once you have studied the types of stretching and the benefits of stretching, you are now ready to design an individualized flexibility program. The following are some guidelines you should follow when designing your program.

★ Determine your needs and set goals based upon the assessment of flexibility.

★ Select exercises that will help you meet your needs and goals.

★ Determine the number of exercises and repetitions of each exercise and how long you will work on each stretch.

★ Determine the time of day to do your stretching routine. Try to make the time consistent or routine.

★ Warm up the joints before stretching by walking, jogging, bicycling, etc. Once you have warmed the muscles you are ready to stretch.

★ Pregnant women should avoid extreme ranges of motion.

You should stretch before and after exercising. Older people should stretch more often than younger people. If you are inactive, you need to start exercising slowly. Do not start exercising without proper stretching. Good flexibility decreases injury. Stretching after a workout is effective for increasing flexibility and to prevent blood pooling in the extremities.

General Flexibility Principles and Guidelines

★ Warm up 3–7 minutes with light aerobic activity (walking, cycling).
★ Use proper technique when exercising.
★ Stretch to a point of mild discomfort, not pain.
★ Stretch daily and before and after activities.
★ Do each stretch 3 to 5 times.
★ Static stretches are the preferred method for safety and to prevent muscle soreness.
★ Proceed with your activity.
★ Following activity, cool down for 3–7 minutes of light aerobic activity, followed with stretching.

Table 5.2 Guidelines for Developing Flexibility (FITT)

	Static	Ballistic	PNF
Frequency	3 to five days a week (everyday if possible) for all three		
Intensity	Slow movement Stretch as far as you can without pain; hold the stretch at end of range of motion	Not recommended Gentle bounce to stretch muscle beyond normal	Same as static
Time	Hold stretch for 15 to 30 seconds; do at least 3 times pausing in between	Gentle bounces for 30 seconds	Hold stretch for 15 seconds and complete at least 3 sets

Principles of Physical Activity

The basic guidelines of the principles of flexibility are as follows:

FIT Principle

Frequency: Stretch 3–7 days a week. Stretching every day is considered the best.

Intensity: Stretch to the point of mild discomfort/feel of stretch, not pain.

Time: Static Stretching: Hold each stretch 10–60 seconds, 2–5 repetitions.

Ballistic Stretching: 10–60 seconds, 2–5 repetitions.

PNF Stretching: 6–10 seconds.

Principle of Overload and Progression

In order to achieve an overload effect, you must stretch the muscle farther than normal. Do not overload the muscle too fast or muscle soreness or injury may occur. Progression is achieved by gradually lengthening the muscle over time.

Principle of Reversibility

Flexibility is lost if you do not continue minimum stretching exercises. Flexibility can be maintained by stretching at least 3 days a week.

Principle of Individuality

Each person has his or her own needs and goals for increasing flexibility. Your bone structure, ligaments, and tendons are unique to you. Everyone must find exercises to overload the muscles that would work for them. It is a personal decision as to the type of stretching used for increasing flexibility.

Principle of Specificity

The exercises you select must be specific to the joints you want to stretch. Stretching programs must be specific to the sport or activity in which you are planning to engage. For example, joggers should stretch the legs while tennis players should stretch their arms, legs, and shoulders. It is best to stretch the major muscles of the body.

Assessment of Flexibility

Accurate measurement of overall body flexibility and range of motion is difficult. Because flexibility measurements must be specific, various tests have been designed to accommodate different joints. Specific tests to evaluate flexibility are found in Labs 5.0 and 5.1. Follow the directions for each test and the scores for the test can be found in the labs.

Safety

★ Warm up prior to flexibility exercises. Cool down after the activity, followed by stretching.

★ Breathe calmly trying not to hold your breath.

★ Never stretch cold muscles.

★ Individuality of stretching: Tailor your flexibility program according to your specific needs. Include all muscle groups.

★ Proper sequence of program: You may order the exercises from top to bottom, bottom to top, or large muscles first.

★ Protect your spine while stretching. You are seeking a neutral position of the lumbar spine (lower back region). While performing the stretching exercises, the lower spine is somewhere between fully flexed and fully extended. It will take much practice to achieve this skill. Working from this neutral position will better isolate the muscle groups being stretched (hamstrings, groin, and quadriceps).

★ Use the correct way to perform flexibility exercises.

★ Do not overstretch.

Stretching Exercises

Many types of exercise place excessive stresses or strains on particular muscles or joints. The following are stretches you should follow in your flexibility portion of your exercise program.

1. **Lateral Head Tilt:** Begin with head in neutral position, slowly tilt the head laterally to the right; neutral position; slowly and gently to the left. Repeat to each side several times.

1. Lateral Head Tilt

2. Upper Arm Stretch

2. **Upper Arm Stretch (Triceps Stretch):**
   Extend left arm overhead, keeping the upper
   portion close to your ear. Bend the elbow
   and reach hand, palm inward, down toward
   the scapula. Place opposite hand on the
   elbow and gently pull the elbow backward.
   Repeat on the opposite side.

3. **Cross Body Stretch:** Cross your left arm in
   front of your body and grasp it with your
   right. Gently pull your arm as close to your
   body as possible. Repeat the stretch with the
   right arm.

1. Lateral Head Tilt

3. Cross Body Stretch

4. Side Stretch

5. Body Rotation

4. **Side Stretch:** Stand with feet shoulder width apart, knees slightly bent, place hands on your waist. Move the upper body to one side and hold the stretch for a few seconds. Repeat on the other side.

5. **Body Rotation:** Stand with feet shoulder width apart, knees slightly bent. Place your arms slightly away from your body and rotate the trunk to one side as far as possible. Hold the position for 10–15 seconds. Repeat on the other side.

6. **Shoulder Hyperextension:** Stand with feet shoulder width apart, knees slightly bent, and arms behind the back. Have a partner grasp you by the wrist and slowly push them inward. Hold final rotation for a few seconds.

7. **Quadriceps Stretch:** Lie on your side and move one foot back by grasping the front of the ankle and flexing the knee. Pull the ankle toward the gluteal region. Hold for a few seconds. Repeat to the other side.

8. **Hip Flexor Stretch:** Raise the right knee off the floor and place the right foot about 3 feet in front of you. Place right hand over the right knee and the left hand over the back of the left hip. Keep the low back flat

6. Shoulder Hyperextension

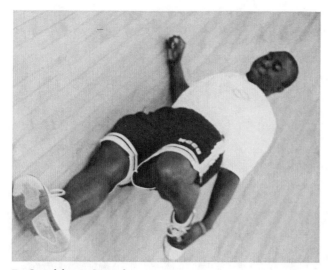

7. **Quadriceps Stretch**

9. **Adductor Stretch**

8. **Hip Flexor Stretch**

10. **Sitting Toe Touch**

and slowly move forward and downward. Apply gentle pressure of the left hip. Repeat on the other side.

9. **Adductor Stretch:** Stand with your feet more than shoulder width apart and place your hands on your thighs slightly above the knee. Bend one knee and slowly go down as far as possible, hold the final position for a few seconds. Repeat on the other side.

10. **Sitting Toe Touch:** Sit on the floor with legs together and straight. Bend at the waist and reach toward the toes. Reach as far as possible. Do not bend at the hips. Keep back straight and head up. Hold for a few seconds.

11. **Butterfly Stretch:** Sit on floor, bring feet in close to your body, allowing the soles of the

11. **Butterfly Stretch**

feet to touch. Using your elbows push your legs downward. Hold for 5 seconds. Relax then gently push the legs down for a greater stretch. Repeat.

12. **Sitting Trunk Rotation and Lower Back Stretch:** Sit on the floor with right leg straight, bend the left knee and place left foot on the floor on the outside of the right knee. Bend your right elbow and place it on the outside of upper left thigh, just about to the knee, to keep the leg stationary. Place left hand behind you, slowly turn your head to look behind you and try to rotate the trunk to the left. Hold 15–30 seconds. Repeat on the opposite side.

13. **Double-Knee-to-Chest Stretch:** Lying on back, bring knees up to a fetal position. Grasp your thigh above the knee, pull the knee toward the chest. Hold for 10–30 seconds, relax, repeat.

14. **Calf Stretch:** Stand 2–3 feet from wall, with feet perpendicular to wall, lean against for 10–30 seconds. Keep feet parallel to each other and make sure rear heel stays on floor. Switch legs and repeat.

15. **Single-Knee-to-Chest Stretch:** Lie down, on your back, flat on the floor. Bend one leg at approximately 100 degrees and gradually pull the opposite leg toward the chest. Place the hands under the thigh above the knee. Switch legs and repeat the exercise.

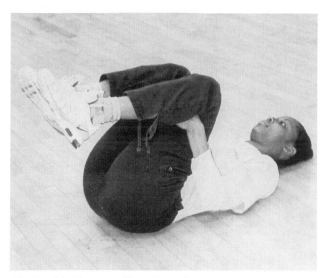

13. Double-Knee-to-Chest Stretch

14. Calf Stretch

12. Sitting Trunk Rotation and Lower Back Stretch

15. Single-Knee-to-Chest Stretch

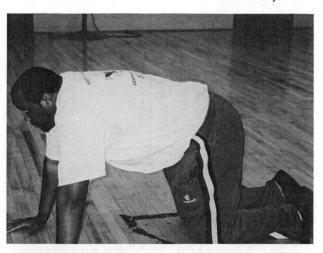

16. **Upper and Lower Back Stretch:** Sit on the floor, soles of the feet touching, bring your feet as close to you as possible. Holding onto your feet, lower your head and upper chest gently toward your chest.

17. **Back Arch and Sway:** (the Cat and the Camel) On all fours, hands and knees in a wide base formation, move head down slowly while arching the back toward the ceiling like a cat. Hold. With head slightly up and eyes looking toward the ceiling, slowly sway back (belly button toward floor). Hold.

17. Back Arch and Sway

18. **Back Extension Stretch:** Lie face down on the floor. Raise your upper body so that you are resting on your elbows. Keep the thighs in contact with the floor at all times. For

18. Back Extension Stretch

16. Upper and Lower Back Stretch

19. Gluteal Stretch

20. Chest Stretch

most people, this will be an adequate range of motion. To increase the degree of stretching, place your hands on the floor in a push-up position and slowly press chest off the floor. Be careful not to go past a point of mild discomfort. Hold.

19. **Gluteal Stretch:** Sit on the floor, bend your right leg and place your right ankle slightly above the left knee. Grasp the left thigh with both hands and gently pull the leg toward your chest. Repeat with the opposite leg.

20. **Chest Stretch:** Place your hands on the shoulders of your partner, the partner will push you down by your shoulders. Hold the final position for a few seconds.

21. **Modified Hurdler Stretch:** Sit with your left leg straight and the sole of your right foot next to your right knee. While keeping the right leg bent and flat, reach as far as possible toward your left foot and hold. Repeat with the other leg.

21. Modified Hurdler Stretch

References

American College of Sports Medicine. (2006). *ACSM resource manual for guidelines for exercise testing and prescription,* 3rd ed. Hagerstown, MD: Lippincott, Williams & Wilkens.

Baechle, T. R. (1994). *Essentials of strength training and conditioning.* Champaign, IL: Human Kinetics.

Corbin, C. B., Welk, G. J., Corbin, W. R., & Welk, K. A. (2006). *Fundamental concepts of fitness and wellness.* 2nd ed. Boston: McGraw-Hill.

Dierking, T. K. & Bemben, M. G. (1998). Delayed onset muscle soreness. *Strength and Conditioning Journal, 21,* 44–48.

Fleck, S. & Kraemer, W. (1997). *Designing resistance training program.* Champaign, IL: Human Kinetics.

Floyd, P. & Parke, J. (1998). *Walk, jog, run for wellness everyone.* Winston-Salem, NC: Hunter Textbooks Inc.

Fox, E. L., Bowers, R. W., & Foss, M. L. (1993). *The physiological basis for exercise and sport,* 5th ed. Madison, WI: Brown & Benchmark.

Harper, T.D. (1997). Protecting the spine during static stretching. *Strength and Conditioning Journal, 19,* 52–53.

Hoeger, W.W.K. & Hoeger, S.A. (2003). *Lifetime fitness and wellness,* 7th ed. United States: Thomson–Wadsworth.

Hoeger, W.W.K. & Hoeger, S.A. (2006). *Principles and labs for physical fitness,* 5th ed. United States: Thomson–Wadsworth.

Liemohn, W., Martin, S.B., & Parker, G.L. (1997). The effect of ankle posture on sit-and-reach test performance. *Journal of Strength and Condition Research, 11,* 239–241.

Mann, D.P. & Jones, M.T. (1999). Guidelines to implementation of a dynamic stretching program. *Strength and Conditioning Journal, 21,* 53–55.

Ninos, J.C. (1996). PNF stretching techniques. *Strength and Conditioning Journal, 18,* 42.

Ninos, J.C. (1997). Stretching the forearm. *Strength and Conditioning Journal, 19,* 64.

Ninos, J.C. (1998). Stretching with age. *Strength and Conditioning Journal, 20,* 69.

Ninos, J.C. (1999). A new method of stretching the iliotisal band. *Strength and Conditioning Journal, 21,* 15–16.

Ninos, J.C. (1999). Starting them young. *Strength and Conditioning Journal, 21,* 48–49.

Ninos, J.C. (1999). When could stretching be harmful? *Strength and Conditioning Journal, 21,* 57–58.

PennState. (1995). Stretching, the truth. *Sportsmedicine Newsletter, 4,* 4–5.

Politano, V., McCormick, M.R., & Jeffreys, A. (1995). *Lifetime physical fitness.* Dubuque, IA: Kendall/Hunt Publishing Company.

Simoneau, G.G. (1998). The impact of various anthropometric and flexibility measurements on the sit-and-reach test. *Journal of Strength and Conditioning Research, 12,* 232–237.

University of California at Berkeley. (1994). Stretching, the truth. *Newsletter of Nutrition, Fitness and Stress Management, 11,* 4–5.

Web Sites

Georgia State University: Flexibility *www.gsu.edu/~www.fit/flexibility*

MedlinePlus *www.nlm.nih.gov/medlineplus*

Name: _____ Section: _____ Date: _____

Lab Activity 5.0
Trunk Flexion (Sit and Reach Test)

Purpose: To measure the flexibility of the lower back and hamstrings.

Procedure:

Warm up before completing the test.

1. Sit with legs extended, knees flat on the floor and feet flat against a vertical surface (box, mat, or feet of another person).
2. Place one hand on top of the other.
3. Bend forward from the waist and reach as far as possible with the fingers (do not bounce). See picture below.
4. Partner will measure the distance the fingertips reach on the measuring stick. (Do not count long fingernails, count the fleshy end of the fingers).
5. Perform test 3 times and record the best score. The score is determined by measuring the number of inches you can reach.
6. Record the highest score.
7. Consult the chart to determine your fitness rating.

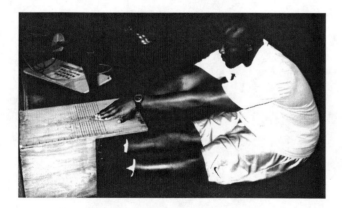

Norms for the Sit and Reach Test

Men	Women	Classification
0 inches	0 inches	Poor
1–3 inches	2–4 inches	Average
4–6 inches	5–7 inches	Good
7 inches or more	8 inches or above	Excellent

1. Record score from sit and reach test _____
2. Record age _____
3. Record sex _____
4. Record fitness level _____

Lab Activity 5.1
Total Body Rotation Test

Purpose: To measure right and left side total body rotation.

Procedures:

1. Tape two 30 inch measuring tapes on a wall (a commercial unit can be mounted on wall).
2. A vertical strip of tape should extend from the floor to a height of 72″ on the wall. The 15″ mark of each tape should be even with the vertical mark.
3. Place another strip of tape on the floor perpendicular to the vertical line and extended 36″ from the wall.
4. Stand sideways an arms length away from the wall with the toes of both feet touching the line on the floor.
5. The arm opposite the wall is held out horizontally from the body; make a fist with the hand.
6. Rotate the trunk, the extended arm goes backward toward the wall; slide the fist along the tape as far as possible (commercial unit has a tab to be slide along the unit). Hold the position for 2 seconds.
7. The farthest point reached is measured to the nearest ½ inch and held for at least two seconds then recorded. The average of the two trials for each side (right and left) is recorded.

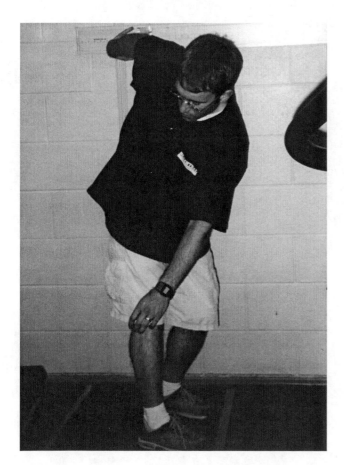

Norms for the Right Body Rotation Test

Men	Women	Classification
22–27 inches	21–29 inches	Excellent
19–21 inches	18–20 inches	Good
16–18 inches	16–17 inches	Average
13–15 inches	14–15 inches	Fair
0–12 inches	3–13 inches	Poor

Norms for the Left Body Rotation Test

Men	Women	Classification
22–28 inches	22–29 inches	Excellent
19–21 inches	19–21 inches	Good
16–18 inches	17–18 inches	Average
13–15 inches	15–16 inches	Fair
0–12 inches	5–14 inches	Poor

Body Composition and Weight Management

Objectives

After completing this chapter, you will be able to do the following:

★ Define body composition.

★ Distinguish between essential and nonessential body fat.

★ Understand the difference between lean body mass and fat weight.

★ Distinguish between obesity and overweight.

★ Learn the causes of obesity.

★ Calculate ideal body weight.

★ Describe and identify eating disorders.

★ Explain basal metabolic rate.

★ Explain the basic nutrients needed by the body.

★ Identify principles of weight management.

Most of us, at one time or another, have been concerned about our body weight. Very few of us seem to be satisfied with our current weight; we either want to lose or, believe it or not, gain weight. Americans look in the mirror and study the roll around the middle, dimples on the hips and thighs, or flabby arms and wonder what to do about them.

The battle against fat has turned into a multimillion dollar business that advertises fad diets, diet pills, spas, and countless gimmicks and gadgets to help lose weight. Commercial weight loss programs tend to let Americans believe they are highly successful in promoting weight loss. Pictures of before and after the programs often make us believe it is an easy process. However, most of the emphasis in these weight loss programs is on weight loss, not appropriate body fat amounts. Our desire to achieve an ideal appearance makes us gullible to these gimmicks and shortcuts. Unfortunately, the average person looks for short-term, quick cures for weight loss rather than making a permanent lifestyle change. Most people who lose weight usually regain it and then some. So why bother?

Overweight and obesity in the United States, in both adults and children, has increased significantly over the last two decades. Nearly one-third of the adults are obese. It is estimated that 16% of children and adolescents are overweight. This is a doubling of the rate among children and tripling of the rate of adolescents. This high prevalence of overweight and obesity is of great concern because excess fat leads to a higher risk of premature death, type 2 diabetes, hypertension, cardiovascular disease, stroke, respiratory dysfunction, and certain kinds of cancer to name a few.

The goal for adults is to achieve and maintain a body weight that optimizes their health. For obese adults, a modest weight loss (10 lbs) has health benefits and the prevention of further weight gain is extremely important. Slowing the rate of weight gain is the goal for children and adolescents. Maintaining a healthy weight through childhood and adolescence may reduce the risk of becoming overweight or obese adults. Eating fewer calories while increasing physical activity will help control weight gain. In order to reverse the trend toward obesity, we need to eat fewer calories, be active, and make wiser food choices. Not all Americans need to lose weight. If you are at a healthy weight you should strive to maintain this weight. Under-weight individuals may need to increase their weight. The following are key recommendations to help prevent weight gain, if overweight or obese:

★ To maintain a healthy body weight, balance calories from food and beverages with calories expended.

★ Make small decreases in food and beverage calories and increase physical activity in order to prevent gradual weight gain over time.

Body Composition

The body is composed of fat mass and lean body mass. **Body composition** is the ratio between fat and lean body mass. **Lean body mass** is composed of all nonfat tissue, muscle, bone, blood, organs, and fluids. **Fat** tissue is found in the organs and adipose cells. Body fat includes essential and storage fat (nonessen-tial). **Essential fats** are needed for normal phys-iological functioning and serve structural and functional roles in the body. Essential fats reside in nerve cells, muscles, and bone mar-row as well as the heart, lungs, and other vital organs. Approximately 3–5% of total body weight in men and 12% of the body weight of women is essential body fat. This is the mini-mum percent of essential body fat the body should possess. Essential fat acts as padding and provides energy for the body. Other func-tions include helping to keep the body warm, storing energy, and protecting the vital organs from injury. Our bodies will not function with-out at least this amount of fat. The higher female percentage of essential fat is directly related to fat deposits in the breasts, uterus,

and other sex specific sites. Women need more essential body fat because of the demands of childbearing. Women have more essential body fat in the hips, thighs, breasts, and uterus. Men store fat in the abdomen, chest, and back, while women deposit fat in the hips.

Storage fat exists primarily within fat cells located just beneath the skin and around the vital organs. Storage fat is fat beyond what is desirable but some of which is necessary. It is the fat that serves as the energy reserve of the body and is just as necessary as essential fat. Storage fat is needed to act as an insulator to retain body heat, padding to protect the vital organs and bones, and to provide energy for the metabolic system. The amount of storage fat varies from person to person and is based on sex, age, hereditary diet, activity level, and metabolism. Having an excess of storage fat means you are consuming more calories than you are expending. When one accumulates excessive nonessential fat, overfatness or obe-sity could occur. Body fat should never be too low or too high.

Obesity

Obesity is having body fat more than 25% of total body weight for men and more than 35% of total body weight for women. Obesity describes an accumulation of body fat and has no one single cause. Obesity is defined as an excess of adipose tissue. The development of obesity has been attributed to several factors: hereditary, sedentary lifestyle, and overeating. One out of every three Americans is overweight or obese.

Obesity is associated with a wide variety of health problems. Obese people have an overall mortality rate greater than nonobese people. They are more likely to develop diabetes. Obe-sity does not occur overnight; it takes months and years to accumulate. As we age we gain extra weight and fat accumulates because we become less active. Our basal metabolic rate (BMR) decreases as we age. **BMR** is the amount of energy expended to sustain the vital func-tioning of the body while at rest. Creeping obe-sity could result in one-half to one pound of fat per year. The prevalence of overweight individ-uals over the past decade has increased sub-stantially (U.S. Surgeon General).

Causes of Obesity

An increase in fat and the development of obesity occurs when the caloric intake is higher than the caloric output. Obesity is caused by a number of factors:

★ Genetics—Obesity is known to run in families. Some individuals are predisposed to gain weight more easily than others. Children of obese parents are more likely to have weight problems, especially if the biological mother is obese. It is difficult to separate genetic components that lead to obesity. You do not have to give in to genetics, just make a determined effort to change your eating habits and lifestyle by including exercise.

★ Set-Point Theory—The **set-point theory** suggests that the body has an internal "set-point" like the temperature set point on a thermostat. In other words, obese individuals are programmed to carry a certain weight. Each of us is born with a predetermined weight. The set-point controls the weight and fat. That is why some people can eat a lot and not gain weight and others seem to gain weight just by looking at the food. This seems to be linked to the person's set-point. There is a link between the amount of stored fat in the body and the body's metabolic rate. When one deprives the body of caloric intake, thereby lowering the set-point, the metabolic rate decreases to protect itself and attempts to maintain a predetermined set. Severe caloric restriction, when dieting, puts the dieter in a state of semi-starvation, thus slowing the metabolic rate. Since the person needs fewer calories to fuel basic functions, less fat is used. The body adjusts its appetite and metabolism back to its previous weight and weight loss ceases. The goal is to raise the metabolic rate through exercise. The best way to lower your set-point and lose unwanted fat is through regular exercise and food selection. When your set-point is reduced, the body increases its resting metabolic rate and burns more calories.

★ Fat Cell Theory—The fat cell theory states that when a person overeats, the fat cells grow larger. Obesity is related to too many fat cells (above average number of fat cells). When the body needs to expand the fat storage, the fat cells send a signal that initiates the formation of new fat cells. Fat cells can increase in number and size. Once fat cells form they become a permanent part of the body. A normal weight person can have 20 to 30 billion fat cells, whereas an obese person may have four times this amount—up to 120 billion. As a fat cell becomes full, it can expand to three times its normal size. Fat cell development is significantly increased during three critical periods of life—during the last three months of pregnancy, first year of life, and the adolescent growth spurt. Overfeeding and overeating during these periods may trigger an acceleration of fat cells that predisposes the individual to obesity as an adult. Restricting the calories in the diet decreases only the size, not the number, of fat cells.

★ Eating Habits—A main cause of obesity is overeating tasty, fat-rich foods. Many college students do not eat properly and eat foods that are high in calories—junk food and desserts. A diet high in sugar promotes obesity to a lesser extent than a diet higher in fat. Caloric intake is an important issue for the obese and overweight.

★ Lack of Physical Activity—Physical activity is important for weight control. Obesity can be caused by the sedentary lifestyle of most Americans. Using energy and maintaining muscle mass, physical activity is an effective adjunct to dietary management. Most experts agree that the main reason for overfatness and obesity is the lack of exercise. When one exercises, the body gains lean tissue and loses fat tissue. Lean tissue burns calories faster than fat tissue, so an increase in lean tissue raises the metabolism. As one exercises, the energy output is increased with more calories being burned at a higher rate. **One pound of stored fat** is equal to **3,500** calories. You will gain 1 pound of fat by eating an extra 3,500 calories. You will lose 1 pound of fat by expending an extra 3,500 calories.

Body Fat Distribution

Genetics play a part in determining where adipose (fat) accumulates. The amount of excess body fat and the location of this excess fat are important in determining an individual's risk of disease and death (Axen & Vermitsky-Axen, 2001). The location of stored fat can influence health risks associated with overweight or obesity. Obesity is characterized according to two patterns—the **android pattern** and the **gynoid pattern.** Male pattern obesity, known as **android,** is characterized by accumulation of fat around the trunk and abdominal region (apple shape). In the **gynoid pattern** (pear shape), found in women, there is an excessive storage of fat in the hips and thighs (Axen & Vermitsky-Axen, 2001). Android-type obesity pattern is associated with greater cardiovascular disease, hypertension, and type II diabetes. The location of fat causes the risk for disease. Some individuals tend to store fat in the abdomen while others tend to store fat in the hips and thighs. It is much healthier not to develop a "beer" belly.

The waist-to-hip ratio **(WHR)** is useful in assessing gynoid and android patterns of fat distribution. A procedure used for years to identify health risk is the **WHR.** The **WHR** is calculated by dividing the circumference of the waist measurement by the circumference of the hip measurement. When the WHR is higher, the pattern of fat distribution is more android. Thus the increased risk is higher for men than women (Axen & Vermitsky-Axen, 2001). The WHR differentiates the "apples" from the "pears." Men need to lose weight if the fat in the waist is larger than the fat in the hips.

Overweight versus Overfatness

Overweight is defined as exceeding an ideal weight according to gender, age, height, and frame. The overweight individual weighs more than does the average person. It is possible for a person to be overweight but lean in regard to body composition. A person can be within the norms for body weight but is overfat. **Overfat** indicates that a person has a high percentage of body fat. The optimal percent for the average man is 10–20% body fat and the optimal percent for the average female is 17–28% body fat.

Assessing Body Composition

Monitoring body composition can be useful for adjusting caloric intake and energy expenditure. A certain amount of fat is present in all of us and there are several ways to assess body fatness. Some methods are more accurate than others. Underwater weighing, skinfold measuring, bioelectric impedance, Bod Pod, DXA, and body mass index are among the ways to measure body composition.

Underwater Weighing. One of the most accurate measurements of body fat is underwater weighing (hydrostatic weighing) and is used in the laboratory. This method is accurate, but complex because it requires time, space, equipment, and skill to administer. If done correctly and the person is able to perform the test adequately, this test is accurate. The person to be weighed sits on a platform attached to a scale. The platform and person are totally submerged into the water. The person exhales the air from the lungs, while underwater, and a weight measurement is taken. The procedure takes approximately 30 minutes and is not feasible for a number of people. The percentage of fat and fat-free weight (lean body mass) are calculated from body density. Fat people tend to weigh less under water and tend to float, and lean people weigh more and tend to sink. Because of the cost, time, and complexity of the method, most fitness programs use other types of measurement.

Bioelectrical Impedence. Another method of analyzing body fat uses a bioelectrical impedence machine but its accuracy is questionable. Bioelectrical impedance analysis is a measurement of the resistance that fat creates as a small electrical current is passed through the body. This new and simple technique predicts body composition by estimating the amount of body water located in lean tissue. This method is comparable to skinfold measurement techniques. A mild electrical current is sent through the body at selected sites. Since fat is a poor conductor of electrical energy, the higher the percentage of body fat the greater the resistance to the passage of electrical energy. Impedence is least in lean body tissue because of the high water content. Although fairly accurate, this method does provide very inaccurate results on some people. This method is more effective with individuals with a high level of body fat.

Skinfold Measurements. Skinfold measurements are one of the least expensive and most economical methods of measuring body composition. Body fat can be measured by use of a caliper which measures the thickness of skin and subcutaneous fat at specific body sites. (see Figures 6.0, 6.1, 6.2, and 6.3.) The measurements yield an estimate of total fat. Men and women tend to develop fat deposits in different body areas; skinfold measurements should be taken at these specific sites. The procedures for assessing the percent body fat can be found in the lab at the end of the chapter. To calculate your ideal body weight complete the following activity.

Determining Ideal Body Weight

Example: A woman weighing 120 pounds has a current body fat of 23%. After evaluating her fitness goals she decides a desirable amount of body fat is 18%.

1. Current body weight × current percent body fat = pounds of fat.

   $120 \times 0.23 = 27.6$ lb

2. Current weight – pounds of fat = lean body pounds

   120 lb – 27.6 lb = 92.4 lb

3. Lean pounds (1.0 – desired percent body fat) = ideal weight

   92.4 lb   (1.0 – 0.18) = ideal weight

   92.4 lb   (0.82) = 112 lb

You can see from these calculations that the ideal body weight is 112 pounds. Subtracting this from the current weight (120 lb – 112 lb = 8 lb) shows the amount of weight to be lost = 8.

Complete Lab 6.1 to determine your desirable body weight.

Body Mass Index. A relatively easy way to measure the body-weight status is to use the person's body weight and height measurement to calculate **body mass index (BMI)**. BMI is defined as weight in kilograms divided by height, in meters, squared (**BMI = wt [kg]/ht [m^2]**). The body mass index is the ratio of body weight to body height. **BMI** is more accurate at approximating body fat than measuring body weight alone. The relationship between BMI and body fat varies according to gender, age, and ethnicity. You can calculate your BMI by following the procedures described in Lab 6.2.

Figure 6.0

Figure 6.1

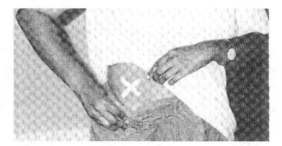

Figure 6.2

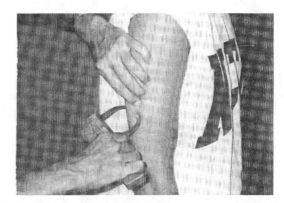

Figure 6.3

The score is valid for both men and women but has its limits. The limits are these:

★ It may overestimate body fat in athletes and others who have a muscular build.

★ It may underestimate body fat in older persons and others who have lost muscle mass.

The BMI score means the following:

	BMI
Underweight	Below 18.5
Normal	18.5–24.9
Overweight	25.0–29.9
Obesity	30.0 & Above

Bod Pod. The Bod Pod is a relatively new device used to measure body composition and compares favorably with hydrostatic weighing. It can be administered relatively easily but is not practical because of its high cost. The Bod Pod is composed of a small chamber in which the person sits. The Bod Pod measures the amount of air displaced by the individual and is determined through computerized pressure sensors. This technique is an accurate assessment technique and could be used as an alternative to underwater weighing for individuals who have special problems.

DEXA. A new method of assessing body composition is the **dual energy X-ray absorptiometry (DEXA)**. **DEXA** uses X-ray energy (low doses) to measure body fat mass, bone density, and fat distribution (Hoeger & Hoeger, 2006). The individual lies on a table and the X-ray scans the body. This method is used in research and medical facilities. It is considered too expensive to be used outside of these two facilities. The DEXA is considered to be the standard technique to assess body composition.

Weight Management

The number of overweight/obese individuals has increased in recent years. Health problems from excess fat are a major concern. Weight management is a multibillion dollar business. Losing weight on a permanent basis is hard to maintain. However, weight loss maintenance can be successful without the use of expensive diets or special foods. To maintain desirable body weight, caloric intake must be balanced by caloric expenditure. Without our conscious knowledge, our bodies perform a balancing act in weight management. The basic principle in weight management is to burn more calories than are consumed. There are three simple strategies to use in weight management: (1) restrict caloric intake, (2) increase caloric expenditure, and (3) a combination of dieting and exercising.

Energy Needs

One pound of body fat represents approximately 3,500 calories. The loss of 1 pound of fat requires a deficit of 3,500 calories. Calories are measures of the energy value of fat. A **Calorie** is the amount of heat needed to raise the temperature of 1 gram of water 1°C. A large calorie or kilocalorie is equal to 1,000 small calories or the amount of heat needed to raise 1 kg of water 1°C.

The nutrients in food that provide energy include carbohydrates, proteins, fats, and alcohol. The caloric content of these nutrients is as follows:

1 gram fat = 9 calories per gram

1 gram protein = 4 calories per gram

1 gram carbohydrates = 4 calories per gram

1 gram alcohol = 7 calories per gram

It is important to think of calories as energy needed to do mechanical work and as the chemical energy stored in the body. Protein and carbohydrates deliver 4 calories of energy per gram. One pound of fat provides a lot more calories than 1 pound of carbohydrates or proteins. Alcohol provides 7 calories of energy per gram. Any excess of calories, no matter the source, can be converted to body fat and stored.

Energy Balance

When the number of calories taken in (eaten) is equal to the number of calories expended (used) you are in a state of energy balance. Caloric expenditure needs to be in balance with caloric intake to maintain body weight and must exceed caloric intake to lose weight. Body weight should remain constant to maintain a stable body weight. There is no

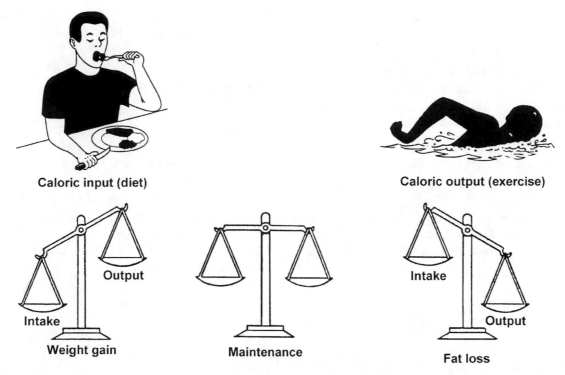

Caloric input (diet)

Caloric output (exercise)

Output

Intake

Intake

Output

Weight gain

Maintenance

Fat loss

Figure 6.5   Balancing calorie input and output.

excess storage fat and no shortfall in energy. A **positive caloric balance exists** when more calories are consumed than are expended. The extra calories are stored and you will gain weight. An increase in the amount of body fat and an increase in total body weight will occur because more energy is consumed than being expended.

If you are attempting to lose weight, you need to burn more calories than you consume. The end result is a **negative caloric balance.** The body has to use its fat store for energy. If we are in a negative caloric balance we lose body fat. More energy is used than consumed. Physical activity results in an increased need for energy and body fat will be lost (Figure 6.5). Most Americans need to eat fewer calories, be more active, and make wiser food choices.

Caloric expenditure decreases with a reduction in **basal metabolic rate (BMR)** as age increases. It is necessary to decrease caloric intake by 2.5% for every 10 years over age 25. As you age, it is important to either increase your physical activity, decrease caloric intake, or both. Caloric expenditure decreases when physical activity decreases. Adding a moderate

level of physical activity will increase your caloric expenditure.

Basal Metabolic Rate (BMR)

It is important to determine the amount of calories needed to support your BMR. The **basal metabolic rate** is the minimum amount of energy needed to maintain the body's vital functions (respiration, heart beat, circulation, and body temperature) during a 24-hour period. The BMR is the percentage of daily caloric intake required for basic body functioning.

The daily caloric intake required for moving the body is referred to as the **working metabolism.** Calories not used while resting or working are stored in the body as fat used for protection, heat insulation, and future energy use. Several factors influence or affect BMR:

★ Gender—Men have a higher BMR than women.

★ Body surface—The greater the body surface area, the higher the BMR.

★ Age—As age increases BMR decreases. BMR declines with age because of decreases in muscle mass.

★ Diet—Low-calorie dieting decreases the BMR.

★ Exercise—Anything you do above the basal baseline will add to your energy expenditure. Exercise has a positive effect on BMR. BMR increases during physical activity and for a period of time after activity ceases.

Lab 6.3 will help you determine your BMR.

Most weight problems are lifestyle problems. It is a known fact that Americans eat more fat, refined sugars, fewer complex carbohydrates and get less exercise. Despite an increased interest in fitness, Americans get far less physical activity than their great-grandparents. The decline in walking, bicycling, and manual labor results in a decrease in daily energy expenditure.

Couple this decline with the tendency to eat fatty processed foods and it is not difficult to see why there are 54 million (or more) overweight Americans. The solution lies in lifestyle management.

Exercise/Physical Activity

Exercise is an important component of weight management. Physical activity and exercise burn calories and increase the metabolism. Weight loss through exercise involves loss of fat tissue and little loss of lean tissue. Establishing a new lifestyle to include daily physical activity takes a great deal of motivation. Exercise habits, for most of us, were established early. Physical activity in adolescence can prevent the formation of excessive fat and result in an increase in lean body weight. Physical activity and caloric reductions can lead to substantial loss of body fat.

Table 6.0 Calories Expended During Certain Activities

Activity*	Calories Expended in 30 Minutes Male (175 lbs)	Calories Expended in 30 Minutes Female (135 lbs)
Biking 12–13.9 mph (moderate effort)	334	258
Circuit training	334	258
Stretching, hatha yoga	167	129
Dancing—general	188	145
Dancing—ballet, modern	251	193
House Cleaning—vigorous (mop, wash car)	188	145
House Cleaning—light (dusting, vacuuming)	104	81
Playing w/kids moderate—walk/run	167	129
Gardening	209	161
Mowing lawn—hand mower	251	193
Running—6 mph	418	322
Jogging	292	225
Basketball—game	334	258
Children's games	209	161
Football	334	258
Frisbee	125	97
Horseback riding	167	129
Skating	292	225
Soccer	292	225
Softball/baseball	209	161
Tennis	292	225
Hiking	251	193
Walking—4 mph, level surface	167	129
Walking—leisure	146	113
Canoeing/rowing—moderate	292	225
Kayaking	209	161
Swimming laps freestyle—moderate	334	258

*Data from *ACSM Resource Manual for Guidelines for Exercise Testing and Prescription Third Edition*

The most efficient way to lose body fat is through a combination of exercise and diet. A moderate increase in physical activity and a moderate decrease in food intake will result in a negative caloric balance. This is a relatively fast and easy method since it focuses on changing eating behavior and activity levels.

Weight loss should be gradual. A pound or two per week is recommended. This approach allows for a long-lasting modification of eating and activity habits. Exercise can make a significant contribution to the loss of body fat. One pound of fat is equal to 3,500 calories and a negative caloric balance of 3,500 calories per week should result in the loss of 1 pound of fat. This can be accomplished through a combination of diet and exercise. For example, reducing the daily caloric intake by 2,100 calories per week (300 calories × 7 days = 2,100) and burning 1,400 calories by moderate to vigorous activity per week would result in the loss of 1 pound in a week (2,100 + 1,400 = 3,500).

Weight Management Guidelines

The American College of Sports Medicine (2006) has made the following specific guidelines for weight control/management:

★ Prolonged fasting and diet programs, which severely restrict caloric intake, are undesirable and can be dangerous.

★ Fasting and diet programs that severely restrict caloric intake result in the loss of large amounts of water, electrolytes, minerals, glycogen stores, and other fat-free tissue (including proteins within fat-free tissues), with minimal amounts of fat loss.

★ Mild caloric restriction (500 to 1,000 calories less than the usual daily intake) results in a smaller loss of water of electrolytes, minerals, and other fat-free tissue and is less likely to cause malnutrition.

★ Dynamic exercise of large muscles helps to maintain fat-free tissue, including muscle mass and bone density and results in loss of body weight. Weight loss resulting from an increase in energy expenditure is primarily in the form of fat weight.

★ A nutritionally sound diet resulting in mild caloric restriction coupled with an endurance exercise program, along with behavioral modifications of existing eating habits, is recommended for weight reduction. The rate of sustained weight loss should not exceed 2 pounds per week.

Table 6.1 Calories Expended During Moderate and Rigorous Activity

Moderate Physical Activity	Approximate Calories/Hr for 154 lb Person[a]
Hiking	370
Light gardening/yard work	330
Dancing	330
Golf (walking and carrying clubs)	330
Bicycling (<10 mph)	290
Walking (3.5 mph)	280
Weight lifting (general light workout)	220
Stretching	180
Vigorous Physical Activity	**Approximate Calories/Hr for 154 lb Person[a]**
Running/jogging (5 mph)	590
Bicycling (>10 mph)	590
Swimming (slow freestyle laps)	510
Aerobics	480
Walking (4.5 mph)	460
Heavy yard work (chopping wood)	440
Weight lifting (vigorous effort)	440
Basketball (vigorous)	440

[a]Calories burned per hour will be higher for persons who weight more than 154 lbs (70 kg) and lower for person who weigh less.
Source: Adapted from the 2005 DGAC Report.

★ To maintain proper weight and optimal body fat levels, a lifetime commitment to proper eating habits and regular physical activity is required.

★ A reduction in dietary fat to less than 30% of total energy intake and emphasis on fruits, vegetables, whole grains, and lean sources of protein is highly recommended.

Eating Disorders

The current emphasis of "thin" is beautiful has increased the frequency of eating disorders. Thin is in and fat is out. Fear of fatness has resulted in an obsession with thinness. The obsession poses a threat to health and well-being. Young adults and adolescent women comprise the majority of people in the United States that have a serious eating disorder. When one believes that being thin is the key to becoming more satisfied with one's self, the individual is susceptible to eating disorders. "Eating disorders are a severe psychological response to body image issues" (Thygerson & Larson, 2006, p. 144).

Bulimia

Bulimia is considered the most common eating disorder. Bulimia involves recurrent episodes of consuming a large amount of food in a short period of time (binge eating) followed by purging (vomiting, laxatives, or fasting) in hope that weight gain will be blunted. Usually binge eating consists of eating high-calorie junk food immediately followed by self-induced vomiting. A typical binge involves consumption of thousands of calories within a 1- to 2-hour period. To avoid gaining weight from this binge, the person follows the binge with purging, primarily by self-induced vomiting supplemented with laxatives and diuretics. The binge eating and, especially, purging is nearly always done in private. The physical and psychological problems resulting from binge eating and purging include esophageal inflammation, erosion of tooth enamel caused by repeated vomiting, the possibility of electrolyte imbalances, and altered mood states, with resulting anxiety and depression.

Bulimia occurs primarily in young women with a morbid fear of becoming fat. Most of these young women are about average and not excessively overfat. Most bulimic individuals are good students, athletes, extremely sociable, and pleasant. Bulimic individuals tend to have problems with interpersonal relationships. Individuals with bulimia suffer from low self-esteem and feel isolated because of their binge eating and purging behavior. They are aware that their binge-purge behavior is not normal but it is beyond their control.

If left untreated, the binge-purge episodes can cause damage to the body. The treatment should focus on the causes of the behavior. Behavior therapy helps the individual learn to cope with personal problems in a more constructive manner. If you know someone who eats large amounts of food, is inactive, yet is not gaining weight, you may suspect this disorder. It may help to discuss bulimia with them and encourage them to seek counseling.

Anorexia Nervosa

Anorexia nervosa is a serious medical and psychological disease in which a person has a deliberate self-starvation due to a morbid fear of becoming fat. The person suffering from anorexia nervosa refuses to maintain a minimal normal weight for age and height. Individuals with this disease have a distorted self-image and a desire to achieve extraordinary thinness. Over a period of time, they lose so much weight that health and life are threatened. No matter how thin they are, they see themselves as fat. In advanced stages, they have lost so much fat and muscle tissue that they have a skeletal appearance.

Anorexia nervosa has become a widespread problem with about 90% of the cases involving females. Anorexia nervosa begins during adolescence and is more prevalent in families that stress high achievement.

It is obvious that an individual is anorectic. The person has an emaciated appearance and looks as though he or she has a life-threatening disease. The person avoids medical help and refuses the advice of family and friends regarding professional assistance. Extreme physical activity behaviors are characteristic of the illness. Because the female has a minimum level of body fat, she fails to menstruate. Anorexia is a subtle disease and individuals with the disease become secretive in their behaviors.

Table 6.2 Checklist of Eating Disorders

Review the following common symptoms and ask yourself if you or someone you know needs help in dealing with the eating disorders.

Symptoms	Anorexia	Bulimia
Excessive weight loss in a relatively short period of time	X	
Continuation of dieting even when pencil thin	X	
Not satisfied with body appearance and always thinks they are fat	X	
Loss of monthly menstrual cycle	X	X
Unusual interest in food and has strange of eating rituals	X	X
Obsession with exercise	X	X
Eating in secret	X	X
Serious depression	X	X
Bingeing		X
Vomiting, use of laxatives or drugs		X
Bingeing with no weight gain		X
Inducing vomiting		X

Young athletes may also be susceptible to an inordinate fear of being fat. Most serious athletes are encouraged to be lean and some overreact by restricting their food intake to excessively low amounts. This behavior has been called **anorexia athletica.** The athlete tends to associate thinness with the ability to perform successfully and be more attractive.

In many instances, the condition starts with an attempt to reduce body fat through caloric reduction and increased physical activity. The person becomes obsessed with body weight and the ability to control body weight. Since anorectics do not supply enough calories to fuel the high energy demands of physical activity, they cannot maintain a reasonable amount of body fat. Anorexia is characterized by extreme weight loss and a variety of psychological disorders, with an obsessive preoccupation with the attainment of thinness.

Individuals with anorexia nervosa will never admit or be convinced they are too thin. As they look into the mirror they see a "fat" person. This person should seek psychological and medical help. The key to treatment is to get the individual to gain weight, his or her their attitude toward food, and resolve underlying personal problems. A checklist of eating disorders and symptoms can be found in Table 6.2.

Underweight

There are a small number of people who are naturally thin and some of them are dissatisfied with their appearance. Being underweight can present as much a problem for young people as obesity does for the obese young person. Some of the causes of underweight include:

★ Smoking, drugs, alcohol
★ Hereditary and metabolic factors
★ Inadequate diet
★ Eating disorders
★ Disease

Many underweight people find it as hard to gain weight as an obese one does to lose weight.

Many very lean people consume large quantities of food, especially those that are rich in calories. These foods are high in fat and sugar. Eating these foods is unhealthy for anyone, whether lean or fat. The best way to gain weight is to combine muscle-building exercises with three well-balanced, nutritious meals and snacks. The amount and type of weight gain should be closely monitored. Table 6.3 contains suggestions on how to gain weight.

The best approach to weight management/weight control is maintaining a moderate lifestyle so that excess weight is not gained.

Table 6.3 How to Gain Weight

- Increase caloric intake by adding more calories per day (increase meal size, number of meals or snacks).
- Eat extra servings of complex carbohydrates (potatoes, rice, pasta, whole wheat bread).
- Consume 1.5 g of protein per pound of body weight per day.
- Increase consumption of dairy products and fruit juices (provides essential nutrients).
- Increase body's lean mass by adding resistance training to the daily routine.
- Eat frequent small meals.
- Eat snacks between meals.
- Exercise to increase muscle mass.

The most important factor in weight maintenance is physical activity. Almost all people who lose weight and keep it off exercise on a daily basis.

Aim for a Healthy Weight—Key Recommendations—Department of Health and Human Services Report

★ Weight loss lowers elevated blood pressure in overweight and obese persons.

★ Weight loss lowers elevated levels of total cholesterol, LDL, and raises low levels of HDL cholesterol in overweight and obese persons.

★ Weight loss lowers elevated blood glucose levels in overweight and obese persons with type 2 diabetes.

★ Weight loss should be about 2 pounds per week.

★ Use low calorie diets for weight loss.

★ Reduce dietary fat and calories.

★ Physical activity should be a comprehensive part of a weight loss program.

★ Weight loss and weight maintenance should employ low calorie diets and increased physical activity.

References

American College of Sports Medicine. (2006). *ACSMs resource manual for guidelines for exercise testing and prescription.* 5th ed. Philadelphia: Lea & Febiger.

Anspaugh, D. J., Hamrick, M. H., & Rosato, F. D. (2000). *Wellness: Concepts and applications,* 4th ed. Boston: McGraw Hill.

Axen, K. & Vermitsky-Axen, K. (2001). *Illustrated principles of exercise physiology.* Upper Saddle River, NJ: Prentice Hall.

Bishop, J. G. & Aldana, S. G. (1999). *Step up to wellness.* Boston: Allyn & Bacon.

Corbin, C. B., Welk, G. J., Corbin, W. R., & Welk, K. A. (2006). *Concepts of physical fitness: Active lifestyles for wellness,* 13th ed. Boston: McGraw-Hill.

Donatelle, R., Snow, C., & Wilcox, A. (1999). *Wellness: Choices for health and fitness,* 2nd ed. Boston: Wadsworth Publishing Company.

Edlin, G., Golanty, E., & McCormack Brown, K. (2000). *Essentials for health and wellness,* 2nd ed. Sudbury, MA: Jones & Bartlett Publishers.

Edlin, G., Golanty, E., & McCormack Brown, K. (2002). *Health and wellness,* 7th ed. Sudbury, MA: Jones & Bartlett Publishers.

Fahey, T. D., Insel, P. M., & Roth, W. T. (1997). *Fit and well.* Mountain View, CA: Mayfield Publishing Company.

Hales, D. (1999). *An invitation to health,* 8th ed. Boston: Brooks/Cole Publishing Company.

Hoeger, W. W. K. & Hoeger, S. A. (2006). *Principles and labs for physical fitness,* 5th ed. United States: Thomson—Wadsworth.

Howley, E. T. & Franks, B. D. (2003). *Health fitness instructor's handbook.* Champaign, IL: Human Kinetics.

Jenkins, F. C. (2001). *Dynamics of fitness and health,* 8th ed. Dubuque, IA: Kendall/Hunt Publishing Company.

Osness, W. H. (1998). *Exercise and fitness for the older adult.* Dubuque, IA: Kendall/Hunt Publishing Company.

Powers, S. K. & Dodd, S. L. (2003). *Total fitness and wellness: Brief edition.* Boston, MA: Benjamin Cummings.

Pruitt, B. E. & Stein, J. J. (1999). *Health styles: Decision for living well,* 2nd ed. Boston: Allyn & Bacon.

Thygerson, A. L. & Larson, K. L. (2006). *Fit to be well.* Boston: Jones & Bartlett Publishing Company, p. 144.

United States Department of Agriculture. (2005). Weight management. Retrieved January 20, 2006 from *www.health.gov/dietaryguidelines/dga2005/document/html.*

United States Department of Health and Human Services. (1996). *Physical activity and health: A report of the Surgeon General.* Atlanta, GA: U.S. Department of Health and Human Services.

United States Department of Health and Human Services. (2000). *Healthy people 2010: National health promotion and disease.* Washington, D.C.: U.S. Government Printing Office.

United States Department of Health and Human Services. (2006). Aim for a healthy weight. Retrieved January 20, 2006 from *www.nhlbi.nih.gov/health/public/heart/obesity/lose_wt/recommen.htm.*

Web Sites

American Obesity Association *www.obesity.org*

Center for Disease Control & Prevention—Obesity & Genetics *www.cdc.gov/genomics/info/perspectives/obesity*

Frontline on Fat *www.pbs.org/wgbh/pages/frontline/shows/fat*

MedlinePlus on Obesity Weight Loss *www.nlm.hih.gov/medlineplus/weightloss/dieting*

National Association of Anorexia Nervosa & Associated Disease *www.anad.org*

National Eating Disorder Association *www.nationaleatingdisorders.org*

Shape-up America *www.shapeup.org*

USDA Food & Nutrition Center *www.nal.usda.gov/fnic*

Weight loss 2000 *www.weightloss2000.com*

Lab Activity 6.0
Skinfold Measurements

Purpose: To estimate your percentage body fat using skinfold measurements.

Procedure:

1. Wear shorts and loose fitting t-shirts (no leotards or sweats) and do not use lotion on the skin.

2. Measure the percent fat on the right side of the body. Measurements are taken from the following sites:

   Males:
   Chest: Diagonal fold halfway between armpit and nipple.
   Abdomen: Vertical fold 1 inch from navel.
   Thigh: Vertical fold on front of the thigh, midway between knee and hip.

   Females:
   Triceps: Vertical fold on the back of the arm, midway between shoulder and elbow.
   Suprailiac: Diagonal fold above crest of hip bone.
   Thigh: Same as males.

3. Measure each site by pinching a fold of skin firmly with the thumb and forefinger, pulling fold slightly away from underlying muscle. Contract the muscle at site and relax.

4. The calipers are held perpendicular to the fold and placed ½ inch below the finger/thumb hold. Take a reading without delay to avoid excessive compression of the skin.

5. Percent fat is obtained by the measurements from the three sites and checking the values in the chart for males and females.

1. Record total body fat percent _____

2. Record your age _____

3. Record your sex _____

4. Record your fitness level _____

Lab Activity 6.1

Determining Your Ideal Body Weight

Purpose: To assist you in determining your desired body weight based on your current weight and body fat percentage.

Procedures:

1. Weigh yourself to determine your present body weight (BW) = _____ lbs.

2. Record your current Percent Fat (%F) (see Lab 6.0) = _____ %.

3. Record your Desired Fat Percentage (DFP) (17% – 25% for women and 9% – 17% for men) DFP = _____ %.

4. Determine your Fat Weight (FW) by multiplying Body Weight by Percent Fat (BW × %F) _____ BW × %F = _____ FW.

5. Determine your Lean Body Mass (LBM) BW – FW = _____ LBW.

6. Recommended Body Weight (RBW) = LBM ÷ (1.0 – DFP) = RBW _____ LBM ÷ (1.0 – DFP) = _____ RBW.

Lab Activity 6.2

Calculating Waist Circumference and Waist-to-Hip Ratio

Purpose: To calculate your waist circumference and waist-to-hip ratio

Procedures:

Waist Circumference

- Remove clothing to make sure the measuring tape is positioned correctly.
- Locate the upper hip bone and the right iliac crest.
- Place a measuring tape around the abdomen at the level of the iliac crest.
- Be sure the tape is snug but does not compress the skin, and is parallel to the floor.
- The measurement is made at the end of breathing out.

You are more likely to develop heart disease, diabetes, high blood pressure and certain cancers if your waist circumference exceeds:
- More than 40 inches (102 cm) for men
- More than 35 inches (88 cm) for women

Waist-to-Hip Ratio

The waist-to-hip ratio (WHR) determines your pattern of fat distribution

$$\frac{\text{Waist circumference (inches)}}{\text{Hip circumference (inches)}} = \underline{\hspace{4cm}} \text{ WHR}$$

Standards for Waist-to-Hip Ratios

Men	< 0.95 (known as "apples")
Women	< 0.8 (known as "pears")

Recording Your Body Composition

Test 1 Date: _____

Assessment	Score	Fitness Rating
Waist circumference	inches	
Waist-to-hip ratio	ratio	
Skinfold	% body fat	

Lab Activity 6.3
Basal Metabolic Rate (BMR)

Purpose: To determine your basal metabolic rate (BMR)

Procedure:

1. Calculating BMR
   a. Convert body weight in pounds to kilograms (see Lab 6.2) (1 kg = 2.2 lbs)
   b. Multiply weight in kg by BMR factor
      1 calorie per kg for men
      0.9 calorie per kg for women
   c. Multiply calories per hour by 24 hours

Example: Female weighing 122 lbs

1. 122 lbs – 2.2 lbs = 55.5 kg.
2. 55.5 kg × 0.9 (calories/kg/hr) = 50 calories/hr.
3. 50 calories/hr × 24 hr = 1198.8 calories/day.
4. BMR = 1198.8 calories/day.

Calculate Your BMR

1. Convert body weight (BW) in pounds to kilograms

    _____ lbs ÷ 2.2 lbs = _____ kg.

2. Multiply weight in kg by BMR factor by Sex (male factor 1.0, female factor 0.9)

    _____ (factor) × _____ kg = _____ calories/hr.

3. Multiply calories per hour by 24 hours per day (number of calories burned per day)

    _____ calories per hr × 24 = _____ calories/day.

4. BMR _____ calories/day.

Nutrition

Objectives

After completing this chapter, you will be able to do the following:

★ Identify the main nutrients and their function.

★ Differentiate between *trans* fats and saturated fats.

★ Explain DRI, EAR, AI, and UL.

★ Explain how to read a food label.

We all have heard the old adage "You are what you eat." This is true that we are what we eat—and it shows in the strength of our muscles, bones, nails, and the sheen of our hair. There are numerous things one can do to enhance our health, none more important than good nutrition. Good nutrition is vital to good health and is absolutely essential. Major causes of morbidity and mortality are related to poor diet and a sedentary lifestyle. **Nutrition** is a science that explores the relationship between our body and the food we eat.

Proper nutrition is important to promoting health and reducing the risk of chronic disease. Very few Americans eat healthy and meet the recommendations of food intake. About 3% of Americans meet four of the five recommendations for the intake of grains, fruits, vegetables, dairy products, and meat and bean food groups. Poor eating habits are usually established during childhood. Approximately 60% of young adults eat too much fat and less than 20% eat fruits and vegetables (Healthier US.Gov, 2006). Physical activity and a high-quality diet that does not provide excessive calories should enhance the health of Americans.

Most Americans can choose from a large array of foods. At least 10,000 to 20,000 new foods are produced each year. Many of these new foods in the typical American diet are high in calories, fat, sugar, saturated fat, and sodium. So what are we suppose to eat? The plethora of claims and counterclaims about nutrition and diets tend to confuse us.

The dietary recommendations for Americans described in this chapter follow the New Food Guide Pyramid. The New Food Guide Pyramid was adopted in 2005 and is the standard guide for American diets.

Eating Right

We have more food choices than our great-great grandparents could ever had imagined. Because of all of the choices it is hard to choose the correct foods. Most Americans consume more calories than is needed but these do not meet the required intake of nutrients. By following the Food Pyramid we need to choose foods that are high in nutrients while keeping calories under control. The essential nutrients needed to form muscles, bones, and other tissues are carbohydrates, fat, protein, vitamins, minerals, and water. Carbohydrates, fat, and protein provide fuel for the body and are measured in calories. Vitamins, minerals, and water, which have no caloric values, are necessary in the diet and are regulatory nutrients. These nutrients are important for normal bodily function and good health. Nutrients are transported throughout the body via the digestive system. A large gap remains between what is recommended and what Americans actually eat.

According to the Dietary Guidelines (USDA, 2005) we should meet the nutrient need through the foods we consume. Food gives us all of the nutrients and other compounds needed to have beneficial effects on health. A diet that complies with the Dietary Guidelines (USDA, 2005) could reduce the risk of chronic disease.

The knowledge of sound nutrition should be the core of a program to maintain a healthy weight or to reverse overweight and overfatness. These classes or components of food are grouped into six categories called **nutrients.** In order to be a nutrient, a food must be able to be digested, absorbed, transported, and metabolized. Fiber and food additives are not considered a nutrient. The classes of nutrients are fat, protein, carbohydrates, vitamins, minerals, and water (Table 7.0).

Table 7.0 The American Diet: Current and Recommended Carbohydrate, Fat, and Protein Intake Expressed as a Percentage of Total Calories

	Current %	Recommended %*
Carbohydrates:	**50%**	**45–65%**
Simple	**26%**	**Less than 25%**
Complex	**24%**	**20–40%**
Fat:	34%	20–35%**
Monounsaturated:	11%	Up to 20%
Polyunsaturated:	10%	Up to 10%
Saturated:	13%	Less than 7%
Protein:	16%	10–35%

*2002 recommended guidelines by the National Academy of Sciences.
**Less than 30% recommended by most health organizations. A higher amount may be indicated for people with metabolic syndrome.

Carbohydrates

Carbohydrates are our main energy food or source of energy and a part of a healthy diet. With the low carb diet plans carbohydrates have gotten a bad rap. They have been described as the cause of obesity. However, carbohydrates are an important part of a healthful diet. Forty-five to 65% of your total calories should be carbohydrates. However, it is important to choose carbohydrates wisely. Carbohydrates should come from the basic food groups—fruits, grains, vegetables, and milk—which are sources of nutrients. Carbohydrates are considered the body's most important source of energy. Carbohydrates are the preferred fuel during exercise of high intensity, such as long distance running.

There are two classifications of carbohydrates—simple and complex. Simple sugars are found in fruit and complex carbohydrates are found in grains, fruit, and stems, leaves, and roots of vegetables. Simple carbohydrates contribute to 20% of the total calories in the average American diet.

Simple Sugars

The most common simple sugars are:

★ Glucose is the most common and is found in all animals and plants. It is a source of energy, commonly referred to as "blood sugar." Excess glucose is stored in adipose tissue.

★ Fructose is one of the sweetest sugars that is found in fruit and honey. It is converted to glucose in the body.

★ Lactose is naturally present in milk. It consists of glucose and the simple sugar galactose. Galactose is converted to glucose in the body.

Complex Carbohydrates

Complex carbohydrates come from grains, legumes, leaves, stems, and roots of plants. The two classes of complex carbohydrates are starch and fiber.

Starch
★ Starch is digestible and is needed to promote growth. Starch is found in nuts, seeds, roots, legumes, pods, potatoes, and grains. Starch is converted to glucose to provide energy.

★ Carbohydrates are the preferred fuel but are stored in limited amounts in the body. This storage form of carbohydrate, called **glycogen,** is found primarily in muscles and the liver. The glycogen in the muscle is used directly by the muscle. Once the stored glycogen is used it is gone.

Fiber

Fiber is the second main type of complex carbohydrates. We should choose foods that are fiber rich. Low intake of fiber tends to reflect low intakes of whole grains, fruits, and vegetables. Diets rich in fiber may reduce the risk of heart disease and some types of cancer. Other disorders that are related to low fiber intake are constipation, hemorrhoids, and hiatal hernia and obesity.

The recommended fiber intake is 14 grams per 1,000 calories consumed per day (USDA, 2005). Americans eat much less than 14 grams per day and this puts us at risk for disease. We can get the proper amount of fiber by eating more fruits, vegetables, grains, and legumes.

There are two classifications of fiber—soluble and insoluble:

- Soluble fiber can be dissolved in water and forms a gel-like substance that sticks to food. It is found primarily in oatmeal, legumes, barley, and some fruits. Soluble fiber has been shown to lower cholesterol.
- Insoluble fiber cannot be dissolved in water. Insoluble fiber cannot be digested by the body. It binds with water and adds bulk to the stool, preventing constipation.

Key Recommendations for Carbohydrates

★ Choose fiber rich fruits, vegetables, and whole grains.

★ Choose and prepare foods and beverages with little added sugars.

★ Limit foods containing large amounts of added sugars (desserts, candy, soda).

★ Total carbohydrates consumed should be 45–65% of total calories.

★ Each gram of carbohydrates supplies 4 calories per gram to the body.

Fats

A healthy diet should include fats and oils; however, the type and total amount of fat is also important and it makes a difference to heart health. It is widely known that high intakes of saturated fats, *trans* fat, and cholesterol increase the risk of coronary heart disease. Both high intakes of fat (35% of total calories) and low intakes of fat (20% of total calories) can affect one's health. A high intake of fat usually increases saturated fat intake and increases the consumption of calories. A low fat intake increases the risk of inadequate intakes of vitamin E and fatty acids and could contribute to unfavorable changes in high density (HDL) cholesterol.

Fats are used as a source of energy for our bodies. They are the most concentrated source of energy. Each gram of fat supplies 9 calories to the body. The recommended total fat intake in the American diet should be between 20 and 25% of calories for adults. Very few Americans consume less than 20% of calories from fat. Most Americans get more than 35% of their calories from saturated fat. It is important that we decrease the intake of saturated and *trans* fats as well as the intake of cholesterol. Consumption of saturated fats should be kept below 10% of the total caloric intake.

In order to meet the 20–35% of calories from fat, the dietary fats should come from sources of polyunsaturated and monounsaturated fatty acids. Omega-6 polyunsaturated fatty acids come from liquid vegetable oil which includes soybean oil, corn oil, and safflower oil. Omega-3 polyunsaturated fatty acids are found in fish and shellfish. Monounsaturated fatty acids include vegetable oils—canola, olive, sunflower—that are liquid at room temperature, and nuts.

Trans fats are found in processed foods (80% of the *trans* fat in the diet). *Trans* fatty acids produced in the partial hydrogenation of vegetable oils account for more than 80% of total intake. The food industry has to play an important role in decreasing *trans* fatty content of food. The most effective way to limit consumption of foods with processed sources of *trans* fatty acid content is to reduce intake of *trans* fats. You can select products that are low in saturated fat, *trans* fat, and cholesterol by reading the food label carefully. *Trans* fats are formed when liquid oils are made into solid fats—lard and margarine—a process known as hydrogenation. *Trans* fat raises the LDL (bad) cholesterol which in turn increases the risk of coronary heart disease (CHD). It is important to choose foods low in saturated fat, *trans* fat, and cholesterol as a part of a healthful diet. The following table indicates the maximum gram amounts of saturated fat that can be consumed to keep saturated fat intake to below 10%. A 2,000 calorie example is included to compare with the food label.

Total Calorie Intake	Limit on Saturated Fat Intake
1,600	18 g or less
2,000	20 g or less
2,200	24 g or less
2,500	25 g or less
2,800	31 g or less

Trans fat content of certain processed foods is listed below:

Food Group	Contribution (percent of total *trans* fats consumed)
Cakes, cookies, crackers, pies, bread, etc.	40%
Animal products	21%
Margarine	17%
Fried potatoes	8%
Potato chips, corn chips, popcorn	5%
Household shortening	4%
Breakfast cereal and candy	5%

Reading the food label allows us to select products low in saturated fat, *trans* fats, and cholesterol. People look at food labels for different reasons. The following label-building skills are intended to make it easier for you to use nutrition labels to make quick, informed food choices. The information at the top section, on the sample label on the next page, is the serving size and number of servings, calories, and nutrient information. The bottom part contains a footnote with Daily Values for 2,000 and 2,500 calorie diets. This footnote provides recommended dietary information for important nutrients including fats, salt, and fiber. On the label

on the next page look for saturated fat, *trans* fat, total fat, and cholesterol. Check the labels and decide which one has the least amount of saturated fat, *trans* fat, and cholesterol.

Fat Intake Recommendations

★ 10% or less of calories consumed should come from saturated fatty acids and *trans* fatty acids should be as low as possible.

★ Total fat intake should be no more than 20–35% of calories.

★ Make food choices that are lean, low fat, or fat-free.

★ Choose products low in saturated and/or *trans* fatty acids.

★ Most fats should come from fish, nuts, and vegetable oils which are polyunsaturated and monounsaturated fatty acids.

Protein

Protein is an important macronutrient in the diet (10–35% of calories). Most Americans consume enough protein and do not need to increase their intake. **Proteins** are used to make up the major structural components of the body. They are used for tissue growth and repair. Proteins build muscles, teeth, hair, bones, nails, nerve cells, and hemoglobin. They are needed to make enzymes, antibodies, and hormones that regulate normal body functions and fight disease. Proteins can be used as an energy source if an insufficient amount of carbohydrates is available. The main sources of proteins are meats, milk, and other dietary products. Just like carbohydrates, a gram of protein is equal to 4 kilocalories. Proteins make up about 20% of the body mass.

Proteins are made up of **amino acids,** which are used for growth and repair. Proteins in food are classified as *complete* or *incomplete*. This refers to the number and proportion of amino acids present in a particular food. Animal proteins, such as red meat and egg whites, are *complete* because of the presence of all necessary amino acids and the appropriate proportion of each. Plant protein is *incomplete* because it does not have all amino acids and would not be present in appropriate proportions. *Complete* and *incomplete* proteins are included in the diet to satisfy needs.

Compare Spreads!*
Keep an eye on Saturated Fat, *Trans* Fat **and** Cholesterol!

Butter **	Margarine, stick †	Margarine, tub †

Nutrition Facts
Serving Size 1 Tbsp (14g)
Servings Per Container 32

Amount Per Serving
Calories 100 Calories from Fat 100

%Daily Value*
Total Fat 11g — 17%
Saturated Fat 7g ← 35%
Trans Fat 0g ←
Cholesterol 30mg → 10%

Nutrition Facts
Serving Size 1 Tbsp (14g)
Servings Per Container 32

Amount Per Serving
Calories 100 Calories from Fat 100

%Daily Value*
Total Fat 11g — 17%
Saturated Fat 2g ← 10%
Trans Fat 3g ←
Cholesterol 0mg → 0%

Nutrition Facts
Serving Size 1 Tbsp (14g)
Servings Per Container 32

Amount Per Serving
Calories 60 Calories from Fat 60

%Daily Value*
Total Fat 7g — 11%
Saturated Fat 1g ← 5%
Trans Fat 0.5g ←
Cholesterol 0mg → 0%

Saturated Fat : 7g	Saturated Fat : 2g	Saturated Fat : 1 g
+ *Trans* Fat : 0g	+ *Trans* Fat : 3g	+ *Trans* Fat : 0.5g
Combined Amt.: 7g	Combined Amt.: 5g	Combined Amt.: 1.5g
Cholesterol: 10 % DV	Cholesterol: 0 % DV	Cholesterol: 0 % DV

*Nutrient values rounded based on FDA's nutrition labeling regulations. Calorie and cholesterol content estimated.

**Butter values from FDA Table of *Trans* Values, 1/30/95.

† Values derived from 2002 USDA National Nutrient Database for Standard Reference, Release 15.

Compare Desserts!*
Keep an eye on Saturated Fat, *Trans* Fat **and** Cholesterol!

Granola Bar ±	Sandwich Cookies ±	Cake, Iced and Filled ±

Nutrition Facts
Serving Size 1 bar (33g)
Servings Per Container 10

Amount Per Serving
Calories 140 Calories from Fat 45

%Daily Value*
Total Fat 5g — 8%
Saturated Fat 1g ← 5%
Trans Fat 0g ←
Cholesterol 0mg → 0%

Nutrition Facts
Serving Size 2 cookies (28g)
Servings Per Container 19

Amount Per Serving
Calories 130 Calories from Fat 45

%Daily Value*
Total Fat 5g — 8%
Saturated Fat 1g ← 5%
Trans Fat 1.5g ←
Cholesterol 0mg → 0%

Nutrition Facts
Serving Size 2 cakes (66g)
Servings Per Container 6

Amount Per Serving
Calories 280 Calories from Fat 140

%Daily Value*
Total Fat 16g — 25%
Saturated Fat 3.5g ← 18%
Trans Fat 4.5g ←
Cholesterol 10mg → 3%

Saturated Fat : 1 g	Saturated Fat : 1 g	Saturated Fat : 3.5g
+ *Trans* Fat : 0 g	+ *Trans* Fat : 1.5g	+ *Trans* Fat : 4.5g
Combined Amt.: 1 g	Combined Amt.: 2.5g	Combined Amt.: 8 g
Cholesterol: 0 % DV	Cholesterol: 0 % DV	Cholesterol: 3 % DV

*Nutrient values rounded based on FDA's nutrition labeling regulations.

± Values for total fat, saturated fat, and *trans* fat were based on the means of analytical data for several food samples from Subramaniam, S., et al., "*Trans*, Saturated, and Unsaturated Fat in Foods in the United States Prior to Mandatory *trans*-Fat Labeling," *Lipids* 39, 11-18, 2004. Other information and values were derived from food labels in the marketplace.

Figure 7.0

Table 7.1   Caloric and Fat Content of Selected Fast Food Items

	Calories	Total Fat (grams)	Saturated Fat (grams)	Percent Fat Calories
Burgers				
McDonald's Big Mac	590	34	11	52
McDonald's Big N' Tasty with Cheese	590	37	12	56
McDonald's Quarter Pounder with Cheese	530	30	13	51
Burger King Whopper	760	46	15	54
Burger King Bacon Double Cheeseburger	580	34	18	53
Burger King BK Smokehouse Cheddar Griller	720	48	19	60
Burger King Whopper with Cheese	850	53	22	56
Burger King Double Whopper	1,060	69	27	59
Burger King Double Whopper with Cheese	1,150	76	33	59
Sandwiches				
Arby's Regular Roast Beef	350	16	6	41
Arby's Super Roast Beef	470	23	7	44
Arby's Roast Chicken Club	520	28	7	48
Arby's Market Fresh Roast Beef & Swiss	810	42	13	47
McDonald's Crispy Chicken	430	21	8	43
McDonald's Filet-O-Fish	470	26	5	50
McDonald's Chicken McGrill	400	17	3	38
Wendy's Chicken Club	470	19	4	36
Wendy's Breast Fillet	430	16	3	34
Wendy's Grilled Chicken	300	7	2	21
Burger King Specialty Chicken	560	28	6	45
Subway Veggie Delight*	226	3	1	12
Subway Turkey Breast	281	5	2	16
Subway Sweet Onion Chicken Teriyaki	374	5	2	12
Subway Steak & Cheese	390	14	5	32
Subway Cold Cut Trio	440	21	7	43
Subway Tuna	450	22	6	44
Mexican				
Taco Bell Crunchy Taco	170	10	4	53
Taco Bell Taco Supreme	220	14	6	57
Taco Bell Soft Chicken Taco	190	7	3	33
Taco Bell Tostada	250	12	5	43
Taco Bell Bean Burrito	370	12	4	29
Taco Bell Fiesta Steak Burrito	370	12	4	29
Taco Bell Grilled Steak Soft Taco	290	17	4	53
Taco Bell Double Decker Taco	340	14	5	37
French Fries				
Wendy's, biggie (5½ oz.)	440	19	7	39
McDonald's, large (6oz.)	540	26	9	43
Burger King, large (5½ oz.)	500	25	13	45
Shakes				
Wendy's Frosty, medium (16 oz.)	440	11	7	23
McDonald's McFlurry, small (12 oz.)	610	22	14	32
Burger King, Old Fashioned Ice Cream Shake, medium (22 oz.)	760	41	29	49
Hash Browns				
McDonald's Hash Browns (2 oz.)	130	8	4	55
Burger King, Hash Browns, small (2½ oz.)	230	15	9	59

*6-inch sandwich with no mayo
Source: Adapted from *Restaurant Confidential* by Michael F. Jacobson and Jayne Hurley (Workman, 2002).

All the amino acids needed can be obtained by food; it is not recommended to take protein supplements. Excessive protein intake can lead to urinary calcium loss. Proteins should account for the smallest intake of calories consumed.

Vitamins

Vitamins are organic compounds that are necessary in the diet and that have specific regulatory functions. Vitamins are not used for fuel but the 13 types of vitamins have a variety of functions. It is vital to consume foods containing the essential vitamins needed for the prevention of disease and the maintenance of good health. Vegetables and fruits are a good source of vitamin A (as carotenoids) and vitamin C, folate, and potassium. Consumption of foods high in vitamin C and vitamin E are associated with the reduced risk for cancer and heart disease. Vitamins C and E and carotenoid-rich foods act as antioxidants, which help prevent cancer and other forms of disease. Vitamins aid in clotting of the blood, in bone formation, and in the synthesis of protein.

Vitamins are classified into two major groups: **fat-soluble** and **water-soluble. Water-soluble** vitamins are not stored but are eliminated from the body by the kidneys. Vitamins B and C must be consumed on a daily basis as they are water-soluble and are eliminated from the body. Vitamins A, D, E, and K are **fat-soluble.** Since these vitamins are soluble in fat it is possible for them to be stored. A small daily intake of vitamins A, D, E, and K is recommended. It is possible to consume too many vitamins and they can accumulate to toxic levels.

People who follow a healthy diet, which includes green and yellow vegetables, citrus fruit, tomatoes, orange fruits, and leafy greens do not need to take vitamin supplements.

Minerals

Minerals have no calories and provide no energy for the body but serve a variety of functions in the body. Minerals are crucial to the maintenance of the water balance in the body. Minerals are available in many foods and play an important role regulating body functions. Three of the most important minerals are calcium, iron, and sodium. Calcium is important to the mineralization of the bone, muscle, nerve, and blood development. Most Americans do not consume adequate amounts of calcium. If diets have inadequate calcium, a condition known as **osteoporosis** may exist in the elderly as well as younger people. **Osteoporosis** is a disease characterized by the loss of bone mass and strength in the bone. Iron is an important mineral and related to the blood carrying adequate oxygen throughout the body. Individuals should strive to eat adequate servings of food rich in iron. Sodium is another mineral that is found in most foods and we do not have to add table salt. Salt intake is recommended for good health but we should not exceed the recommended intake of 2,400 mg per day. Most processed foods have a high content of salt and we consume well above the recommended levels. Salt should not be more than 4 to 6 grams per day (1 teaspoon is equal to 3 grams of table salt).

Water

Water is essential and a critical component of a healthy diet. It is a major component of all food we eat. Most of the body is made up of water, approximately 60% of an adult's total body weight. Water contains no calories, provides no energy to the body, and provides no nutrients but is extremely important to health and survival. One must consume water on a regular basis to maintain water balance and it is critical to many bodily functions. Water is necessary for energy production, digestion, and maintaining the proper environment inside and outside cells. Water is necessary to maintain body temperature control and elimination of waste products from the body. It carries oxygen and nutrients to the cells via the blood, regulates temperature through perspiration, and lubricates the joints. Most water intake comes from beverages; however, solid foods also make a significant contribution. Most fruits and vegetables are more than 80% water.

How much water is enough? We are advised to drink at least eight glasses of water every day. Water is needed before, during, and after physical activity. Total water intake includes fluids from other beverages and moisture found in foods. If you are physically active in hot environments you may need more water; however, most people consume adequate fluid in response to thirst. Do not rely on thirst to regulate your fluid intake. Plain tap water is the preferred source of water. Water consumption should occur throughout the day. It is possible to consume too much water but this rarely occurs. Individuals should limit their intake of caffeinated beverages.

Dietary Reference Intake (DRI)

A basis of the premise of the Dietary Guidelines is that our diets should provide nutrients needed for growth and health. Individuals are encouraged to achieve the most recent nutrient intake recommendations of the Institute of Medicine, known as the Dietary Reference Intakes (DRI). The DRI nutrient list can be found in Appendix A.

The Dietary Guidelines suggest that the nutrients we consume should come primarily from foods. Foods contain the vitamins and minerals as well as other natural substances such as carotenoids, flavonoids, isoflavones, and protease inhibitors that could provide protection against chronic health conditions (USDA, 2005). The Dietary Guidelines give science-based advice on food and physical activity choices for health. The Dietary Guidelines describe a healthy diet as one that:

★ Emphasizes fruits, vegetables, whole grains, and fat-free or low-fat milk and milk products

★ Includes lean meats, poultry, fish, egg whites, and nuts

★ Is low in saturated fats, *trans* fats, cholesterol, salt, and added sugars

The general term "DRIs" includes four general guidelines for establishing adequate amounts of nutrient intake in the diet. These are Estimated Average Requirement (EAR), Recommended Dietary Allowance (RDA), Adequate Intake (AI), and Upper Intake Level (UL).

Table 7.2   Dietary Reference Intakes (DRIs): Recommended Dietary Allowances (RDA) and Adequate Intakes (AI) for Selected Nutrients

	Recommended Dietary Allowances (RDA)													Adequate Intakes (AI)					
	Thiamin (mg)	Riboflavin (mg)	Niacin (mg NE)	Vitamin B₆ (mg)	Folate (mcg DFE)	Vitamin B₁₂ (mcg)	Phosphorus (mg)	Magnesium (mg)	Vitamin A (mcg)	Vitamin C (mg)	Vitamin E (mg)	Selenium (mcg)	Iron (mcg)	Calcium (mg)	Vitamin D (mcg)	Fluoride (mg)	Pantothenic acid (mg)	Biotin (mg)	Choline (mg)
Males																			
14–18	1.2	1.3	16	1.3	400	2.4	1,250	410	900	75	15	55	11	1,300	5	3	5.0	25	550
19–30	1.2	1.3	16	1.3	400	2.4	700	400	900	90	15	55	8	1,000	5	4	5.0	30	550
31–50	1.2	1.3	16	1.3	400	2.4	700	420	900	90	15	55	8	1,000	5	4	5.0	30	550
51–70	1.2	1.3	16	1.7	400	2.4	700	420	900	90	15	55	8	1,200	10	4	5.0	30	550
>70	1.2	1.3	16	1.7	400	2.4	700	420	900	90	15	55	8	1,200	15	4	5.0	30	550
Females																			
14–18	1.0	1.0	14	1.2	400	2.4	1,250	360	700	65	15	55	15	1,300	5	3	5.0	25	400
19–30	1.1	1.1	14	1.3	400	2.4	700	310	700	75	15	55	18	1,000	5	3	5.0	30	425
31–50	1.1	1.1	14	1.3	400	2.4	700	320	700	75	15	55	18	1,000	5	3	5.0	30	425
51–70	1.1	1.1	14	1.5	400	2.4	700	320	700	75	15	55	8	1,200	10	3	5.0	30	425
>70	1.1	1.1	14	1.5	400	2.4	700	320	700	75	15	55	8	1,200	15	3	5.0	30	425
Pregnant	1.4	1.4	18	1.9	600	2.6	*	+40	750	85	15	60	27	*	*	3	6.0	30	450
Lactating	1.5	1.6	17	2.0	500	2.8	*	*	1,300	120	19	70	10	*	*	3	7.0	35	550

*Values for these nutrients do not change with pregnancy or lactation. Use the value listed for women of comparable age.
Source: Adapted from *Recommended Dietary Allowances,* 10th Edition, and the *Dietary Reference Intakes series.*

Estimated Average Requirement

The EAR determines the inadequacy for a nutrient in the diet. The EAR is the amount of nutrients needed to meet the nutrient requirement of one-half of the healthy people in a specific population (Hoeger & Hoeger, 2006). This means that at least 50% of a specific population (age and gender) have met their nutrient requirements.

Recommended Dietary Allowance

The RDA is the daily allowance of a nutrient considered adequate to meet the nutrient needs of healthy people. The RDA recommendation is found on the food label and is designated as percent daily values. The RDA as recommended is usually higher than what is required.

Adequate Intake

The AI values are used when a firm RDA cannot be established. The AI value is an approximation of observed nutrient intakes of a group of healthy people.

Upper Intake Level

The UL reflects the maximum level of daily nutrient intake that seems to be safe and without adverse effects. Supplements and fortified foods may cause intakes to exceed safe levels of nutrients. An individual should not exceed the recommended UL per day.

MyPyramid

The USDA released new dietary guidelines and a revised MyPyramid Food Guide Pyramid. MyPyramid is a food guidance system. The food system provides options to help Americans make healthy food choices and to be active every day. The different food groups are highlighted with different colors—orange for grains; green for vegetables; red for fruits; blue for milk; purple for meat and beans; and yellow for oils. The width of the bands at the bottom of each color represents specific daily amounts from each food group and limits for calories from fat, added sugars, and alcohol. The icon climbing the stairs indicates the right balance between food and physical activity. Please visit *www.mypyramid.gov* for more information and activities—a food plan is available at this site.

MyPyramid Plan offers you a chance to get your own food plan at an appropriate calorie level. A color MyPyramid can be found on the inside cover of the back page.

As shown in Figure 7.2, the food label, each gram of fat provides 9 calories, 1 gram of carbohydrates provides 4 calories, and 1 gram of protein provides 4 calories. When figuring the percent of each nutrient of individual food you may find Table 7.1 helpful. Multiply the total fat grams by 9 and divide by the total calories in that food (per serving). Then multiply by 100 to get the percentage.

The equation shows that 73% of the total calories comes from fat.

As we read the labels we should be wary of the "fat-free" products. These products use weight and not percent of total calories, as a measure of fat. Many of these products are high in fats.

Recommended Dietary Intake of Nutrients

★ Consume a diet with a variety of nutrients—dense food and beverages.

★ Limit intake of saturated and *trans* fats, cholesterol, added sugars, salt, and alcohol.

★ Meet recommended intakes within energy needs by adopting a balanced eating pattern.

★ Individuals with dark skin should consume extra vitamin D from vitamin D-fortified foods.

Nutrition for Athletes

The beneficial effects of nutrition on exercise and performance are well documented. This is especially true for athletes. What an athlete eats and drinks can affect exercise performance. The athlete who wants to optimize exercise performance needs to have good nutrition and

---

Table 7.3   Determining Fat Content of Food

Percent fat calories = (grams of fat) × 9 – calories per serving × 100
Percent fat calories = 13 grams of fat × 9 – 60 calories per serving × 100
Percent fat calories = 117 – 160 (60 × 100) = .73 (73% of calories come from fat)

Figure 7.1

GRAINS
Make half your grains whole

Eat at least 3 oz. of whole-grain cereals, breads, crackers, rice, or pasta every day

1 oz. is about 1 slice of bread, about 1 cup of breakfast cereal, or ½ cup of cooked rice, cereal, or pasta

VEGETABLES
Vary your veggies

Eat more dark-green veggies like broccoli, spinach, and other dark leafy greens

Eat more orange vegetables like carrots and sweetpotatoes

Eat more dry beans and peas like pinto beans, kidney beans, and lentils

FRUITS
Focus on fruits

Eat a variety of fruit

Choose fresh, frozen, canned, or dried fruit

Go easy on fruit juices

MILK
Get your calcium-rich foods

Go low-fat or fat-free when you choose milk, yogurt, and other milk products

If you don't or can't consume milk, choose lactose-free products or other calcium sources such as fortified foods and beverages

MEAT & BEANS
Go lean with protein

Choose low-fat or lean meats and poultry

Bake it, broil it, or grill it

Vary your protein routine — choose more fish, beans, peas, nuts, and seeds

---

For a 2,000-calorie diet, you need the amounts below from each food group. To find the amounts that are right for you, go to MyPyramid.gov.

| Eat 6 oz. every day | Eat 2½ cups every day | Eat 2 cups every day | Get 3 cups every day; for kids aged 2 to 8, it's 2 | Eat 5½ oz. every day |

Find your balance between food and physical activity

- Be sure to stay within your daily calorie needs.
- Be physically active for at least 30 minutes most days of the week.
- About 60 minutes a day of physical activity may be needed to prevent weight gain.
- For sustaining weight loss, at least 60 to 90 minutes a day of physical activity may be required.
- Children and teenagers should be physically active for 60 minutes every day, or most days.

Know the limits on fats, sugars, and salt (sodium)

- Make most of your fat sources from fish, nuts, and vegetable oils.
- Limit solid fats like butter, stick margarine, shortening, and lard, as well as foods that contain these.
- Check the Nutrition Facts label to keep saturated fats, *trans* fats, and sodium low.
- Choose food and beverages low in added sugars. Added sugars contribute calories with few, if any, nutrients.

MyPyramid.gov
STEPS TO A HEALTHIER YOU

USDA

U.S. Department of Agriculture
Center for Nutrition Policy and Promotion
April 2005
CNPP-15

USDA is an equal opportunity provider and employer.

Table 7.4   MyPyramid Food Intake Pattern Calorie Levels

MyPyramid assigns individuals to a calorie level based on their sex, age, and activity level.

The chart below identifies the calorie levels for males and females by age and activity level. Calorie levels are provided for each year of childhood, from 2–18 years, and for adults in 5-year increments.

	MALES				FEMALES		
Activity level	Sedentary*	Mod. active*	Active*	**Activity level**	Sedentary*	Mod. active*	Active*
AGE				**AGE**			
2	1000	1000	1000	2	1000	1000	1000
3	1000	1400	1400	3	1000	1200	1400
4	1200	1400	1600	4	1200	1400	1400
5	1200	1400	1600	5	1200	1400	1600
6	1400	1600	1800	6	1200	1400	1600
7	1400	1600	1800	7	1200	1600	1800
8	1400	1600	2000	8	1400	1600	1800
9	1600	1800	2000	9	1400	1600	1800
10	1600	1800	2200	10	1400	1800	2000
11	1800	2000	2200	11	1600	1800	2000
12	1800	2200	2400	12	1600	2000	2200
13	2000	2200	2600	13	1600	2000	2200
14	2000	2400	2800	14	1800	2000	2400
15	2000	2600	3000	15	1800	2000	2400
16	2400	2800	3200	16	1800	2000	2400
17	2400	2800	3200	17	1800	2000	2400
18	2400	2800	3200	18	1800	2000	2400
19–20	2600	2800	3000	19–20	2000	2200	2400
21–25	2400	2800	3000	21–25	2000	2200	2400
26–30	2400	2600	3000	26–30	1800	2000	2400
31–35	2400	2600	3000	31–35	1800	2000	2200
36–40	2400	2600	2800	36–40	1800	2000	2200
41–45	2200	2600	2800	41–45	1800	2000	2200
46–50	2200	2400	2800	46–50	1800	2000	2200
51–55	2200	2400	2800	51–55	1600	1800	2200
56–60	2200	2400	2600	56–60	1600	1800	2200
61–65	2000	2400	2600	61–65	1600	1800	2000
66–70	2000	2200	2600	66–70	1600	1800	2000
71–75	2000	2200	2600	71–75	1600	1800	2000
76 and up	2000	2200	2400	76 and up	1600	1800	2000

*Calorie levels are based on the Estimated Energy Requirements (EER) and activity levels from the Institute of Medicine Dietary Reference Intakes Macronutrients Report, 2002.
SEDENTARY = less than 30 minutes a day of moderate physical activity in addition to daily activities.
MOD. ACTIVE = at least 30 minutes up to 60 minutes a day of moderate physical activity in addition to daily activities.
ACTIVE = 60 or more minutes a day of moderate physical activity in addition to daily activities.

(1) **Serving Size**: Serving sizes are standardized to make it easier to compare similar food followed by the number of grams

(2) **Calories and Calories from Fat**: Provides the number of calories per serving (2 servings with 250 calories per serving would be 500 calories)

(3) **The Nutrients**: (Limit these nutrients) Fat, saturated fat, *trans* fat, cholesterol, sodium, sugars. How many calories are there, in the sample label, from fat in ONE serving?
Answer: 110

(4) **The Nutrients**: (Get enough of these) These nutrients include dietary fiber, vitamin A, vitamin C, calcium, and iron

(5) **Footnote**: Note the * used after the heading "%Daily Value" on the Nutrition Facts label. **% DVs are based on a 2,000 calorie diet—** This statement must be on all food labels. DVs are recommended levels of daily intake for a 2,000 calorie diet.

Sample label for
Macaroni & Cheese

Nutrition Facts

Serving Size 1 cup (228g)
Servings Per Container 2

Amount Per Serving

Calories 250   Calories from Fat 110

	% Daily Value*
Total Fat 12g	**18%**
Saturated Fat 3g	**15%**
Trans Fat 3g	
Cholesterol 30mg	**10%**
Sodium 470mg	**20%**
Total Carbohydrate 31g	**10%**
Dietary Fiber 0g	**0%**
Sugars 5g	
Protein 5g	

Vitamin A	4%
Vitamin C	2%
Calcium	20%
Iron	4%

* Percent Daily Values are based on a 2,000 calorie diet. Your Daily Values may be higher or lower depending on your calorie needs.

		Calories:	2,000	2,500
Total Fat	Less than		65g	80g
Sat Fat	Less than		20g	25g
Cholesterol	Less than		300mg	300mg
Sodium	Less than		2,400mg	2,400mg
Total Carbohydrate			300g	375g
Dietary Fiber			25g	30g

(6) **Percent Daily Value (% DV)**: The DVs are based on the Daily Value recommended for key nutrients but only for a 2,000 calorie daily diet—not 2,500 calories. **5% or less is low and 20% DV or more is high.** Look at the amount of Total Fat in one serving listed on the sample nutrition label. Is 18% DV contributing a lot or little to your fat limit of 100% DV? 18% is not yet high but if you ate two servings you would double that amount, eating 36% of your daily allowance for Total Fat. That leaves you with 64% (100% – 36% = 64%) for **all** other foods for the day.

Figure 7.2   How to Read the Food Label

hydration. The following is a sample of key recommendations for nutrition and athletic performance:

★ Adequate energy needs to be consumed (food) during high-intensity exercise.

★ Carbohydrates are important to replace muscle glycogen and maintain blood glucose.

★ Increase protein requirements during exercise—this is met through the diet alone.

★ Do not restrict fat—fat is important in the diets of athletes and provides energy, fat-soluble vitamins, and essential fatty acids.

★ Avoid dehydration—dehydration decreases performance.

★ Before exercise the athlete's meals/snacks should be low fat and fiber but high intake of carbohydrates.

★ During exercise the athlete should replace fluids and carbohydrates for maintenance of blood glucose levels.

★ After exercise the meals should provide adequate energy and carbohydrates to ensure rapid recovery.

★ Vitamins and minerals should come from a variety of foods—supplements should not be required (American College of Sports Medicine et al., 2000).

A food composition table can be found in Appendix A.

References

American College of Sports Medicine, American Dietetic Association & Dietitians of Canada (2000). Nutrition and athletic performance. *Medicine & Science in Sports & Exercise,* Electronic version. *www.acsm-msse.org*

Corbin, C. B., Welk, G. J., Corbin, W. R. & Welk, K. A. (2006). *Fundamental concepts of fitness and wellness,* 2nd ed. Boston: McGraw-Hill.

Corbin, C. B., Welk, G. J., Corbin, W. R., & Welk, K. A. (2006). *Concepts of physical fitness:*

Pop Quiz

Which should you choose?
Select a product for an answer!

Serving size = 1 Tablespoon* (g = grams; mg = milligrams)

Product	Calories	Total Fat g	Saturated Fat g	*Trans* Fat g	Combined Saturated and *Trans* Fats g	Cholesterol mg
Margarine, 80% fat, stick [†]	100	11	2	3	5	0
Butter **	100	11	7	0	7	30
Margarine, 60% fat, tub [‡]	80	9	1.5	0	1.5	0
Margarine, 70% fat, stick [†]	90	10	2	2.5	4.5	0

*Nutrient values rounded based on FDA's nutrition labeling regulations. Calorie and cholesterol content estimated.
**Butter values from FDA Table of *Trans* Values. Dated 1/30/95.
[†] Values derived from 2002 USDA National Nutrient Database for Standard Reference. Release 15.
[‡] Prerelease values derived from 2003 USDA National Nutrient Database for Standard Reference. Release 16.

Answers:
Margarine, 80% fat, stick [†] Look for another option. This choice does not contain the lowest combined amount of Saturated and *Trans* Fat.
Butter** Look for another option. This choice contains the highest combined amount of Saturated and *Trans* Fat, and the highest amount of Cholesterol.
Margarine, 60% fat, tub [‡] Congratulations! This choice has the lowest combined amount of saturated and *Trans* fat 0 g of Cholesterol.
Margarine, 70% fat, stick [†] Look for another option. This choice does not contain the lowest combined amount of Saturated and *Trans* Fat.

Active lifestyles for wellness, 13th ed. Boston: McGraw-Hill.

Corbin, C. B., Welk, G. J., Corbin, W. R., & Welk, K. A. (2006). *Concepts of fitness and wellness: A comprehensive lifestyle approach,* 6th ed. Boston: McGraw-Hill.

Hoeger, W. W. K. & Hoeger, S. A. (2003). *Lifetime fitness and wellness,* 7th ed. United States: Thomson—Wadsworth.

Hoeger, W. W. K. & Hoeger, S. A. (2006). *Principles and labs for physical fitness,* 5th ed. United States: Thomson—Wadsworth.

Nicholas Institute of Sports Medicine and Athletic Trauma. (2005). *NISMAT sports nutrition corner: Carbohydrate.* Retrieved February, 15, 2006 from *www.nismat.org/nutricor/carbohydrate.*

U.S. Food and Drug Administration. (2004). *How to understand and use the nutrition facts label.* Retrieved February, 13, 2006 from *www.cfsan.fda.gov.*

USDA. (2005). *MyPyramid. www.mypyramid.gov.*

Web Sites

Fast Food Finder *www.olen.com/food*

Mayo Clinic Diet and Nutrition Resource Center *www.mayohealth.org/mayo/common/htm/diet/page.htm*

MyPyramid *www.mypyramid.gov*

USDA Food and Nutrition Information Center *www.nal.usda.gov/fnic*

Nutrition Analysis Tool, University of Illinois *www.nat.uiuc.edu*

Lab Activity 7.0
MyPyramid Food Guide

Purpose: To make an accurate assessment of your nutritional intake.

Procedures:

1. Go to *http://www.nutrition.gov.* This will bring you to the MyPyramid page of the Department of Agriculture. On the right side of the page click on "I want to see the MyPyramid Food Guidance System." You will be asked to submit your age, sex, and activity level. Once you have completed this, click on the Submit button.

2. The next page will list the food items and amount. You are to fill out the table that is left blank.

3. Choose "Proceed to Food Intake". Enter a food from your MyPyramid worksheet in the text box and click "Search." Add a food that you have eaten that day by clicking on it from the list. Repeat until you have included all foods and beverages eaten/drunk for that day.

4. Choose "Select Quantity"—choose the serving size and the amount of servings consumed. Click "Save and Analyze."

5. On "Analyze Your Food Intake" page choose Meeting Dietary Guidelines. When prompted, choose "Maintain Current Weight" and record your findings on the table below. Use the back button to return to the previous page, and choose the recommendations for "gradually achieving and maintaining a healthy weight." Record your findings. How do these two options differ? Which do you think most pertains to you?

6. At the top of the window, choose "Analyze Your Food Intake" to return to this page. Choose "Calculate Nutrient Intake from Foods." Complete the table with the recommended amounts and your actual intake of the nutrients listed.

7. Go to MyPyramid Worksheet and complete the form. Set a goal for each day and determine how you did each day.

Results:

1. Write a one-page description of your daily nutritional intake. Use the following questions to write the paper.
   a. Did your dietary expectations differ from that of the USDA? Are you meeting the Dietary Guidelines recommendations?
   b. Are you currently at a healthy weight? What dietary changes do you need to make or attain a healthier weight?

2. If your total fat percentage is 30%, which foods contributed to your high fat intake?

3. Do you need to make any changes to improve the nutritional quality of your diet? Do you need to eat more fruits and vegetables? Do you eat too much salt, sugar, or fat? Should you replace your whole or 2% milk with skim milk?

Ollie American's Diet

Read the following description of Ollie American's diet and analyze it by answering the following questions about food groups, servings, and daily activity.

Ollie American gets up in the morning and heads for school. On the way to school, he stops at a convenience store and grabs a 32-ounce soda and a bag of chips. He sips the soda and eats the chips on the way to school. He feels energized and ready to face the day. Around mid-morning he starts to feel a little tired and goes to the vending machine during a break in class. He buys a can of soda and a candy bar to last him through the morning. At lunch, Ollie American is starving, so he and his friends head for a local fast-food place. Ollie orders a large hamburger with everything on it, a large order of fries, and a soda.

After class, Ollie heads for home. For relaxation, he spends a couple of hours playing a video game. Since this is Monday evening football night, Ollie is having some friends over to watch the game. The group puts their money together to order several large pepperoni pizzas. They decide to stop at the store on the way home to purchase some beer and chips to go with the pizza. During the game, Ollie has about half of a large pizza, a half bag of chips, and has four cans of beer.

Ollie has noticed that he is starting to gain weight. He is six feet tall and weighs 230 pounds.

1. What is Ollie's body mass index (BMI)? _____

   BMI = (705 × body weight) ÷ by (height × height)

2. According to Ollie's BMI, is he considered obese? _____

3. Estimate the food groups and number of servings of each for Ollie's diet.

Food Group	Foods Eaten	Number of Servings
Bread, cereal, rice, pasta		
Vegetables		
Fruits		
Milk, yogurt, cheese		
Meat, fish, poultry, eggs		

4. What food items are contributing to Ollie's weight gain?

5. What suggestions would you make to help Ollie choose a more healthy diet and lose weight?

Critical Thinking about Tobacco Advertising

Despite the well-known detrimental health effects of smoking, efforts to prevent people from starting to smoke or help them quit are hampered by tobacco industry advertising. Consider the following:

- Tobacco is heavily marketed. Of all products, only automobiles are marketed more intensely than tobacco products.
- In 1998, tobacco companies spent 18 million dollars a day to advertise their products. Many advertisements have special appeal to young people.
- Children and teenagers make up the majority of new smokers.
- About 85 percent of adolescent smokers buy Marlboro, Newport, or Camel cigarettes, the three most heavily advertised brands. With the introduction of the cartoon character Joe Camel, the RJ Reynolds's share of the adolescent's cigarette market increased significantly.
- Tobacco advertising is increasingly aimed at young women, as in the Virginia Slims slogan, "You've come a long way, baby!" Women's groups are combating this type of advertising with "Virginia Slam" campaigns.
- Tobacco products are advertised and promoted more in communities with a high percentage of ethnic minorities.*

Your instructor will divide the class into groups. Discuss the following questions. Appoint a recorder to write your best ideas on the board.

1. What techniques are used by tobacco advertisements to encourage people to smoke?

2. What are the best ways to prevent young people from starting to smoke?

3. What are your best ideas for reducing tobacco usage in the United States?

---

*U.S. Department of Health and Human Services, Centers for Disease Control and Prevention, Office on Smoking and Health, 11 April 2001.

Name: _____ Section: _____ Date: _____

Health

Make a quick list of your activities during the last 48 hours. List any activities that promote or detract from your health including the foods you ate at each meal.*

Promote Health   **Detract from Health**

Based on the above list, write three intention statements for maintaining good health in the future.

1.

2.

3.

*Exercise contributed by Paul Delys, counselor and professor, SDSU and Cuyamaca College, San Diego, CA.

Fitness Equipment and Facilities

Objectives

After completing this chapter, you will be able to do the following:

★ Describe the various types of cardio and weight training equipment that can be used when exercising.

★ Discuss what you should look for when selecting a health or fitness club.

★ Explain how shoes should be selected for exercising.

★ Explain what to look for when buying fitness equipment.

The rapid growth in the fitness and wellness programs during the past decade has spurred the growth of exercise equipment and facilities. The consumer has seen a barrage of media advertisement ranging from pills to help you lose weight or improve your memory to exercise equipment and fitness centers. The stereotypical image of healthy and fit young men and women appears in magazines and on television.

The interest in fitness and exercise is seen in the expenditures for sport equipment and exercise equipment. The sale of exercise equipment has become big business. Sales of fitness equipment, shoes, clothing, and home exercise equipment have skyrocketed in the last 15–20 years. Stationary bicycles, treadmills, stairclimbers, rowing machines, diet and exercise books, and weight training equipment seem to be the most popular types of equipment. Corporate fitness programs have increased in number, recreational programs in the community have risen, and the number of fitness facilities has increased, including facilities just for women.

In order not to be taken by fraud, it is essential for the consumer to become educated by taking a critical look at the products or services you plan to purchase. You need to become an informed consumer. How do you determine fact from fiction when purchasing exercise equipment or determining which fitness center to join? Do your homework—research the equipment in the library or seek the advice of a reputable professional. Be sure the professional is not connected with the facility or receives a profit from product sales but is one who knows the product you want to buy. Shop around and make a careful selection of the product. Realize that it is easy to be "taken in" by advertisement that projects the image that appeals to the consumer.

Fitness Equipment

The fitness equipment or facilities you choose will depend upon the type of activity in which you plan to engage. Consider the requirements of your activity when evaluating fitness products. Make sure you judge the product according to function, not looks, price, or fanciness. Your choice of exercise equipment often affects the likelihood of continued use, risk of injury, and enjoyment. The equipment should fit well and be without defects. Just following a few guidelines, when purchasing equipment, will prolong participation with the equipment.

★ Always try out equipment before buying it. Read all of the product information. Ask a professional for recommendations and try out the equipment at a gym before you decide to purchase the equipment.

★ Price. Prices of equipment can range from $2.00 for a jump rope to $100,000 for highly specialized aerobic or computer driven isokinetic devices. You do not need to purchase an expensive piece of equipment to see fitness results. Before buying expensive fitness equipment, ask yourself if you would use the equipment often enough to justify the cost.

★ Quality. You need to buy good quality equipment; however, the good quality does not have to be expensive. Like buying an automobile, review *Consumer Report* for their rating of fitness equipment. When buying equipment check for a warranty, money back guarantee, and repair cost. When buying equipment be sure it is beneficial, but remember, does it do what you what it to do? For example, does the cardiorespiratory

equipment allow you to work within your target heart rate range? Does the muscular strength equipment allow the exercised muscle to be worked through a full range of motion and overloaded enough to create muscular strength gains?

★ Safety. Check the instruction booklet to make sure you are using equipment correctly and safely. Make periodic checks on the equipment to ensure it is in good working condition. Replace all worn parts on a regular basis.

★ Exercise Style. Are you going to buy the equipment just to have it sit, collect dust, or be a clothes hanger? Will sitting on a stationary bicycle for 30 minutes be boring? Are you motivated to use your free weights? How often will you use the equipment? If you honestly think you can answer these questions positively, then go ahead and purchase the equipment. If you only use the equipment occasionally, you will be better off joining a gym. If you work hard and push the equipment to the maximum, buy a model that can handle the stress.

Home Exercise Equipment

More and more of us are purchasing equipment to turn our homes into fitness centers. The convenience of working out at home would dictate a careful choice of equipment. Among the more popular pieces of home equipment are treadmills, rowing machines, stationary bicycles, stairclimbers, ski machines, multi-gyms, and weight systems.

Treadmills

Treadmills provide the jogger/runner or walker the same benefits of jogging/running or walking out-of-doors.

"At its heart a treadmill is a looped belt propelled by an electric motor and supported by a sturdy deck whose incline is adjustable. (Some inexpensive treadmills have no motor—your feet moves the belt, but they are generally less stable and are not suitable for running.) Electronic controls and displays let you change speed and incline and monitor progress." (Treadmills, 2002, p. 13)

Costs range from a few hundred dollars to thousands of dollars. The more common brands are Precor, Tunturi, Reebok, ClubTrack, Star Trac, Image, HealthRider, Trimline, Pro-Form, Nordic Track, Vision Fitness, True Vision, and Keys Fitness. No matter the type you choose, be sure the belt is long enough to accommodate your jogging/running or walking stride. The belt starts and stops gradually, there is a wide range of motor speeds, handrails are positioned such that moving arms do not hit them, the deck is shock absorbent, and the machine is stable (Treadmills, 2002). Treadmills allow you to control your workout by varying the speed at which you jog/run or walk.

★ *Types:* motorized, nonmotorized

★ *Exercises:* walking, jogging, running

★ *Readouts:* speed, distance, incline, time elapsed, heart rate, calories expended

★ *Other options:* upper body resistance levers, speed, running bed incline, programmable workouts, pace

★ *Primary benefits:* cardiovascular and aerobic fitness

★ *Secondary benefits:* lower body endurance

★ *Check:* stable running bed, height/stability of side rails, width of running belt, length of running surface

Stationary Exercise Bikes

There are many different exercise bikes available to the consumer. Some of the more common brands are Schwinn, Lifecycle, Monarch, Tunturi, and Cybex. Most good stable bikes range in price between $200 and $1,000. Bicycles that are computerized with heart rate, speed, calories burned, and so forth, are usually found in fitness centers and cost up to $5,000.

There are three types of exercise bikes you can purchase. These are the single-action, dual-action, and recumbent. The "single-action" bike has a flywheel that creates the resistance and the resistance can be changed with a twist of a knob. The "single action" bike will last longer but it is more expensive. The "dual-action" bikes have you use your legs and arms at the same time. These bikes use a fan to create resistance. The resistance on the bike can be increased by pumping the arms and legs faster. The dual-action bike allows you to exercise only your arms if you are so inclined. These bicycles require a higher energy expenditure. The "recumbent" bike allows you to sit in a recumbent position. In this position the person exercises the hamstring muscles; it is useful for individuals with back problems or who have poor balance.

★ *Types:* friction belt, electronically braked, air resistance

★ *Readouts:* power, work, heart rate, calories expended

★ *Other options:* upper body exercise, coaster pedals, programmable workouts, arm action only, arm and leg action, recumbent design

★ *Primary benefits:* cardiovascular and aerobic fitness

★ *Secondary benefits:* lower body endurance or upper body endurance

★ *Check:* strength of construction, body fit, padded seat, padded handlebars, 15+ lb flywheel, ease of setting resistance level

Rowing Machines

The most common home models of rowing machines are DP, Sears, and Tunturi, and the cost ranges from $200 to $800 for home machines. Commercial machines range between $1,000 and $5,000. Rowing machines are designed to imitate the movements of rowing a boat. The machines have a sliding seat and movable handles. The person exercising presses his/her feet against stationary footplates with the legs while the seat slides backward and simultaneously pulls the handles to create a rowing motion. The legs bend and the seat slides forward in a continuous motion. In order to get the benefit from the machine, the motion must continue for at least 20 minutes.

★ *Types:* air resistance, fluid resistance, user resistance

★ *Readouts:* power, work, calorie expenditure

★ *Other options:* resistance dials, special design (a pull handle connected to a bladed wheel or blade in a container of water)

★ *Primary benefits:* cardiovascular and aerobic fitness

★ *Secondary benefits:* lower body endurance and upper body endurance

★ *Check:* stability, contoured seat, padded seat, foam-padded hand grips, resistance control seat that moves back and forth smoothly, programmable workouts, uniform resistance

Ski Machine

The ski machine is a simulation of cross-country skiing and has many of the same aerobic benefits. The ski machines are manufactured by NordicTrack, Precor, DP, Vitamaster, and Tunturi. The ski machine ranges in price from $300 to $3,000 for models used in the fitness facilities. The ski machine has two flat boards that slide back and forth in a groove on rollers. The arms are involved by using a rope and pulley action. This allows you to work both the upper and lower body. Some machines have variable resistance, may have an incline, and have some type of monitor that can show heart rate, resistance, calories expended, and speed of movement.

★ *Types:* manual

★ *Exercises:* cross-country skiing

★ *Readouts:* heart rate, speed of movement, distance, calories expended, elapsed time

★ *Other Options:* resistance dials and wheels

★ *Primary benefits:* cardiovascular and aerobic fitness

★ *Secondary benefits:* upper and lower body muscular strength and endurance

★ *Check:* stability, contour of handgrips, size of foot bindings, location of monitor for readouts, noise level

Stairclimber

The stairclimber is a popular type of exercise machine. It is simply a set of levers, attached to a type of resistance device, that allows your legs to pump as if you were climbing stairs. The models that allow you to push the steps straight down are safer and reduce the chance of an injury. There are different models available and they vary in resistance, drive train, flywheel, or wind resistance. The stairs are linked in some models while other models have dual-action, which allows you to work both the arms and legs at the same time. Another type of model has a series of stairs that rotate, like an escalator going in the wrong direction.

Some of the more typical home models are sold at Sears and sporting good stores with brand names such as Tunturi, DP, and Precor. Stairmaster and Lifestep make the commercial

units, which are usually more expensive. Stair-climbing machines can cost between $200 and $5,000.

★ *Types:* dependent (linked pedals) or independent (unlinked pedals)

★ *Readouts:* number of steps, steps per minute, energy expenditure, floors climbed, heart rate, elapsed time

★ *Other options:* hydraulic shocks (for occasional use), flywheel resistance (for heavy use), adjustable step height, upper body components

★ *Primary benefits:* cardiovascular and aerobic fitness

★ *Secondary benefits:* lower body endurance

★ *Check:* stability of steps and supports, step pedal size, amount of time allowed for stepping, easy-to-reach controls, noise level, comfortable handles

Elliptical Exercisers

Elliptical exercise machines,

"represent the marriage of a stairclimber and cross-country ski machine. Your feet,

on pedals move in flattened circles; your arms, grasping the handlebars, move back and forth . . . the machine resists the motion of your arms and legs with a fly-wheel that is braked in one of two ways. On most machines designed for home use, the resistance comes courtesy of a band around the flywheel's rim. Most health club ellipticals have a magnetic resistance, which makes pedaling feel smoother." (Elliptical Exercisers, 2002, p. 16)

Cost can range from $500 to over $2,000. The more common models are Reebok, Nordic Track, ProForm, FitnessQuest, Life Fitness, True Vision, and Vision Fitness. Theoretically, elliptical exercise is a very good concept. An individual can participate in a full body, weight-bearing workout without suffering vertical pounding on the joints. The movement mechanics of elliptical exercise machines are easy to perfect and the calories burned per session can rival that of a treadmill. However, at this time, the best elliptical machines are found in fitness facilities; they are larger, built better, and are much more expensive than machines constructed for home use. Elliptical exercise machines can provide someone with an adequate workout. Individual's, whose knees cannot withstand the vertical pounding of running, may find the ellipticals beneficial. However, elliptical exercisers manufactured for home use are inferior to industrial models. As a result "treadmills offer a more varied exercise program because of their range of speeds and inclines" (Elliptical Exercisers, 2002, p. 16).

★ *Types:* motorized and manual

★ *Exercise:* walking

★ *Readouts:* speed, distance, incline, time elapsed, heart rate, calories expended

★ *Other options:* preset program

★ *Primary benefits:* cardiorespiratory and aerobic fitness

★ *Secondary benefits:* upper and lower body endurance

★ *Check:* machine stability, stability of foot pedals and arm rails, step pedal size, movement arm width, noise level, and comfortable handles

Free Weights (Barbells, Dumbells)

Free weights are the most economical device you can use to build muscular strength and muscular endurance. "A set, with a variety of weights, costs as little as $50" (Gym Dandy, 2001, p. 49). Free weights are weights that are not attached to a machine. Most often they come in the form of a barbell (designed for two-handed lifts), or dumbbell (designed for one-handed lifts), which can be adjusted to provide various amounts of resistance. Free weights work by allowing the lifter to move the loads through various movements and ranges of motion. Increasing or decreasing the amount of the load lifted varies resistance. Bars come in a variety of lengths and widths.

> Two things to consider closely regarding bars are tensile strength and the construction of the sleeves. Tensile strength is the maximum strength capacity the bar can handle before it bends or breaks. The higher the tensile strength, the better the bar . . . the sleeves should rotate smoothly and be self-lubricating. For this reason they have ball bearings, or brass brushings. (Pauletto, 1991, p. 17)

Collars, which are used to secure the weights to the bars, "should fasten securely to the bar. The best type is a spin-lock collar that spins on, that you secure by tightening the levers" (Pauletto, 1991, p. 17).

The best plates are machine-finished Olympic plates constructed out of cast iron. These plates are usually more accurate in their weight and fit tighter on the bars. The plates "should be painted or have another long-lasting finish. When buying additional plates, try to buy the same brand you already have. Different brands of plates weigh the same, but might be different in shape and diameter" (Pauletto, 1991, p. 18).

> All benches and racks should sit solidly on the floor. The seats of all bench-type apparatus should be low enough so that you can sit comfortably with your feet on the floor . . . depending on your needs, you may want your equipment to be versatile enough so that you can perform a variety of exercises on them, especially if your space and budget are limited (e.g., a bench that can change into an incline when you adjust the seat and stands). (Pauletto, 1991, p. 18)

Advantages

★ *Cost:* You can purchase a full Olympic set for as little as $300 (including a bench).

★ *Unlimited variety:* You can work virtually every muscle in the body from any angle with a set of free weights.

★ *Whole-body workout:* You can work more than one muscle group at once—for example, lifting a barbell over your head works muscles in your arms, shoulders, and upper back.

★ *One size fits all:* Because of the adjustability of barbells and dumbbells, free weights can be adapted to almost anyone.

Disadvantages

★ *Injury:* Injury is possible if proper technique is not followed.

★ *Spotter:* A partner, or spotter, may be needed when performing certain lifts.

★ *Skill required:* When performing lifts, you must balance and control the load while moving it, therefore, greater skill is needed.

Resistance Machines

Because most resistance machines guide the direction of the movement "the exercises tend to require less coordination than free weights, making them easier and safer for inexperienced users" (Gym Dandy, 2001, pp. 48–52). Nautilus, Cybex, Paramount, Body Master, Bow Flex, and Total Gym are some of the more popular resistance machines on the market today. If used properly, machines can be very effective in developing muscular strength and endurance. Resistance machines may be classified by the manner in which they provide resistance to the muscles.

Weight Stack System—"A stack of metal plates, kept in line by a vertical bar or track, is lifted by a cable routed through pulleys and levers. Resistance is varied by moving a pin that determines how many plates are lifted" (Gym Dandy, 2001, p. 48).

Hydraulic Piston System—"Cylinders that look and act like a car's shock absorbers are attached to the machine's frame and the levers you push and pull. Resistance comes from fluid in the cylinders that's forced from one chamber to another as the piston moves in and out. Resistance is varied by changing the point at which the piston is attached to the levers or by adjusting the valves" (Gym Dandy, 2001, p. 48).

Flexible Rod and Rubber Band Systems— "Rods—bent like an archer's bow—or thick rubber bands are attached to the machine's frame and the cable or lever you push or pull. Resistance is varied by using a fewer or more rods or bands, or thinner rods or bands" (Gym Dandy, 2001, p. 49).

Advantages

★ *Safety:* There's less chance of injury when you work out with machines, since most of

them guide your motions, control weights' movements, and make you maintain the correct posture. Since you are seated, your lower back is protected. You cannot get trapped under the actual weights.

★ *Muscle isolation:* Because the machine controls the movement pattern of the load, and balances the load, it is easier to isolate individual muscles.

★ *Ease of use:* Machines are not as intimidating and are a good way to get started.

★ *Calibrated resistance:* The machines are designed so that the resistance varies appropriately as you move through the arc.

Disadvantages

★ *Cost:* Machines are generally more expensive than free weights.

★ *Size and specifications:* One size does not fit all. Machines are constructed to fit a certain body type and if your body type does not fit within the specifications you may have difficulty performing various exercises through their full range of motion.

★ *Portability:* Portability is limited. Some of the machines are so large they require a large amount of floor space. They are harder to store and are extremely heavy.

A lot of the people have turned their homes into mini-gyms with the purchase of home exercise equipment. Before doing the same, consider the following suggestions offered by The American Academy of Orthopaedic Surgeons:

★ Get medical advice on the type of equipment that is best suited to fit your needs.

★ Match the equipment to specific goals.

★ Avoid impulse buying.

★ Test the equipment before you buy it and wear your workout clothes during the test.

★ Pay attention to how your muscles and joints feel while using the equipment.

★ Don't equate the amount of money spent on exercise equipment with the quality of a workout.

★ Realistically evaluate advertisements for exercise equipment. There is no single piece of equipment that can offer a balanced, total workout that includes strength, flexibility, and cardiorespiratory endurance (Brown, 1999, p. 6).

Regardless of the intent of your exercise program, there are some reasons to be cautious in your expectations of what home exercise devises can do. Are you going to have the discipline to make your purchase worth the money? There is a general agreement that attics, bedrooms, and garages across the country are filled with little-used equipment. Americans like to buy things, use them for a short period of time, then put them away never to be used again. The repetitive nature of the exercise machines can bore most people to the point of not using them. So, before purchasing home equipment, be sure you are committed to working out and you will use the equipment.

Gyms, Fitness Clubs, Spas

Joining a fitness club or gym has become popular among a lot of people. Clubs or gyms offer many benefits including equipment, qualified instructors, a supportive environment, fitness assessment, and a variety of classes. It is not necessary to join a fitness center in order to improve your fitness level. A university may have similar equipment and offer the same service at a less expensive price. Various authors have recommended criteria by which fitness facilities may be evaluated (Hoeger & Hoeger, 1995; Kusinitz & Morton, 1995; Prentice, 1997). If you want to join a private fitness center you should consider the following guidelines.

★ *Types of facilities:* Make yourself familiar with the different types of facilities available such as spas, YMCA, gyms, etc.

★ *Location of facilities:* Where is the facility located? Is it accessible to your work or house? Is parking adequate?

★ *Equipment available:* Does the center have enough equipment, including weights and aerobic equipment? Is there sufficient locker space? Is the equipment in good condition? Does the equipment suit your fitness goals?

★ *Programs offered:* What type and quality of programs are offered? Are these programs appropriate for you? Can programs be designed for specific medical needs?

★ *Qualification of personnel:* Do they have a background in physical education, exercise physiology, kinesiology, athletic training, or physical therapy? Are they certified by the American College of Sports Medicine (ACSM) as exercise leaders, fitness instructors, or exercise specialists or the National Strength Coaches Association (NSCA) as Certified Strength and Conditioning Specialists (CSCS) or personal trainers?

★ *Accessibility of personnel:* Are instructors easily accessible or must members seek them out for help and/or instruction?

★ *Hours of operation:* What are the hours of operation? Is the facility open 7 days a week? When is it most crowded? Is it coed? Are the classes crowded? Are there long lines for the equipment you plan to use? When is the least crowded time period?

★ *Types of membership and payments:* Do they have a no-contract, pay-as-you-go plan? Did you read the fine print of the contract? Were you rushed into signing the contract? Do they have a trial membership? Did you read and understand every word of the contract?

★ *Club's/Spa's reputation/length of time in business:* How long has the club been in business? Is it a well-established business? How do they rate with the Better Business Bureau? Did you confer with members about the operation of the business?

Exercise Clothing and Shoes

You have planned your exercise program, purchased equipment, or joined a fitness club, so what do you wear for exercise class. The clothes and shoes should be functional and should be selected for the weather and activity. The right apparel allows for freedom of movement and is appropriate for the type of activity. Shop carefully for exercise clothing and ask yourself the following questions:

★ Will your movements be restricted, or will you be able to move freely?

★ Does the clothing fit your body properly?

★ Will the fabric allow your skin to breathe in hot weather or keep you warm in cold weather?

★ Will the clothing keep you comfortable and dry?

★ Is the clothing durable?

★ Can the clothing easily be seen by traffic—night and day? (Wear bright colors and reflective fabrics that are visible.)

Hot Weather Clothing

Selecting clothing for hot-humid weather is relatively easy. Your clothes should be lightweight, light-colored, and loose-fitting. The clothing should be chosen for its breathability and for maximal body heat dissipation. The clothing should be able to wick (draw moisture away from the skin) to permit sweat to evaporate. Regulating your body temperature in hot-humid weather is crucial. You should wear lightweight tops (tank type) to allow for evaporation. Clothing that is light in color aids in reflecting radiant heat energy. It is advisable to wear a hat, which helps block some of the heat from the sun.

Hot weather exercise tips: According to the American College of Sports Medicine (ACSM, 2000) there are strategies you can use to prevent heat-related problems when you exercise. The strategies are:

Choose clothing that will effectively allow heat loss and sweat to evaporate. Reschedule your exercise session for a cooler time in the day, i.e., evenings or mornings. Move the exercise session to cooler, breezier locations or move indoors with fans and air conditioning. Lastly, slow the intensity, or add rest periods in order to maintain, not exceed, the target heart rate that you normally utilize.

Cold Weather Clothing

When exercising in cold weather, wear clothes that retain heat but allow the sweat to evaporate. Dressing in cold weather means dressing in layers. You should dress in thin layers of clothes that can be removed easily when you begin to perspire, or added should you get chilled. Three loose fitting layers will help trap the heat and insulate the body. A hat should be worn during cold weather because you can lose up to 30% of your body heat through your head.

Shoes

Before a discussion of shoes can begin, some foot basics are necessary to help you understand how your foot may move during an activity session. Hiser (1999) discusses three types of foot positions/movements: *supination, the neutral position,* and *pronation.* A **supinated foot** means you have a tendency to put the pressure/weight of your body on the outside edges of your feet; consequently you wear down the outsides of the soles of your shoes. If you have calluses on the ball of your foot, you probably supinate your foot when you strike the ground. In the **neutral position,** your pressure/weight is more balanced and is distributed equally; therefore, the soles of your shoes wear evenly. The last position, **pronation,** means you distribute your pressure/weight on the insides of your feet when you strike the ground; therefore, the inside soles of your shoes wear out. If you have calluses on the insides of your feet, you probably pronate your foot. Either way, if you *pronate* or *supinate* your foot when you move, avoid shoes that have limited flexion at the ball of the foot. Hold your shoe up at eye level and look at the inside or outside soles of your shoes. On which side is it more worn out? Do you *supinate, pronate,* or are you *neutral?*

Footwear is the most important piece of equipment you can and should buy. The technology of shoe design in the 1990s was incredible; exercise shoes have been improving over the past two decades. Researchers and exercise specialists have been studying shoe design to prevent injury and improve performance (Bishop, 1995; Hiser, 1999; Mangili & Mazzeo, 1999; Miller & Allen, 1995; Prentice, 1997). Shoes are now made either for specific activities or for cross training. Aside from the specific components of a shoe (Figures 8.0 and 8.1), each component has a purpose and is designed to absorb, spread out, or negate the forces that react and have an impact on your body. Every time your foot (heel or toe) strikes the ground, the ground reaction forces, or impact vibrations, are sent back up your leg. These vibrations are transmitted up through your foot, into the ankle, shin, knee, hip, and up into the pelvis and spine. Your feet may have to absorb the impact of these vibrations up to three times your body weight. Consequently, it is very important to try to match the shoe to the type of activity in which you are going to participate.

What should you look for when purchasing footwear for exercise? Shoes should provide good support to your feet and help absorb and spread out the impact of these shock forces, prevent chronic stress injuries, and help to make your workout session more comfortable. The main difference between high-impact and low-impact shoes is the amount of shock absorption you are going to need. If you are going to participate in high-impact, or combination activity, it may be worth the extra expense to pay for extra cushioning. **Cross-training shoes** allow you to participate in a variety of activities while still using the same shoe; they are an ideal shoe if you are just getting started. Look for a shoe that has flexibility in the midsole, shock absorption, and good lateral support. A shoe known as "mid-cut," neither low-cut or high top, provides the added lateral support. Most cross-trainers and aerobic shoes are manufactured with a mid-cut. Shoes specifically made for just walking, or just running are not a good alternative choice because they do not provide lateral support or have extra padding in the forefoot.

Running shoes should have cushioned insoles, good shock-absorbing qualities at the midsole and the heel, and a flexible midsole. Running shoes have rubber outsoles with an elevated-flared heel that provides lateral stability and prevents heel strike (heel bruises) and a great deal of flexibility in the forefoot. The treads on most running shoes are rough; therefore, they can cause problems during aerobic dance activities because they are designed to grip the ground surface so that the runner has traction at push off. These rough treads are inappropriate for aerobic dance, step, and hi/low impact classes. These classes are usually conducted on a smooth surface, such as a carpet or dance floor. Aerobic dance is a series of movements with changes of direction accompanied by music; the threads on running shoes could cause injury due to abrupt stops. **Walking shoes** have heels that tend to be lower, less padded, and more beveled. **Aerobic dance shoes** should be lightweight, flexible in the forefoot, and have straight, nonflared heels to allow for lateral movements. However, if you are a larger person, you are putting a lot of weight and force on the foot. As a result you may want to purchase a somewhat heavier, sturdier shoe which may be better for you than a lightweight shoe. **Court shoes** (racquetball, tennis, handball, volleyball, and basketball) have support for lateral movements and have flat firm soles. Mid-cut or high-top shoes have the most stability and side-to-side support.

Parts of a Shoe

In the following discussion, brand names may be mentioned; however, any one company is not being promoted over another. This information will help you make sound choices when selecting the most appropriate shoe to fit your needs (Bishop, 1995; Hiser, 1999; Mangili & Mazzeo, 1999; Miller & Allen, 1995; Prentice, 1995).

★ **Heel counter**—The heel counter is the portion of the shoe that controls the movement of the heel; it stops it from slipping inside the shoe and provides support and stability of the heel.

★ **Achilles tendon pad**—A cushioned heel padding to prevent Achilles tendon irritation.

★ **Arch support**—A durable yet soft supportive material.

★ **Shoe uppers**—The upper portion of the shoe is made up of nylon and leather. The uppers must have extra support in the saddle area. If made of leather, it should have vent holes, or mesh for ventilation.

★ **Stabilizing strap(s)**—These help provide additional support, side-to-side, in the front of the foot. They can be anchored to the shoe in a variety of ways. Some wrap around the front and the ankle portions of the shoe and over the laces for additional support.

★ **Toe box**—The front part of the shoe nearest the toe is the toe box. There should be plenty of room in the toe box to fit your toes comfortably. Your toes need room to spread out when your foot hits the ground. You need at least one thumb-width of room between your toes and the end of the shoe.

★ **Sole**—The sole must provide for shock absorption and it must be durable. There are three layers on the sole:

  ★ *Outsole*—The outsole is the hard rubber part that touches the ground and provides traction. If you are exercising on a carpeted or smooth surface, choose a smoother tread which will allow for easy pivoting.

  ★ *Midsole*—The layer of shock absorbing material located between the insole and outsole which cushions the midfoot and toes. Manufacturers such as Nike, Asic,

Saucony, Rhyka, New Balance, Adidas, and Reebok all use unique types of shock absorption systems in the midsole of their shoes. These systems include encapsulated nitrogen air, a honeycombed inset, and compressed synthetic foams. Midsoles should be flexible so that your foot can "roll down" comfortably with each step you take. Try on the shoes, with socks you will be wearing, and try to bend the shoe with your foot. Remember each person's foot has its own unique anatomy and the structure of the midsole and its shock absorption system may or may not feel right on your foot. Remember to keep in mind pronation and supination.

★ **Insole**—The insert in the shoe on which the foot rests and contains additional cushioning and arch and heel support.

Americans are interested in health and fitness; however, it is essential to be an intelligent consumer of fitness products and services. Reading and understanding this chapter should help you make informed decisions concerning fitness products and services. As an informed consumer, you will know what questions to ask before purchasing products or services. Strategies include: research the product or service before buying; check with experts on the product or service about your needs or goals; seek reliable sources of information; try out the product and ask questions about services; and make sure you read all contracts carefully.

References

American College of Sports Medicine. (2000). *ACSM's guidelines for exercise and prescription*, 6th ed. Philadelphia, PA: Lippincott, Williams & Wilkins.

Bishop, J. G. (1995). *Fitness through aerobics*, 3rd ed. Scottsdale, AZ: Gorsuch Scarisbrick.

Brown, J. M. (1997). Serious treadmills for serious exercisers. *PennState Sports Medicine Newsletter, 5*, 2–3.

Brown, J. M. (1999). Choosing home exercise equipment. *Georgia Tech Sports Medicine and Performance Newsletter, 1*, 6–7.

Elliptical Exercisers. (2002). *Consumer Reports, 66*, 16–17.

Gym Dandy. (2001). *Consumer Reports, 66*, 48–52.

Tennis

Flexibility: More rigid than running type, firm sole
Uppers: Leather or leather with nylon
Heel flare: None
Cushioning: Less than running types
Soles: Polyurethane
Tread: Flattened

Aerobic

Flexibility: Rates in between running and tennis types
Uppers: Leather or leather with nylon
Heel flare: Very little
Cushioning: Rates in between running and tennis types
Soles: Rubber or polyurethane
Tread: Needs to be flat, may have pivot dot

Running

Flexibility: Ball of foot is flexible
Uppers: Nylon or nylon mesh
Heel flare: Flared for greater stability
Cushioning: Heel and sole well padded
Soles: Made of carbon-based material for greater durability
Tread: Grip is enhanced by deep grooves

Illustrations modified from Payne WA, Hahn DB: *Understanding your health,* ed. 4, St. Louis, 1995, Mosby.

Figure 8.0 Choosing an appropriate athletic or fitness shoe.

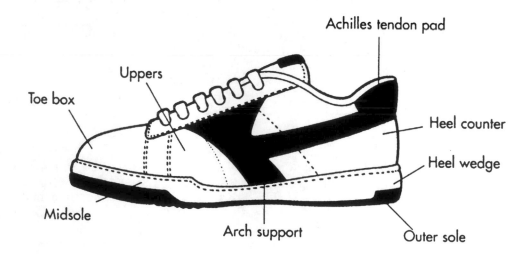

Illustrations modified from Payne WA, Hahn DB: *Understanding your health,* ed. 4, St. Louis, 1995, Mosby.

Figure 8.1 Parts of a well-designed shoe.

Hiser, J. (1999). *Winning edge series: Racquetball.* Boston: McGraw-Hill.

Hoeger, W.W.K. & Hoeger, S.A. (1995). *Lifetime physical fitness and wellness: A personalized program,* 4th ed. Englewood, CO: Morton.

Kusinitz, I. & Morton F. (1995). *Your guide to getting fit,* 3rd ed. Mountain View, CA: Mayfield Publishing.

Mangili, L.M. & Mazzeo, K.S. (1999). *Step training plus: The way to fitness,* 2nd ed. Englewood, CO: Morton.

Miller, D.K. & Allen, T.E. (1995). *Fitness: A lifetime commitment,* 5th ed. Boston: Allyn & Bacon.

Pauletto, B. (1991). *Strength training for coaches.* Champaign, IL: Leisure Press.

Payne, W.A. & Hahn, D.B. (1995). *Understanding your health,* 4th ed. St Louis: Mosby.

Prentice, W.E. (1991). *Fitness for college and life,* 3rd ed. St. Louis: Mosby.

Prentice, W.E. (1997). *Fitness for college and life,* 5th ed. St. Louis: Mosby.

Shultz, M. (2000). Run for your money. *Durham Herald-Sun,* March 5, G-1.

Treadmills. (2002). *Consumer Reports, 67,* 13–15.

Web Sites

American Alliance for Health, Physical Education, Recreation and Dance (AAHPERD) *www.aahperd.org*

CDC National Center for Chronic Disease Prevention and Health Promotion *www.cdc.gov/nccdphp*

American College of Sports Medicine *www.acsm.org*

President's Council on Physical Fitness *www.fitness.gov/*

Healthy People 2010 Web Sites

CDC *www.cdc.gov*

FDA *www.fda.gov*

NIH *www.nih.gov*

Substance Abuse and Mental Health Services Administration *www.samhsa.gov*

Planning Your Own Exercise Program

Objectives

After completing this chapter, you will be able to do the following:

★ Identify the steps for putting together a successful personal fitness program.

★ Name and define the five health-related components of fitness.

★ Name and define the three components of an exercise session.

★ Use the components of fitness and principles of physical activity to design a physical fitness program.

With continuing research, suggestions and recommendations for developing personal exercise programs have been established, reviewed, analyzed, re-evaluated, and modified over the years. The first American

College of Sports Medicine's (ACSM) position statement on exercise prescription released in 1978 stated that:

> People should exercise 3–5 days/week, for a duration of 15–60 minutes/session, at an intensity of 60–90% of maximal heart rate using activities such as swimming, biking, cross-country skiing and jumping rope. These recommendations did not allow for muscle skeletal health, nor did they provide any relationship between patterns of physical activity and health promotion and the prevention of disease. The first set of recommendations addressed body composition and cardiorespiratory fitness only. (Nieman, 2003, p. 230–232)

The ACSM re-evaluated their guidelines on a regular basis and worked cooperatively with the Centers for Disease Control (CDC) and published new guidelines in 1995. These guidelines recommended that everyone participate in moderate-intensity level activities, preferably on a daily basis. The recommended duration is for 30 minutes, which can be conducted in segments and accumulated throughout the day, or in a single 30-minute session (Nieman, 2003).

These 1995 guidelines and recommendations are different from those published 17 years earlier in 1978 in three ways. One, for individuals with very low fitness levels, the detrained state, the minimum target heart rate intensity was lowered to 40%. Two, it is now recommended that people participate in some type of activity 5–7 days per week rather than 3–5 days per week. Three, with respect to the duration of the activity, the 1995 guidelines added the choice of accumulation time periods (8–10 minute segments) instead of one 30-minute period.

In 1998, the ACSM position was revised regarding the guidelines for quantity and quality. This revision states "the minimal training intensity threshold is 55–65% of the maximum heart rate, especially for the unfit" (Nieman, 2003, p. 233). Since these reports, other agencies and groups sponsored by the U.S. government have supported these suggestions and have issued guidelines of their own. The American Cancer Society (ACS) and the American Heart Association (AHA) are two such organizations that list physical inactivity as a major health concern, and the need for exercise programs as ways to deter sedentary disease. In 1993, the International Consensus Conference on Physical Activity Guidelines for Adolescents issued a similar statement for their findings and suggested that physical activity should be a part of general lifestyle behaviors at least 3 or more times a week for at least 20 minutes or more (Nieman, 2003).

In 1996 the U.S. Preventive Services Task Force recommended to all their health care providers that they advise their clients/patients that to avoid sedentary diseases such as high blood pressure, obesity, diabetes, and coronary heart disease, they add physical activity to their lives on a daily basis (Nieman, 2003). Lastly, the National Institute of Health (NIH) listed five major suggestions with respect to physical activity:

★ Everyone should have at least 30 minutes of activity of moderate intensity preferably on a daily basis.

★ By adding more time, or changing the intensity, additional health benefits can be achieved.

★ People with chronic diseases and disorders who want to participate in physical activity should contact their physician and be provided with appropriate assessments in order to develop an exercise program.

★ If you are male over 40 or female over 50 and you have previously been inactive, consult your physician before participating in an activity program.

★ Strength training (resistance training/weight lifting) should be added to your exercise program at least twice a week (Nieman, 2003).

At this point, we have evaluated our cardiorespiratory endurance, muscular strength and endurance, flexibility, and body composition and received scores for each of the health-related fitness components (Chapters 3, 4, 5, 6). Based upon these scores, we need to develop and implement a personalized physical fitness program. By keeping the aforementioned guidelines in mind, it is easier to understand that a physical activity program can be developed on personal interest, and be implemented in a variety of ways.

A well-rounded exercise program should be implemented through participation in exercise sessions. Each session should include a warm-up, exercise workout, and a cool-down. Each of

these are discussed in Chapter 2 as well. The total session should not last more than 1 hour for beginning exercisers. As your fitness level improves, the total time may exceed 1 hour if time is available.

Warm-Up

Recommended time: 5–10 minutes

"A warm-up is defined as a group of exercises performed immediately before an activity which provides the body with a period of adjustment from rest to exercise" (Nieman, 2003, p. 236). This can be accomplished by performing "light calisthenics, jogging, stationary cycling, or exercises that provide a rehearsal for the actual performance activity" (Nieman, 2003, p. 236).

Actual Workout

Recommended time is 10–60 minutes

This is the actual exercise session and it may be purely aerobic, purely anaerobic, or a combination of the two. Depending upon the type of activity, and the level of condition of the participant, the length of the session may vary.

Cool-Down

Recommended time is 5–15 minutes.

The cool-down is the warm-up in reverse. Its purpose is to slowly return the heart rate and body temperature to their pre-exercise states. Slow walking, jogging, swimming, and/or per-

forming your exercise at a much lower intensity can accomplish this. If flexibility exercises are added to the cool-down session, the session could run up to 25 minutes. "The major reason for performing flexibility exercises after the aerobic phase is to more safely and effectively stretch the warm muscle groups and joints involved in the aerobic exercise" (Nieman, 2003, p. 255). Individuals participating in anaerobic exercise sessions may perform flexibility exercises as part of the warm-up, or after the cool-down. For more information regarding designing and implementing flexibility programs, see Chapter 5.

There are, however, many people who have limited amounts of time in which to exercise and do not have time to drive to the gym, work out, and drive back to work. The previously reviewed guidelines suggest that there are many ways to improve health and physical fitness, and by utilizing nontraditional methods of adding physical activity to your daily life, you can also begin to reap the benefits. By following the suggested guidelines, you can still plan a well-rounded exercise program that provides health protection benefits as well as improvements in physical fitness and the quality of life. Recommended time allotments for each component of a well-rounded exercise program are presented in Table 9.0 if you have limited blocks of time in your schedule. Either way, long blocks of time or shorter segments, attention should be given to effective exercise strategies in order to ensure safety and maximize results from the physical fitness program.

Table 9.0 Time Allotments for Program Components

Components	Recommended Time
Warm-Up (includes light jogging, brisk walking, swimming, etc. and stretching exercises)	5–10 minutes
Muscle Conditioning (Strength and Endurance)	15–30 minutes
Cardiovascular Endurance	20–30 minutes
Cool-Down (stretching exercises)	5–10 minutes

Designing a Program

The key to any successful fitness program is designing a program that you will enjoy and one that will meet your needs. The following guidelines will help you design a program that is right for you (ACSM, 2000; Corbin et al., 2002; Nieman, 2003; Prentice, 1997).

★ **Set realistic goals.** This is a crucial first step in a successful fitness program. Your goals might be related to specific activities that you enjoy and you will be more motivated to stay with your goals if they are important to you.

★ **Select specific activities.** Select activities for your program based upon your age, health, present level of fitness, goals, motivation, and previous exercise experience. Choose activities based upon the ability to help you reach your goals. You need to select activities that support your commitment to exercise and not turn the program into a chore. One strategy would be to select a different activity to develop each component. Enjoyment is the key to exercise adherence—if exercise is fun, you are more likely to continue it. Add variety to your program through **cross training.** This concept uses a variety of activities to develop one fitness component. Adding variety could include bicycling on Monday, Wednesday, Friday and swimming on Tuesday and Thursday.

★ **Determine the frequency, intensity, and duration (time) FIT.** You should note your target heart rate, how frequently you want to work out, and how long your workouts will be. Slowly progress week by week by adding small amounts of time, short distances, or intensity levels.

★ **Make a commitment.** You must believe in the importance of exercise in order to continue to do it. The benefits you receive must be worth the price you will pay for your commitment.

★ **Start and continue your program.** Pace yourself and allow your body to adjust to the program. Slowly progress from week to week. In order to continue try the following activities:

   ★ Vary activities in your program to prevent boredom.

   ★ Exercise with others.
   ★ Make time to exercise.
   ★ Change activities periodically.
   ★ Reward yourself.
   ★ Set aside a regular time and place to exercise.
   ★ Plan for obstacles (weather, soreness, illness, etc.).
   ★ Make exercise a part of your daily routine.

★ **Chart your progress.** Track your progress through the use of an exercise log. Record information from each session so you can see what you are doing. Design a weekly exercise schedule. Keep a record of workouts (frequency, intensity, duration, heart rate, etc.).

★ **Plan your program.** Put your plan in writing and design a weekly exercise schedule. Try out the exercise program and make changes in the program, if necessary. Regularity and consistency are the keys to a successful program.

★ **Evaluate your program.** After you have tried your program for at least 6 weeks, take time to evaluate. Consider the following:

   ★ Were you able to complete your program? If not, what obstacles got in your way?
   ★ Did you enjoy the activities? Which ones would you change?
   ★ Have you noticed any changes in your fitness level?
   ★ How would you change your program to improve it?

★ **Form a habit of exercise.** Regular exercise needs to be a lifestyle behavior change. A well-rounded program must include each of the components that were evaluated. The actual fitness program is composed of individual workouts or exercise sessions. Each session consists of four specific phases to be completed in a safe way to ensure the benefits of any program. The four phases of exercise are performed for a particular purpose and the time spent on each varies.

The following programs are examples of the application of the theories and concepts discussed in this chapter. Regardless of the program (whether it be aerobic, anaerobic, or a combination of both), the critical factor in obtaining results is consistency of participation over time.

Combination Program

Nieman (2003) suggests a combination program for aerobic conditioning, flexibility, and muscular fitness as follows:

Time needed: 1–1.5 hours

Warm-up: 5–10 minutes

Aerobic exercise: 20–30 minutes of moderate to vigorous activity

Cool-down: 5–10 minutes of mild to moderate aerobic activity

Flexibility: 5–10 minutes of static (nonbouncing movements) stretching, emphasizing all major muscle groups and joints

Muscular strength and endurance:
20–30 minutes of weight lifting, one set of 8–12 repetitions of 8–10 different exercises utilizing the major muscle groups (biceps, triceps, pectoralis major, deltoids, latissimus dorsi, abdominals quadriceps, hamstrings, gluteus muscles, gastroc/soleus) (p. 257)

This program could also be completed over a 2-day period. Day one would consist of the warm-up, aerobic exercise, the cool-down, and flexibility. Day two would consist of a warm-up, muscular strength and endurance, and a cool-down.

Aerobic Conditioning Program

A typical aerobic program may consist of the following: warm-up (5–20 minutes) of easy to moderate activities, the workout (10–60 minutes), and the cool-down (10–25 minutes) of easy to moderate activity. Table 9.1 illustrates a typical aerobic fitness program (the workout session) using the ACSM's frequency, intensity, and time **(FIT)** guidelines for the beginner, intermediate, and advanced participants.

Table 9.1   A Typical Aerobic Conditioning Program

F.I.T. Guidelines	Low Fitness (Beginner)	Average Fitness (Intermediate)	High Fitness (Advanced)
Frequency (# of sessions per week)	3	3–4	5 or more
Intensity (% of heart rate reserve [HRR])	40–59%	60–74%	75–85%
Intensity (% of Max heart rate)	60%	70%	80%
Time (minutes/session)	10–19 minutes	20–29 minutes	30–60 minutes

Note: With respect to the intensity levels, if the participant is unable to maintain the level for the required time, decrease the percentage. If the participant feels that these levels are not at a high enough intensity, increase the percentage. However, whether increasing or decreasing percentages, it is important to use small increments; it is recommended that 5 percentage points be the limit.

Modified from Nieman, D. (2003). *Exercise testing and prescription: A health related approach (5th ed.)* Boston, MA: McGraw-Hill, p. 237.

Resistance Training Program

Nieman (2003) recommends that a typical strength-training program for muscular strength and endurance consist of the following:

Warm-up: 5–20 minutes of easy to moderate activities

Workout: 10–60 minutes

Cool-down: 10–25 minutes of easy to moderate activities

Table 9.2 illustrates a typical strength-training program (the weight lifting session) using the ACSM's progression model for muscular strength, muscular endurance, and/or for hypertrophy (the increase in muscular size).

Different Systems of Resistance Training

The following are different systems of resistance training (Fleck & Kraemer, 1997), which may be employed in the performance of the ACSM's program, or to add variation to whatever program you choose to use.

1. **Single set system:** Each weight lifting exercise is performed for one set of a specific number of repetitions.

2. **Multiple-set system:** Several sets of an exercise performed using the same amount of resistance. The sets may be performed using any amount of resistance, for any number of repetitions and sets.

3. **Light-to-heavy system:** In this system, you progress from light resistance to heavy resistance. You perform one set with your lightest load and highest number of repetitions. Next, you add weight and perform fewer repetitions. This procedure continues until you perform your fewest number of repetitions with your heaviest weight.

4. **Heavy-to-light:** This is a reversal of the light-to-heavy system. You progress from your heaviest weight (and fewest number of repetitions) to your lightest weight (and highest number of repetitions).

5. **Triangle program:** This program combines the light-to-heavy and heavy-to-light systems within the same workout. First you perform the light-to-heavy system, immediately followed by the heavy-to-light system.

6. **Super-set system:** There are two types of super sets. In one type, multiple sets of two

Table 9.2 Progression Models in Resistance Training for Healthy Adults

	Loading	Volume	Frequency
Strength			
Beginner	60–70% 1 RM	1–3 sets, 8-12 reps	2–3x/week
Intermediate	70–80% 1 RM	Multiple sets, 6–12 reps	2–4x/week
Advanced	1 RM periodized	Multiple sets, 1–12 reps, periodized	4–6x/week
Endurance			
Beginner	50–70% 1 RM	1–3 sets, 10–15 reps	2–3x/week
Intermediate	50–70% 1 RM	Multiple sets, 10–15 reps or more reps	2–4x/week
Advanced	30–80% 1 RM periodized	Multiple sets, 10–25 reps or more, periodized	4–6x/week
Hypertrophy			
Beginner	60–70% 1 RM	1–3 sets, 8–12 reps	2–3x/week
Intermediate	70–80% 1 RM	Multiple sets, 6–12 reps	2–4x/week
Advanced	70–100% 1 RM periodized	Multiple sets, 1–12 reps periodized	4–6x/week

Note: 1 RM: One repetition maximum. Periodized refers to planned variation in the volume, intensity of training, and/or exercise selection.

Note: Under "strength" (Advanced level) a participant may work from 85-100 percent of the 1 RM. Under "strength" (Beginner level), at the highest load, 70%, when you can perform 3 sets of 12 repetitions at 70% intensity for at least 2–3 consecutive workout sessions, increase the weight anywhere from 2-10%.

Note: It is important to work the larger muscles prior to the smaller muscles, the multiple joint exercises prior to the single joint exercises, and work from higher intensity exercises to lower intensity.

Modified from: American College of Sports Medicine. Position stand on progression models in resistance training for healthy adults. *Med Sci Sports Exer 34:364-380, 2002*. In Nieman, D. (2003). *Exercise Testing and Prescription: A health related approach (5th ed.)* Boston, MA: McGraw-Hill, p. 258.

exercises for the same body part, but opposing muscle groups, are performed without any rest in between (biceps vs. triceps). In the second type, several exercises for the same muscle, or body part, are performed in rapid succession.

7. **Circuit program:** A sequence of resistance training exercises performed one after the other, with minimal rest (15–30 seconds) between each of the exercises.

8. **Split-routine system:** In this system, the body is divided (split) and various parts of the body are worked on alternate days. Two of the more common split systems are upper body (one day perform exercises for the upper body)/lower body (one day perform exercises for the lower body), and push (performing all pushing exercises one day)/pull (performing all pulling exercises one day). Split routines can be 4-day, 5-day, or 6-day. For example, a 4-day top/bottom split routine would entail performing upper body exercises on Monday and Thursday, and lower body exercises on Tuesday and Friday. Wednesday, Saturday, and Sunday the lifter rests.

You will start your program with a lot of energy and good intentions, but somewhere down the line you may become a fitness dropout. If this happens, review the guidelines set forth in this chapter. Be sure that you choose activities that are enjoyable, can be done at home or on campus, fit into your budget, and are a natural extension of your daily routine. Remember, any activity is better than none at all. You do not have to join a spa or club or buy expensive equipment or clothing; all you need to do is find at least 15 minutes and just **MOVE!!** To help plan your program several sample programs are provided and will help you complete Lab 9.0.

References

American College of Sports Medicine. (2000). *ACSM's guidelines for exercise testing and prescription*, 6th ed. Philadelphia, PA: Lippincott, Williams & Wilkins.

Corbin, C. B., Lindsey, R., & Welk, G. (2002). *Concepts of fitness and wellness*. Boston: McGraw-Hill.

Fleck, S. & Kraemer, W. (1997). *Designing resistance training programs*. Champaign, IL: Human Kinetics.

Hoeger, W. W. K. & Hoeger, S. A. (1992). *Lifetime physical fitness and wellness*, 3rd ed. Englewood, CO: Morton Publishing Company.

Nieman, D. C. (2003). *Exercise testing and prescription: A health-related approach*, 5th ed. Boston: McGraw-Hill.

Politano, V., McCormick, M. R., and Jeffreys, A. (1995). *Lifetime physical fitness*. Dubuque, IA: Kendall/Hunt Publishing Company.

Prentice, W. E. (1997). *Fitness for college and life*, 5th ed. St. Louis: Mosby.

Lab Activity 9.0
Designing an Exercise Program

Purpose: To monitor and improve your fitness level through personal assessment and a self-designed exercise program.

Procedures:

1. Review the sample programs provided, and use the information presented within the chapter, then construct your own program and exercise session.

2. Fill out the blank charts completely.

Current Body Weight: _____   Current Body Composition: (LMM) _____

Projected Body Weight: _____   (Adipose) _____

Calculate Target Heart Rate Range using Maximum Heart Rate: _____ to _____ bpm
(See Chapter 3 for formula)   Beginner   Advanced

Calculate Target Heart Rate Reserve (using resting heart rate): _____ to _____ bpm
                                                                 Beginner   Advanced

Sample Flexibility Fitness Program

MAJOR MUSCLE: Arms: Biceps, triceps; **Shoulders:** Deltoid; **Chest:** Pectoralis; **Upper/Lower Back:** Latissimus Dorsi & Erector Spinae; **Hip/buttocks:** Gluteus; **Groin:** Hip adductors; **Front of Thighs:** Quadriceps; **Back of Thighs:** Hamstrings; **Calf/Achilles Tendon:** Nemius/Soleus; **Stomach/Waist:** Abdominal/Obliques

Date _____

Warm-up		You Select Your Choice			
	Body Part	**Specific Stretch**	**Hold Time 15–30 secs.**	**Repetitions**	**Number of Sets**
Abdominal/obliques	Stomach/waist		15–30	2	1
Biceps	Upper arm		15–30	2	1
Triceps	Upper arm		15–30	2	1
Deltoids	Shoulder		15–30	2	1
Pecs	Chest		15–30	2	1
Lats	Back		15–30	2	1
Erector Spinae	Back		15–30	10	2
Glutes	Buttocks		15–30	5	2
Hip Adductors	Groin		15–30	5	2
Hamstrings	Back of thighs		15–30	10	2
Quadriceps	Front of thighs		15–30	10	2
Gastroc	Calf		15–30	10	2
Achilles	Heel to bottom of calf		15–30	10	2
Cool-down					

Flexibility Fitness Program

MAJOR MUSCLES: Same as in sample program

Date _____

Warm-up		You Select Your Choice			
	Body Part	**Specific Stretch**	**Hold Time 15–30 secs.**	**Repetitions**	**Number of Sets**
Abdominal/obliques	Stomach/waist				
Biceps	Upper arm				
Triceps	Upper arm				
Deltoids	Shoulder				
Pecs	Chest				
Lats	Back				
Erector Spinae	Back				
Glutes	Buttocks				
Hip Adductors	Groin				
Hamstrings	Back of thighs				
Quadriceps	Front of thighs				
Gastroc	Calf				
Achilles	Heel to bottom of calf				
Cool-down					

Sample Cardiorespiratory Fitness Program
(Aerobic Conditioning)

Fitness Component	Current Level (B, I, or A)	Specific Exercise	Location	Frequency	Intensity	Duration
Warm-up						
Aerobic Activity	Beginner	Swimming	Pool	M, W, F	Low level 60% of Max	25 minutes
	Intermediate	Step Class	Aerobic Gym	T/TH	Mid level 70% of Max 60% of reserve	45 minutes
	Advanced	Cycling	Wellness Center	M, W, F	Adv level 80% of Max 70% of reserve	60 minutes
Cool-down						

Cardiorespiratory Fitness Program
(Aerobic Conditioning)

Fitness Component	Current Level (B, I, or A)	Specific Exercise	Location	Frequency	Intensity	Duration
Warm-up						
Aerobic Activity						
Cool-down						

Sample Muscular Strength and Endurance Program

MAJOR MUSCLES: Biceps/Triceps, Deltoids, Pecs, Lats, AB/Obliques, Gluteus, Quads, Hams, Gastroc/Achilles

Warm-up: Cycle 5–8 minutes

Date	Seat Setting	Exercise	Weight	Repetitions	# of Sets
3/21/03		Squat	150 lbs	12	3
3/21/03	Flat	Flys	45 lbs	12	3
3/21/03	Flat	Bench Press	100 lbs	12	3
3/21/03	2 chest 3 seat	Seated Row	75 lbs	12	3
3/21/03	3	Lat Pull Down	50 lbs	12	3
3/21/03	3	Seated Lateral Raises	40 lbs	12	3
3/21/03	4 seat back	Leg Extension	40 lbs	12	3
3/21/03	3 leg piece	Leg Curl	40 lbs	12	3
3/21/03		Bicep Curl	25 lbs	12	3
3/21/03	3 back piece 4 seat	Tricep Extension	30 lbs	12	3
3/21/03	3 seat 2 foot piece	AB Crunch	15 lbs	15	5
3/21/03	3	Rotary Torso	15 lbs	15	3
3/21/03		Calf Raises	15 lbs	15	3

Please note: This program was designed with a young male in mind. A beginner should not attempt these weights, number of repetitions, and number of sets.

Cool-down: Cycle for 5–8 minutes, stretch 5–10 minutes

Muscular Strength and Endurance Program

MAJOR MUSCLES: Same as in sample program

Warm-up:

Date	Seat Setting	Exercise	Weight	Repetitions	# of Sets

Cool-down:

Appendix

Food Composition Table

Food	Amount	Weight (g)	Calories	Protein (g)	Fat (g)	Sat. Fat (g)	Cholesterol (g)	Carbohydrate (g)	Fiber (g)	Calcium (mg)	Iron (mg)	Sodium (mg)	Vit A (IU)	Thiamin (Vit B₁) (mg)	Riboflavin (Vit B₂) (mg)	Niacin (mg)	Vit C (mg)	Folate (mcg)
Apples, fresh, w/peel, lrg	1 ea	150	88	0.3	1	0.1	0	23	4.1	10	0.3	0	80	0.03	0.02	0.1	9	4.2
Applesauce, swnd, w/o salt, cnd	1 cup	255	194	0.5	0	0.1	0	51	3.1	10	0.9	8	28	0.03	0.07	0.5	4	1.53
Apricots, pitted, fresh, whole	3 ea	114	55	1.6	0	0	0	13	2.7	16	0.6	1	2978	0.03	0.05	0.7	11	9.8
Apricots, w/skin, in heavy syrup, cnd, whole	½ cup	120	100	0.6	0	0	0	26	1.9	11	0.4	5	1476	0.02	0.03	0.5	4	2.04
Asparagus, spears, ckd w/o salt	4 ea	60	14	1.6	0	0	0	3	1	12	0.4	7	323	0.07	0.08	0.6	6	87.6
Avocado, Calif, fresh	½ ea	120	212	2.5	21	3.1	0	8	5.9	13	1.4	14	734	0.13	0.15	2.3	9	78.6
Bagel, plain, 3½" diameter	1 ea	68	187	7.1	1	0.1	0	36	1.6	50	2.4	363	0	0.37	0.21	3.1	0	59.84
Banana, fresh, med	1 ea	140	129	1.4	1	0.3	0	33	3.4	8	0.4	1	113	0.06	0.14	0.8	13	26.74
Bar, granola, hard	1 ea	24	113	2.4	5	0.6	0	15	1.3	15	0.7	71	36	0.06	0.03	0.4	0	5.52
Beans, black, mature, ckd w/o salt	1 cup	172	227	15.2	1	0.2	0	41	15	46	3.6	2	10	0.42	0.1	0.9	0	255.9
Beans, chickpea/garbanzo, mature, ckd	1 cup	164	269	14.5	4	0.4	0	45	12.5	80	4.7	11	44	0.19	0.1	0.9	2	282.0
Beans, frijoles/refried, cnd	½ cup	145	136	8	2	0.7	12	23	7.7	51	2.4	434	0	0.04	0.02	0.5	9	15.95
Beans, green, snap/string, ckd	½ cup	65	23	1.2	0	0	0	5	2.1	30	0.8	2	433	0.05	0.06	0.4	6	21.64
Beans, kidney, red, mature, cnd	1 cup	185	157	9.7	1	0.1	0	29	11.8	44	2.3	631	0	0.19	0.16	0.8	2	93.61
Beans, lima, fordhook, immature, ckd f/fzn w/o salt, drained	½ cup	85	85	5.2	0	0.1	0	16	4.9	19	1.2	45	162	0.06	0.05	0.9	11	18.02
Beans, mung, mature, sprouted, raw	½ cup	52	16	1.6	0	0	0	3	0.9	7	0.5	3	11	0.04	0.06	0.4	7	31.62
Beans, pinto, mature, ckd w/o salt	1 cup	171	234	14	1	0.2	0	44	14.7	82	4.5	3	3	0.32	0.16	0.7	4	294.1
Beef, chuck arm pot roast, brsd, choice, ¼" trim	3 oz	85	296	22.9	22	8.6	84	0	0	8	2.6	50	0	0.06	0.2	2.7	0	7.65
Beef, corned, cnd	3 oz	85	212	23	13	5.3	73	0	0	10	1.8	855	0	0.02	0.12	2.1	0	7.65
Beef, ground, hamburger patty, brld, well done, 16% fat	3 oz	85	225	24.3	13	5.3	84	0	0	8	2.4	70	0	0.06	0.27	5	0	9.35
Beef, ground, hamburger patty, brld, well done, 18% fat	3 oz	85	238	24	15	5.9	86	0	0	10	2.1	76	0	0.05	0.2	5.1	0	9.35
Beef, liver, fried	3 oz	85	184	22.7	7	2.3	410	7	0	9	5.3	90	30689	0.18	3.52	12.3	20	187
Beef, T-bone steak, brld, choice, ¼" trim	3 oz	85	263	19.7	20	7.7	57	0	0	7	2.3	54	0	0.08	0.18	3.4	0	5.95
Beef, top sirloin steak, lean, brld, choice, ¼" trim	3 oz	85	172	25.8	7	2.6	76	0	0	9	2.9	56	0	0.11	0.25	3.6	0	8.5
Beer	12 fl-oz	360	148	1.1	0	0	0	13	0.7	18	0.1	18	0	0.02	0.09	1.6	0	21.6
Beer light	12 fl-oz	354	99	0.7	0	0	0	5	0	18	0.1	11	0	0.03	0.11	1.4	0	14.51
Beets, cnd, drained, diced	½ cup	80	25	0.7	0	0	0	6	1.4	12	1.5	155	9	0.01	0.03	0.1	3	24.16
Biscuits, homemade	1 ea	35	124	2.5	6	1.5	1	16	0.5	82	1	203	29	0.12	0.11	1	0	21.35
Blueberries, fresh, bilberries	½ cup	73	41	0.5	0	0	0	10	2	4	0.1	4	73	0.04	0.04	0.3	9	4.67
Brandy, 86 proof	1 oz	28	70	0	0	0	0	0	0	0	0	0	0	0	0	0	0	0
Bread, banana, prep f/recipe w/veg shortening	1 pce	50	169	2.2	6	1.5	22	28	0.7	9	0.7	99	46	0.09	0.1	0.7	1	5.5
Bread, cracked wheat	1 pce	25	65	2.2	1	0.2	0	12	1.4	11	0.7	134	0	0.09	0.06	0.9	0	15.25
Bread, French	1 pce	35	96	3.1	1	0.2	0	18	1	26	0.9	213	0	0.18	0.12	1.7	0	33.25
Bread, mixed grain	1 pce	26	65	2.6	1	0.2	0	12	1.7	24	0.9	127	0	0.11	0.09	1.1	0	20.8
Bread, pita pocket, white	1 ea	60	165	5.5	1	0.1	0	33	1.3	52	1.6	322	0	0.36	0.2	2.8	0	57
Bread, pumpernickel	1 pce	32	80	2.8	1	0.1	0	15	2.1	22	0.9	215	0	0.1	0.1	1	0	25.6
Bread, rye	1 pce	25	65	2.1	1	0.2	0	12	1.5	18	0.7	165	2	0.11	0.08	1	0	21.5
Bread, white, f/recipe w/2% milk	1 pce	25	71	2	1	0.3	1	12	0.5	14	0.7	90	20	0.1	0.1	0.9	0	22.75
Bread, whole wheat	1 pce	25	62	2.4	1	0.2	0	12	1.7	18	0.8	132	0	0.09	0.05	1	0	12.5
Broccoli, med stalk, 8" long, ckd w/o add salt	1 ea	140	39	4.2	0	0.1	0	7	4.1	64	1.2	36	1943	0.08	0.16	0.8	104	70
Broccoli, spear, raw, 5" long	1 ea	114	32	3.4	0	0.1	0	6	3.4	55	1	31	1758	0.07	0.14	0.7	106	80.94
Brownie, chocolate, w/walnuts, prep f/rec	1 ea	20	93	1.2	6	1.5	15	10	0.4	11	0.4	69	153	0.03	0.04	0.2	0	5.8
Brussels Sprouts, ckd, drained	½ cup	78	30	2	0	0.1	0	7	2	28	0.9	16	561	0.08	0.06	0.5	48	46.8
Buns, hamburger	1 ea	40	114	3.4	2	0.5	0	20	1.1	56	1.3	224	0	0.19	0.12	1.6	0	38
Buns, hot dog/frankfurter	1 ea	40	114	3.4	2	0.5	0	20	1.1	56	1.3	224	0	0.19	0.12	1.6	0	38
Burger/Patty, vegetarian, Gardenburger, original	1 ea	71	130	8	3	1	11	18	5	84	0	290	50	0.11	0.15	1.1	0	10.08

Food	Amount	Weight (g)	Calories	Protein (g)	Fat (g)	Sat. Fat (g)	Choles-terol (g)	Carbo-hydrate (g)	Fiber (g)	Calcium (mg)	Iron (mg)	Sodium (mg)	Vit A (IU)	Thiamin (Vit B_1) (mg)	Ribo flavin (Vit B_2) (mg)	Niacin (mg)	Vit C (mg)	Folate (mcg)
Burger/Patty, vegetarian, soy	1 ea	71	142	14.9	6	1	0	6	3.3	21	1.5	390	0	0.64	0.43	7.1	0	55.38
Butter, salted	1 Tbs	5	36	0	4	2.5	11	0	0	1	0	41	153	0	0	0	0	0.15
Buttermilk, skim, cultured	1 cup	245	99	8.1	2	1.3	9	12	0	285	0.1	257	81	0.08	0.38	0.1	2	12.25
Cabbage, ckd w/o add salt, drained, shredded	½ cup	85	19	0.9	0	0	0	4	2	26	0.1	7	112	0.05	0.05	0.2	17	17
Cabbage, raw shredded	½ cup	45	11	0.6	0	0	0	2	1	21	0.3	8	60	0.02	0.02	0.1	14	19.35
Cake, angel food, cmrd prep	1 pce	60	155	3.5	0	0.1	0	35	0.9	84	0.3	449	0	0.06	0.29	0.5	0	21
Cake, carrot, w/cream cheese icing	1 pce	96	419	4.4	25	4.7	52	45	1.2	24	1.2	236	3310	0.13	0.15	1	1	11.52
Cake, chocolate, w/chocolate icing, ⅛th	1 pce	69	253	2.8	11	3.3	29	38	1.9	30	1.5	230	59	0.02	0.09	0.4	0	11.73
Cake, devils food, marshmallow iced	1 pce	99	408	3.5	21	5.8	52	52	1.2	47	1.3	338	0				0	
Cake, pound, w/butter	1 pce	30	116	1.7	6	3.5	66	15	0.1	10	0.4	119	182	0.04	0.07	0.4	0	12.3
Cake, white, w/chocolate icing	1 pce	71	259	1.8	8	3.7	13	46	0.8	55	0.5	219	166	0.05	0.07	0.3	0	2.11
Calamari/Squid, fried, mixed species	1 cup	150	262	26.9	11	2.8	390	12	0	58	1.5	459	52	0.08	0.69	3.9	6	21
Candy Bar, Almond Joy, fun size	1½ oz	42	196	1.8	11	7.3	2	24	2	26	0.6	61	5	0.01	0.06	0.2	0	
Candy Bar, Mars almond	1 ea	50	234	4.1	12	3.6	8	31	1	84	0.6	85	94	0.02	0.16	0.5	0	9.5
Candy Bar, Milky Way, 2.1 oz bar	1 ea	60	254	2.7	10	4.7	8	43	1	78	0.5	144	65	0.02	0.13	0.2	1	6
Candy Bar, Special Dark sweet chocolate	1 ea	41	226	2	13	8.3	0	25	2	11	1	3	14	0.01	0.03	0.2	0	0.82
Candy, caramels, plain/chocolate	1 oz	28	107	1.3	2	1.8	2	22	0.3	39	0	69	9	0	0.05	0.1	0	1.4
Candy, hard, all flvrs	1 oz	28	110	0	0	0	0	27	0	1	0.1	11	0	0	0	0	0	0
Candy, kisses, milk chocolate	1 oz	28	144	1.9	9	5.2	6	17	1	53	0.4	23	52	0.02	0.08	0.1	0	2.24
Candy, M & M's peanut chocolate	1 oz	28	144	2.7	7	2.9	3	17	1	28	0.3	13	26	0.03	0.05	1	0	9.8
Candy, M & M's plain chocolate	1 oz	28	138	1.2	6	3.7	4	20	0.7	29	0.3	17	57	0.02	0.06	0.1	0	1.68
Candy, milk chocolate, w/almonds	1 oz	28	147	2.5	10	4.8	5	15	1.7	63	0.5	21	21	0.02	0.12	0.2	0	3.36
Carrots, ckd w/o add salt, drained, slices	½ cup	73	33	0.8	0	0	0	8	2.4	23	0.5	48	17924	0.02	0.04	0.4	2	10.15
Carrots, raw, whole, 7½″ long	1 ea	81	35	0.8	0	0	0	8	2.4	22	0.4	28	22784	0.08	0.05	0.8	8	11.34
Catsup/Ketchup	1 Tbs	15	16	0.2	0	0	0	4	0.2	3	0.1	178	152	0.01	0.01	0.2	2	2.25
Cauliflower, ckd, drained	½ cup	63	14	1.2	0	0	0	3	1.7	10	0.2	9	11	0.03	0.03	0.3	28	27.72
Celery, raw, med stalk, 8″ long	1 ea	40	6	0.3	0	0	0	1	0.7	16	0.2	35	54	0.02	0.02	0.1	3	11.2
Cereal, 100% Bran, rte, dry	½ cup	33	89	4.1	2	0.3	0	24	9.8	23	4.1	229	0	0.79	0.89	10.5	31	23.43
Cereal, All-Bran, rte, dry	¼ cup	21	55	2.6	1	0.1	0	16	6.8	74	3.1	43	525	0.27	0.29	3.5	10	63
Cereal, Alpha-Bits, rte, dry	1 cup	28	110	2.2	1	0.1	0	24	1.2	8	2.7	178	1235	0.36	0.42	4.9	0	98.84
Cereal, bran flakes, rte, dry	¾ cup	30	96	2.8	1	0.1	0	24	5.3	17	8.1	220	750	0.38	0.43	5	0	99.9
Cereal, Cheerios	1 cup	23	84	2.4	1	0.3	0	18	2	42	6.2	218	958	0.29	0.33	3.8	12	76.59
Cereal, Chex, corn, rte, dry	1 cup	28	105	2	0	0.1	0	24	0.5	94	8.4	270	0	0.35	0	4.7	6	93.24
Cereal, Chex, Wheat, rte, dry	1 cup	46	159	4.8	1	0.2	0	37	5.1	92	13.8	412	0	0.34	0.06	4.6	6	92
Cereal, corn flakes, rte, dry	1 cup	25	91	1.6	0	0.1	0	22	0.7	1	7.8	266	625	0.32	0.35	4.2	12	88.25
Cereal, Corn Pops, rte, dry	1 cup	28	107	1	0	0.1	0	26	0.4	2	1.7	111	700	0.36	0.39	4.7	14	98.84
Cereal, Cream of Wheat, quick, ckd w/ water	1 cup	244	132	3.7	0	0.1	0	27	1.2	51	10.5	142	0	0.24	0	1.5	0	109.8
Cereal, Crispy Rice, rte, dry	¾ cup	22	87	1.4	0	0	0	19	0.3	4	0.6	161	971	0.41	0.46	5.4	12	108.6
Cereal, Frosted Flakes, rte, dry	1 cup	35	135	1.4	0	0.1	0	32	0.7	1	5.1	226	847	0.42	0.49	5.6	17	105
Cereal, Frosted Mini Wheats, rte, dry	1 cup	55	186	5.2	1	0.2	0	45	5.9	20	15.4	2	0	0.38	0.44	5.4	9	110
Cereal, granola, rte, dry	½ cup	57	257	6	10	1.3	0	38	3.6	43	1.8	92	0	0.18	0.06	0.6	0	8.55
Cereal, Grape Nuts, rte, dry	½ cup	57	205	6.2	1	0.2	0	46	5	19	15.9	348	737	0.37	0.42	4.9	0	98.04
Cereal, Honey Bran, rte, dry	½ cup	30	102	2.6	1	0.2	0	25	3.3	14	4.8	173	1323	0.39	0.45	5.3	16	20.1
Cereal, Life, plain, rte, dry	1 cup	44	167	4.3	2	0.3	0	35	2.8	134	12.3	240	16	0.55	0.62	7.3	0	146.9
Cereal, Mueslix, five grain muesli, rte, dry	1 cup	82	289	6.2	5	0.7	0	63	5.6	67	8.9	107	2488	0.75	0.84	9.8	1	196.8
Cereal, Nutri-Grain, Wheat, rte, dry	1 oz	28	101	2.4	0	0.1	0	24	1.8	8	0.8	190	0	0.36	0.42	4.9	15	98.84
Cereal, oatmeal, unsalted, ckd w/water ½ cup	120	74	3.1	1	0.2	0	13	2	10	0.8	1	19	0.13	0.92	0.2	0	4.8	
Cereal, raisin bran, rte, dry	1 cup	49	155	3.9	1	0.1	0	38	6.4	22	9	299	623	0.31	0.35	4.2	0	82.81
Cereal, Shredded Wheat, sml biscuits, rte, dry	1 cup	19	68	2.1	0	0.1	0	15	1.9	7	0.8	2	0	0.05	0.05	1	0	9.5
Cereal, Smacks, rte, dry	1 cup	37	141	2.4	1	0.4	0	32	1.3	4	2.5	70	1028	0.52	0.59	6.8	21	136.9

Food	Amount	Weight (g)	Calories	Protein (g)	Fat (g)	Sat. Fat (g)	Cholesterol (g)	Carbohydrate (g)	Fiber (g)	Calcium (mg)	Iron (mg)	Sodium (mg)	Vit A (IU)	Thiamin (Vit B_1) (mg)	Riboflavin (Vit B_2) (mg)	Niacin (mg)	Vit C (mg)	Folate (mcg)
Cereal, Special K, rte, dry	1 cup	21	78	4.3	0	0	0	15	0.7	3	5.9	169	508	0.36	0.4	4.7	10	63
Cereal, Total, wheat, rte, dry	1 cup	33	116	3.3	1	0.2	0	26	2.9	284	19.8	218	1375	1.55	1.87	22.1	66	439.8
Cereal, Wheaties, rte, dry	1 cup	29	106	3.1	1	0.2	0	23	2	53	7.8	215	725	0.36	0.41	4.8	14	96.57
Cheese Puffs/Cheetos	1 oz	28	155	2.1	10	1.8	1	15	0.3	16	0.7	294	74	0.07	0.1	0.9	0	33.6
Cheese Spread, low fat, low sod	1 pce	34	61	8.4	2	1.5	12	1	0	233	0.1	2	92	0.01	0.13	0	0	3.06
Cheese, American, proc, shredded	1 oz	28	105	6.2	9	5.5	26	0	0	172	0.1	401	339	0.01	0.1	0	0	2.18
Cheese, blue	1 oz	28	99	6	8	5.2	21	1	0	148	0.1	391	202	0.01	0.11	0.3	0	10.19
Cheese, cheddar, diced	1 oz	28	113	7	9	5.9	29	0	0	202	0.2	174	297	0.01	0.11	0.1	0	5.1
Cheese, feta	1 oz	28	74	4	6	4.2	25	1	0	138	0.2	313	125	0.04	0.24	0.3	0	8.96
Cheese, monterey jack, shredded	1 oz	28	105	6.9	8	5.3	25	0	0	209	0.2	150	266	0	0.11	0	0	5.1
Cheese, mozzarella, part skm mlk, low moist, shredded	1 oz	28	78	7.7	5	3	15	1	0	205	0.1	148	197	0.01	0.1	0.2	0	2.77
Cheese, parmesan, grated	1 Tbs	5	23	2.1	2	1	4	0	0	69	0	93	35	0	0.02	0.3	0	0.4
Cheese, ricotta, part skm	1 oz	28	39	3.2	2	1.4	9	1	0	76	0.1	35	121	0.01	0.05	0	0	3.67
Cheese, Swiss, shredded	1 oz	28	105	7	8	5	26	1	0	269	0.1	73	237	0.01	0.1	0	0	1.79
Cheesecake	1 pce	85	273	4.7	19	8.4	47	22	0.4	43	0.5	176	465	0.02	0.16	0.2	0	15.3
Cherries, sweet, fresh	10 ea	75	54	0.9	1	0.2	0	12	1.7	11	0.3	0	160	0.04	0.04	0.3	3	3.15
Chicken, broiler/fryer, breast, rstd	1 ea	98	193	29.2	8	2.1	82	0	0	14	1	70	91	0.06	0.12	12.5	0	3.92
Chicken, broiler/fryer, dark meat, w/o skin, rstd	3 oz	85	174	23.3	8	2.3	79	0	0	13	1.1	79	61	0.06	0.19	5.6	0	6.8
Chicken broiler/fryer, drumstick, rstd	1 ea	52	112	14.1	6	1.6	47	0	0	6	0.7	47	52	0.04	0.11	3.1	0	4.16
Chicken broiler/fryer, meat only, w/o skin, rstd	3 oz	85	162	24.6	6	1.7	76	0	0	13	1	73	45	0.06	0.15	7.8	0	5.1
Chips, corn	1 oz	28	151	1.8	9	1.3	0	16	1.4	36	0.4	176	26	0.01	0.04	0.3	0	5.6
Chips, tortilla, chili & lime	18 pce	28	110	2	2		0	22	2	60	3.6	200	0	0.02		0.4	2	
Chips, tortilla, plain	1 oz	28	140	2	7	1.4	0	18	1.8	43	0.4	148	55	0.07	0.05	0.4	0	2.8
Cod, batter fried	3½ oz	100	173	17.4	8	1.6	50	7	0.2	29	0.7	91	30	0.02	0.1	2.3	0	8.71
Cod, stmd/poached	3½ oz	100	102	22.4	1	0.1	46	0	0	9	0.3	80	28	0	0.05	2.2	3	6.6
Coffee, brewed	¾ cup	180	4	0.2	0	0	0	1	0	4	0.1	4	0	0	0	0.4	0	0.18
Collards, ckd w/o add salt	½ cup	95	25	2	0	0	0	5	2.7	113	0.4	9	2973	0.04	0.1	0.5	17	58.35
Cone, ice cream, wafer/cake type	1 ea	115	480	9.3	8	1.4	0	91	3.4	29	4.1	164	0	0.29	0.41	5.1	0	117.3
Cookie, chocolate chip, prep w/marg f/rec	2 ea	20	98	1.1	6	1.6	6	12	0.6	8	0.5	72	127	0.04	0.04	0.3	0	6.6
Cookie, chocolate sandwich, creme filled	4 ea	40	189	1.9	8	1.5	0	28	1.3	10	1.6	242	1	0.03	0.07	0.8	0	17.2
Cookie, fig bar	4 ea	56	195	2.1	4	0.6	0	40	2.6	36	1.6	196	18	0.09	0.12	1	0.	15.12
Cookie, oatmeal raisin, prep f/rec	2 ea	26	113	1.7	4	0.8	9	18	0.8	26	0.7	140	167	0.05	0.04	0.3	0	7.8
Cookie, peanut butter, prep f/rec	2 ea	24	114	2.2	6	1.1	7	14	0.5	9	0.5	124	144	0.05	0.05	0.8	0	13.2
Cookie, shortbread, cmrd, plain	4 ea	32	161	2	8	2	6	21	0.6	11	0.9	146	28	0.11	0.11	1.1	0	18.88
Cookie, vanilla, wafer type, 12–17% fat	10 ea	40	176	1	6	1.5	20	29	0.8	19	1	125	11	0.11	0.13	1.2	0	20
Coriander, raw	¼ cup	4	1	0.1	0	0	0	0	0.1	4	0.1	1	111	0	0	0	7	0.41
Corn, yellow, vac pack, cnd	½ cup	83	66	2	0	0.1	0	16	1.7	4	0.3	226	200	0.03	0.06	1	0	40.92
Cornbread prep f/dry mix	1 ea	60	188	4.3	6	1.6	37	29	1.4	44	1.1	467	123	0.15	0.16	1.2	0	33
Cornmeal, yellow, degermed, enrich, dry	½ cup	120	439	10.2	2	0.3	0	93	8.9	6	5	4	496	0.86	0.49	6	0	224.4
Cottage Cheese, 2% fat	½ cup	113	101	15.5	2	1.4	9	4	0	77	0.2	459	79	0.03	0.21	0.2	0	14.8
Cottage Cheese, creamed, sml curd	½ cup	105	109	13.1	5	3	16	3	0	63	0.1	425	171	0.02	0.17	0.1	4	12.81
?? drained	1 cup	135	134	27.7	3	0.3	120	0	0.2	136	1.1	450	7	0.11	0.11	1.8	0	57.38
Crackers, cheese	1 ea	10	50	1	3	0.9	1	6	0.4	15	0.5	100	16	0.06	0.04	0.5	0	8
Crackers, graham, plain/honey, 2½ square	2 ea	14	59	1	1	0.2	0	11	0.8	3	0.5	85	0	0.03	0.04	0.6	0	8.4
Crackers, matzoh, plain, svg	1 ea	25	111	2.8	0	0.1	0	23		4	0.9	1	0	0.11	0.08	1.1	0	32.76
Crackers, rye, wafers	2 ea	14	47	1.3	0	0	0	11	3.2	6	0.8	111	1	0.06	0.04	0.2	0	6.3
Crackers, saltine	1 ea	11	48	1	1	0.3	0	8	0.3	13	0.6	143	0	0.06	0.05	0.6	0	13.64

Food	Amount	Weight (g)	Calories	Protein (g)	Fat (g)	Sat. Fat (g)	Cholesterol (g)	Carbohydrate (g)	Fiber (g)	Calcium (mg)	Iron (mg)	Sodium (mg)	Vit A (IU)	Thiamin (Vit B_1) (mg)	Riboflavin (Vit B_2) (mg)	Niacin (mg)	Vit C (mg)	Folate (mcg)
Crackers, standard, reg, snack type, round	1 ea	3	15	0.2	1	0.1	0	2	0	4	0.1	25	0	0.01	0.01	0.1	0	2.31
Crackers, triscuit	1 ea	5	24	0.5	1	0.2	0	3	0.5		0.2	26		0.01	0.01	0.1	0	0.36
Crackers, wheat	1 ea	2	9	0.2	0	0.1	0	1	0.1	1	0.1	16	0	0	0.06	0	0	3.7
Cream Cheese	1 oz	28	98	2.1	10	6.2	31	1	0	22	0.3	83	400	0.01	0.02	0	0	0.34
Cream, light	1 Tbs	15	29	0.4	3	1.8	10	1	0	14	0	6	95	0	0.02	0	0	0.56
Cream, whipping, heavy	1 Tbs	15	52	0.3	6	3.5	21	0	0	10	0	6	221	0	0.14		0	
Croissant, butter	1 ea	57	231	4.7	12	6.6	38	26	1.5	21	1.2	424	424	0.22	0.01	1.2	2	35.34
Cucumber, w/o skin, raw, sliced	½ cup	60	7	0.3	0	0	0	2	0.4	8	0.1	1	44	0.01	0.08	0.1	2	8.4
Dates, fresh, whole	10 ea	83	228	1.6	0	0.2	0	61	6.2	27	1	2	42	0.07		1.8	0	10.46
Dinner, chicken, cacciatore, w/noodles, low cal, fzn	1 ea	308	311	22.5	10	2.4	59	33	3.4	29	3.2	934	732	0.28	0.4	8	26	32.22
Doughnut, cake	1 ea	47	198	2.3	11	1.7	17	23	0.7	21	0.9	257	27	0.1	0.11	0.9	0	22.09
Doughnut, raised, glazed	1 ea	60	242	3.5	14	3.5	4	27	0.7	26	1.2	205	8	0.22	0.13	1.7	0	25.8
Egg Substitute, Egg Beaters, new	¼ cup	61	30	6	0	0	0	1	0	20	1.1	125	300	0	0.85	0	0	32.0
Egg Whites, raw	1 ea	33	16	3.5	0	0	0	0	0	2		54	0		0.15	0	0	0.99
Egg Yolks, raw, lrg	1 ea	17	61	2.8	5	1.6	218	0	0	23	0.6	7	331	0.03	0.11	0	0	24.82
Eggs, hard ckd/bld, lrg	1 ea	50	78	6.3	5	1.6	212	1	0	25	0.6	62	280	0.03	0.26	0.1	0	22
Eggs, scrambled, plain, lrg	1 ea	64	106	7.1	8	2.4	225	1	0	45	0.8	179	436	0.03	0.28	0.1	0	19.2
Eggs, whole, Fried	1 ea	46	52	6.2	7	1.9	211	1	0	25	0.7	162	394	0.03	0.24		0	17.48
Entree, lasagna, w/meat, prep f/rec	1 pce	220	352	20.7	14	7.2	52	36	2.5	243	2.8	351	902	0.21	0.3	3.8	13	17.82
Entree, macaroni & cheese, prep f/rec w/margarine	½ cup	100	215	8.4	11	4.4	21	20	0.6	181	0.9	543	430	0.1	0.2	0.9	1	5.15
Entree, meatloaf, beef	1 pce	111	232	20.2	14	5.6	107	5	0.2	37	2.1	185	148	0.06	0.28	3.3	1	14.28
Entree, quiche, lorraine	1 pce	242	724	20.5	56	25.9	304	34	1	318	2.6	303	1323	0.36	0.67	2.8	1	26.48
Entree, spaghetti, w/meatballs, prep f/rec	1 cup	248	332	18.6	12	3.3	74	39	7.7	124	3.7	1009	1587	0.25	0.3	4	22	9.99
Entree, spaghetti, w/tomato sauce & cheese, prep f/rec	1 cup	250	260	8.8	9	2	8	37	2.5	80	2.2	955	1075	0.25	0.17	2.2	12	8
Figs, dried, unckd	1 ea	21	54	0.6	0	0	0	14	2.5	30	0.5	2	28	0.01	0.02	0.1	0	1.57
Fish Sticks/Portions, heated f/fzn, 4×1×.5	2 ea	56	152	8.8	7	1.8	63	13	0	11	0.4	326	59		0.1	1.2	0	10.19
Flour, all purpose, white, bleached, enrich	1 cup	125	455	12.9	1	0.2	0	95	3.4	19	5.8	2	0	0.98	0.62	7.4	0	192.5
Flour, whole wheat	1 cup	120	407	16.4	2	0.4	0	87	14.6	41	4.7	6	0	0.54	0.26	7.6	0	52.8
Frankfurter/Hot Dog, beef & pork, 10 pack	1 ea	57	182	6.4	17	6.1	28	1	0	6	0.7	638	0	0.11	0.07	1.5	0	2.28
Frankfurter/Hot Dog, beef, 8 pack	1 ea	57	180	6.8	16	6.9	35	1	0	11	0.8	585	0	0.03	0.06	1.4	0	2.28
Frankfurter/Hot Dog, turkey	1 ea	45	102	6.4	8	2.7	48	1	0	48	0.8	642	0	0.02	0.08	1.9	0	3.6
Frozen Yogurt, vanilla/strawberry, nonfat, sml scoop	4 oz	113	112	5.6	0	0.1	2	22	0	196	0.1	75	7	0.05	0.23	0.1	1	11.99
Fruit Cocktail, in heavy syrup, cnd	1 cup	245	179	1	0	0	0	46	2.5	15	0.7	15	502	0.04	0.05	0.9	5	6.37
Fruit Cocktail, in juice	1 cup	248	114	1.1	0	0	0	29	2.5	20	0.5	10	756	0.03	0.04	1	7	6.2
Fruit Punch, prep f/pwd	1 cup	240	89	0	0	0	0	23	0.2	38	0.1	34	0	0	0	0	28	0.24
Fudge, chocolate, prep f/rec	1 oz	28	107	0.5	2	1.4	4	22	0.2	12	0.1	17	53	0.04	0.02	0.2	0	0.56
Grapefruit, pink, fresh, 3¾" diameter	½ ea	123	37	0.7	0	0	0	9	1.7	14	0.1	1	319	0.05	0.02	0.2	47	15.01
Grapes, tokay/empress/red flame, fresh	10 ea	50	36	0.3	0	0.1	0	9	0.5	6			36	0.08	0.03		5	1.95
Haddock, fillet, brd, fried	3 oz	85	184	17.1	9	1.9	65	7	0.2	53	1.5	145	69	0.06	0.09	3.7	0	11.6
Halibut, Greenland, fillet, bkd/brld	3 oz	85	203	15.7	15	2.6	50	0	0	3	0.7	88	51	0.08	0.09	1.6	0	0.85
Honey, strained, extracted	1 Tbs	21	64	0.1	0	0	0	17	0	1	0.1	1	0		0.01	0	0	0.42
Hot Cocoa/Choc, prep f/rec w/whole milk	1 cup	250	192	9.8	6	3.6	20	29	2	315	1.1	128	515	0.1	0.44	0.4	2	15
Hummus/Hummos, raw	1 cup	246	421	12.1	21	3.1	0	50	12.5	123	3.9	600	62	0.23	0.13	1	19	146.1
Instant Breakfast, prep f/dry mix w/nonfat milk	1 cup	282	216	15.7	1	0.7	9	36	0.2	407	4.8	268	2343	0.4	0.42	5.5	31	118.2

Food	Amount	Weight (g)	Calories	Protein (g)	Fat (g)	Sat. Fat (g)	Cholesterol (g)	Carbohydrate (g)	Fiber (g)	Calcium (mg)	Iron (mg)	Sodium (mg)	Vit A (IU)	Thiamin (Vit B$_1$) (mg)	Riboflavin (Vit B$_2$) (mg)	Niacin (mg)	Vit C (mg)	Folate (mcg)
Instant Breakfast, prep f/whole milk	1 cup	281	280	15.4	9	5.4	38	36	0.2	396	4.9	262	2151	0.41	0.47	5.5	31	117.7
Jam/Preserves, pkt	1 ea	14	39	0.1	0	0	0	10	0.2	3	0.1	4	2	0	0	0	1	4.62
Jelly	1 Tbs	18	51	0	0	0	0	13	0.2	1	0	5	3	0	0	0	0	0.18
Juice, apple, unswtnd, cnd/btld	½ cup	124	58	0.1	0	0	0	14	0.1	9	0.5	4	1	0.03	0.02	0.1	1	0.12
Juice, cranberry cocktail	1 cup	253	144	0	0	0	0	36	0.3	8	0.4	5	10	0.02	0.02	0.1	90	0.51
Juice, grape, unswtnd, btld/cnd	½ cup	127	77	0.7	0	0	0	19	0.1	11	0.3	4	10	0.03	0.05	0.3	0	3.3
Juice, grapefruit, unswtnd, cnd	½ cup	124	47	0.6	0	0	0	11	0.1	9	0.2	1	9	0.05	0.02	0.3	36	12.9
Juice, grapefruit, unswtnd, prep f/fzn cone	1 cup	247	101	1.4	0	0	0	24	0.2	20	0.3	2	22	0.1	0.05	0.5	83	8.89
Juice, lemon, fresh	1 Tbs	15	4	0.1	0	0	0	1	0.1	1	0	0	3	0.1			7	1.94
Juice, orange, prep f/fzn	½ cup	125	56	0.9	0	0	0	13	0.2	11	0.1	1	98	0.1	0.02	0.3	49	54.75
Juice, prune, w/o pulp	½ cup	88	60	0.7	0	0	0	14	0.5	2	0.9	4	54				3	
Juice, tomato, w/salt, cnd	1 cup	244	41	1.9	0	0	0	10	1	22	1.4	881	1357	0.11	0.08	1.6	45	48.56
Kale, ckd w/o add salt, drained	½ cup	55	15	1	0	0	0	3	1.1	40	0.5	13	4070	0.03	0.04	0.3	23	7.32
Kiwifruit/Chinese Gooseberries, fresh, med	1 ea	76	46	0.8	0	0	0	11	2.6	20	0.3	4	133	0.02	0.04	0.4	74	28.88
Lamb, leg, whole, lean, rstd, choice, ¼" trim	3 oz	85	162	24.1	7	2.3	76	0	0	7	1.8	58	0	0.09	0.25	5.4	0	19.55
Lamb, loin chop, lean, brld, choice, ¼" trim	3 oz	84	181	25.2	8	2.9	80	0	0	16	1.7	71	0	0.09	0.24	5.8	0	20.16
Lemonade, white, fzn cone	12 oz	340	615	1	1	0.1	0	160	0	24	2.4	14	0	0.09	0.33	0.3	60	34
Lentils, sprouts, stir fried	1 cup	124	125	10.9	1	0.1	0	26	4.8	17	3.8	12	51	0.27	0.11	1.5	16	83.08
Lentils, unsalted, ckd	1 cup	200	232	18	1	0.1	0	40	15.8	38	6.7	4	16	0.34	0.15	2.1	3	361.6
Lettuce, butterhead, Boston/bibb, leaf, raw	2 pce	15	2	0.2	0	0	0	0	0.2	5	0	1	146	0.01	0.01	0	1	11
Lettuce, romaine, raw, chpd	1 cup	55	8	0.9	0	0	0	1	0.9	20	0.6	4	1430	0.06	0.06	0.3	13	74.64
Lobster, northern, stmd	1 cup	145	142	29.7	1	0.2	104	2	0	88	0.6	551	126	0.01	0.1	1.6	0	16.1
Lunchmeat Spread, liverwurst, cnd	1 oz	28	87	3.6	7	2.5	33	2	0.5	3	2.3	193	3818				0	1
Lunchmeat, bologna, beef & pork	1 pce	28	88	3.3	7	3	15	1	0	3	0.4	285	0	0.05	0.04	0.7	0	1.4
Lunchmeat, bologna, turkey	2 pce	57	113	7.8	8	2.9	56	1	0	48	0.9	500	0	0.03	0.09	2	0	3.99
Lunchmeat, roast beef, deli style, pouch	3 oz	85	96	17.2	3	1.1	41	1	0	5	1.6	860	0				0	
Lunchmeat, turkey breast, rstd, fat free	1 pce	28	24	4.2	0	0.1	9	1	0	3	0.3	334	0				0	0
Mayonnaise, imit, low cal	1 Tbs	15	35	0	3	0.5	4	2	0	0	0	75	0	0	0	0	0	0.38
Mayonnaise, soybean oil, w/salt	1 tsp	5	36	0.1	4	0.6	3	0	0	1	0	28	14	0	0	0	0	
Melon, cantaloupe/musk, med 5" diameter	¼ ea	239	84	2.1	1	0.2	0	20	1.9	26	0.5	22	7705	0.09	0.05	1.4	101	40.63
Melon, honeydew, fresh, wedge, ⅛ melon	1 pce	129	45	0.6	0	0	0	12	0.8	8	0.1	13	52	0.1	0.02	0.8	32	7.74
Milk Shake, chocolate, fast food	10 fl-oz	340	432	11.6	13	7.9	44	70	2.7	384	1.1	330	316	0.2	0.83	0.5	1	11.9
Milk, evaporated, whole, w/add vit A, cnd	½ cup	126	169	8.6	10	5.8	37	13	0	329	0.2	133	500	0.06	0.4	0.2	2	9.95
Milk, low fat, 1%, w/add vit A	1 cup	244	102	8	3	1.6	10	12	0	300	0.1	123	500	0.1	0.41	0.2	2	12.44
Milk, low fat, 2%, chocolate	1 cup	250	179	8.1	5	3.1	17	26	1.2	284	0.6	150	500	0.09	0.41	0.3	2	12
Milk, low fat, 2%, w/add vit A	1 cup	244	121	8.4	5	2.9	18	12	0	297	0.1	122	500	0.1	0.4	0.2	2	12.44
Milk, nonfat/skim, w/add vit A	1 cup	245	86	8	0	0.3	4	12	0	302	0.1	126	500	0.09	0.34	0.2	2	12.74
Milk, whole, 3.3%	1 cup	244	150	8	8	5.1	33	11	0	291	0.1	120	307	0.09	0.4	0.2	3	12.2
Milkshake, strawberry, fast food	10 fl-oz	340	384	11.6	10	5.9	37	64	1.4	384	0.4	282	408	0.15	0.66	0.6	3	10.2
Mixed Vegetables, cnd, drained	1 cup	182	86	4.7	0	0.1	0	17	5.5	49	1.9	271	21198	0.08	0.09	1.1	9	42.95
Muffin, English, plain	1 ea	57	134	4.4	1	0.1	0	26	1.5	99	1.4	264	0	0.25	0.16	2.2	0	46.17
Muffin, English, plain, tstd	1 ea	52	133	4.4	1	0.1	0	26	1.5	98	1.4	262	0	0.2	0.14	2	0	38.48
Muffin, wheat bran, prep f/rec w/whole milk	1 ea	45	130	3.2	6	1.2	16	19	3.2	84	1.9	265	363	0.15	0.2	1.8	4	23.4
Mushrooms, raw, pces/slices	1 cup	35	9	1	0	0	0	1	0.4	2	0.4	1	0	0.03	0.15	1.4	1	4.2
Mustard Greens, ckd w/o add salt, drained	½ cup	70	10	1.6	0	0	0	1	1.4	52	0.5	11	2122	0.03	0.04	0.3	18	51.38

Food	Amount	Weight (g)	Calories	Protein (g)	Fat (g)	Sat. Fat (g)	Cholesterol (g)	Carbohydrate (g)	Fiber (g)	Calcium (mg)	Iron (mg)	Sodium (mg)	Vit A (IU)	Thiamin (Vit B1) (mg)	Riboflavin (Vit B2) (mg)	Niacin (mg)	Vit C (mg)	Folate (mcg)
Nuts, almonds, dried, unblanched, whole	1/2 cup	36	208	7.7	18	1.4	0	7	4.2	89	1.5	0	4	0.09	0.29	1.4	0	10.44
Nuts, Brazil, dried, shelled, 32 kernels	1 oz	28	184	4	19	4.5	0	4	1.5	49	1	1	0	0.28	0.03	0.5	0	1.12
Nuts, cashews, dry rstd, salted	1 cup	137	786	21	63	12.5	0	45	4.1	62	8.2	877	0	0.27	0.27	1.9	0	94.8
Nuts, coconut, unswtnd, dried	1/2 cup	65	429	4.5	42	37.2	0	16	10.6	17	2.2	24	0	0.04	0.06	0.4	1	5.85
Nuts, peanuts, oil rstd, unsalted, chpd	1 oz	28	163	7.4	14	1.9	0	5	1.9	25	0.5	0	0	0.07	0.03	4	0	35.2
Nuts, pecans dried, halves	1 oz	28	193	2.6	20	1.7	0	4	2.7	20	0.7	0	22	0.18	0.04	0.3	0	6.16
Nuts, walnuts, black, dried, chpd	1 oz	28	170	6.8	16	1	0	3	1.4	16	0.9	0	83	0.06	0.03	0.2	1	18.34
Oil, canola	1 Tbs	218	1927	0	218	15.5	0	0	0	0	0	0	0	0	0	0	0	0
Oil, corn	1 Tbs	15	133	0	15	1.9	0	0	0	0	0	0	0	0	0	0	0	0
Oil, olive	1 Tbs	15	133	0	15	2	0	0	0	0	0.1	0	0	0	0	0	0	0
Oil, peanut	1 cup	216	1909	0	216	36.5	0	0	0	0	0.1	0	0	0	0	0	0	0
Oil, safflower, greater than 70% linoleic	1 Tbs	15	133	0	15	0.9	0	0	0	0	0	0	0	0	0	0	0	0
Oil, soybean	1 tsp	5	44	0	5	0.7	0	0	0	0	0	0	0	0	0	0	0	0
Okra, bindi, ckd w/o add salt f/raw, drained, pods	8 ea	85	27	1.6	0	0	0	6	2.1	54	0.4	4	489	0.11	0.05	0.7	14	38.85
Olives, w/o pits, ripe, lrg, cnd	10 ea	44	51	0.4	5	0.6	0	3	1.4	39	1.5	384	177	0	0	0	0	0
Olives, w/o pits, ripe, sml, cnd	10 ea	32	37	0.3	3	0.5	0	2	1	28	1.1	279	129	0	0	0	0	0
Onions, yellow, ckd w/o add salt, drained, chpd	1/2 cup	105	46	1.4	0	0	0	11	1.5	23	0.3	3	0	0.04	0.02	0.2	5	15.75
Oranges, fresh, med	1 ea	180	85	1.7	0	0	0	21	4.3	72	0.2	0	369	0.16	0.07	0.5	96	54.54
Oysters, eastern, brd, fried, med	1 ea	45	89	3.9	6	1.4	36	5	0.1	28	3.1	188	136	0.07	0.09	0.7	2	13.95
Oysters, eastern, raw, wild	1/2 cup	120	82	8.5	3	0.9	64	5	0	54	8	253	120	0.12	0.11	1.7	4	12
Pancake, buckwheat, prep f/incomplete dry mix, 4"	1 ea	27	56	2.1	2	0.5	18	8	0.6	69	0.5	144	63	0.05	0.07	0.4	0	4.59
Pancake, plain, homemade, 4"	1 ea	73	166	4.7	7	1.5	43	21	1.1	160	1.3	320	143	0.15	0.21	1.1	0	27.74
Papaya, fresh, med	1/2 ea	227	89	1.4	0	0.1	0	22	4.1	54	0.2	7	645	0.06	0.07	0.8	140	86.26
Pasta, egg noodles, enrich, ckd	1/2 cup	80	106	3.8	1	0.2	26	20	0.9	10	1.3	6	16	0.15	0.07	1.2	0	51.2
Pasta, macaroni noodles, enrich, ckd	1/2 cup	70	99	3.3	0	0.1	0	20	0.9	5	1	1	0	0.14	0.07	1.2	0	49
Pasta, spaghetti noodles, enrich, salted, ckd	1 cup	140	197	6.7	1	0.1	0	40	2.4	10	2	140	0	0.29	0.14	2.3	0	98
Pasta, spaghetti noodles, whole wheat, ckd	1 cup	125	155	6.7	1	0.1	0	33	5.6	19	1.3	4	0	0.14	0.06	0.9	0	6.25
Pastry, cinnamon danish	1 ea	110	443	7.7	25	6.2	23	49	1.4	78	2.2	408	13	0.33	0.29	3.2	0	68.2
Peaches, fresh, sliced	1/2 cup	85	37	0.6	0	0	0	9	1.7	4	0.1	6	455	0.01	0.03	0.8	6	2.89
Peaches, in heavy syrup, cnd	1/2 tsp	96	71	0.4	0	0	0	19	1.2	3	0.3	6	319	0.01	0.02	0.6	3	3.07
Peaches, in juice, cnd, whole	1/2 tsp	77	34	0.5	0	0	0	9	1	5	0.2	3	293	0.01	0.01	0.4	3	2.62
Peanut Butter, smooth, salted	1 Tbs	32	190	8.1	16	3.3	0	6	1.9	12	0.6	149	0	0.03	0.03	4.3	0	23.68
Pears, bartlett, fresh, med	1 ea	180	106	0.7	1	0	0	27	4.3	20	0.4	0	36	0.04	0.07	0.2	7	13.14
Pears, in heavy syrup, cnd, halves	1/2 ea	103	76	0.2	0	0	0	20	1.6	5	0.2	5	0	0.01	0.02	0.2	1	1.24
Pears, in juice, cnd, halves	1/2 ea	77	38	0.3	0	0	0	10	1.2	7	0.2	3	5	0.01	0.01	0.2	1	0.92
Peas, cnd, drained	1/2 cup	85	59	3.8	0	0.1	0	11	3.5	17	0.8	214	653	0.1	0.07	0.6	8	37.65
Peas, green, ckd f/fzn w/o add salt, drained	1/2 cup	80	62	4.1	0	0	0	11	4.4	19	1.3	70	534	0.23	0.08	1.2	8	46.88
Peppers, bell, green, sweet, raw, med	1 ea	200	54	1.8	0	0.1	0	13	3.6	18	0.9	4	1264	0.13	0.06	1	179	44
Peppers, bell, red, sweet, raw, sml	1 ea	74	20	0.7	0	0	0	5	1.5	7	0.3	1	4218	0.05	0.02	0.4	141	16.28
Peppers, bell, yellow, sweet, raw, lrg	1 ea	186	50	1.9	0	0.1	0	12	1.7	20	0.9	4	443	0.05	0.05	1.7	341	48.36
Pickles, dill	1 ea	135	24	0.8	0	0.1	0	6	1.6	12	0.7	1731	444	0.02	0.04	0.1	3	1.35
Pickles, sweet, med	1 ea	35	41	0.1	0	0	0	11	0.4	1	0.2	329	44	0.01	0.01	0.1	0	0.35
Pie, apple, bkd f/fzn, 1/8th of 8"	1 pce	118	280	2.2	13	4.5	0	40	1.9	13	0.5	314	146	0.03	0.21	0.3	4	25.96
Pie, bluberry, prep f/rec, 1/8th of 9"	1 pce	158	387	4.3	19	4.6	0	53	2.2	11	1.9	292	66	0.24	0.21	1.9	1	36.34
Pie, cherry, prep f/rec, 1/8th of 9"	1 pce	118	319	3.3	14	3.5	0	45	1.8	12	2.2	225	483	0.17	0.15	1.5	1	31.86
Pie, chocolate cream, rts, 1/6th of 8"	1 pce	175	532	4.5	34	8.7	9	59	3.5	63	1.9	238	0	0.06	0.19	1.2	0	22.75
Pie, lemon meringue, rts, 1/6th of 8"	1 pce	140	375	2.1	12	2.5	63	66	1.7	78	0.9	204	245	0.09	0.29	0.9	4	18.2
Pie, pecan, rts, 1/6th of 8"	1 pce	138	552	5.5	26	4.9	44	79	4.8	23	1.4	585	242	0.13	0.17	0.3	2	37.26

Food	Amount	Weight (g)	Calories	Protein (g)	Fat (g)	Sat. Fat (g)	Cholesterol (g)	Carbohydrate (g)	Fiber (g)	Calcium (mg)	Iron (mg)	Sodium (mg)	Vit A (IU)	Thiamin (Vit B_1) (mg)	flavin (Vit B_2) (mg)	Niacin (mg)	Vit C (mg)	Folate (mcg)
Pie, pumpkin, rts, 1/6th of 8"	1 pce	114	239	4.4	11	2	23	31	3.1	68	0.9	321	3915	0.06	0.17	0.2	1	22.8
Pineapple, chunks, fresh	½ cup	78	38	0.3	0	0	0	10	0.9	5	0.3	1	18	0.07	0.03	0.3	12	8.27
Pineapple, in heavy syrup, cnd, tidbits	½ cup	128	100	0.4	0	0	0	26	1	18	0.5	1	18	0.12	0.03	0.4	9	5.89
Pineapple, in juice, cnd	½ cup	125	75	0.5	0	0	0	20	1	18	0.3	1	48	0.12	0.02	0.4	12	6
Popcorn, air popped, plain	1 cup	6	23	0.7	0	0	0	5	0.9	1	0.2	0	12	0.01	0.01	0.1	0	1.38
Popcorn, ckd in oil, salted	1 cup	11	55	1	3	0.5	0	6	1.1	1	0.3	97	17	0.01	0.01	0.2	0	1.87
Pork, bacon/cracklings, brld/pan fried/rstd	2 pce	15	86	4.6	7	2.6	13	0	0	2	0.2	239	0	0.1	0.04	1.1	0	0.75
Pork, cured, ham, reg, 11% fat, rstd	3 oz	85	151	19.2	7	2.7	50	0	0	7	1.1	1275	0	0.62	0.28	5.2	0	2.55
Pork, ham, whole, rstd	3 oz	85	232	22.8	15	5.5	80	0	0	12	0.9	51	8	0.54	0.27	3.9	0	8.5
Pork, ribs, spareribs, brsd	3 oz	85	337	24.7	26	9.5	103	0	0	40	1.6	79	8	0.35	0.32	4.7	0	3.4
Potato Chips, plain, salted	10 pce	20	107	1.4	7	2.2	0	11	0.9	5	0.3	119	0	0.03	0.04	0.8	6	9
Potatoes, au gratin, prep w/milk & butter f/dry mix	1 cup	245	228	5.6	10	6.3	37	31	2.2	203	0.8	1076	522	0.05	0.2	2.3	8	16.17
Potatoes, baked, w/flesh & skin, long	1 ea	202	220	4.6	0	0.1	0	51	4.8	20	2.7	16	0	0.22	0.07	3.3	26	22.22
Potatoes, hash browns, prep f/fzn	½ cup	78	170	2.5	9	3.5	0	22	1.6	12	1.2	27	0	0.09	0.02	1.9	5	5.07
Potatoes, mashed, w/whole milk	½ cup	105	81	2	1	0.3	2	18	2.1	27	0.3	318	20	0.09	0.04	1.2	7	8.61
Potatoes, sweet, flesh, bkd in skin, med, peeled	1 ea	146	150	2.5	0	0	0	35	4.4	41	0.7	15	31860	0.11	0.19	0.9	36	33
Pretzels, hard, salted, twisted	1 oz	28	107	2.5	1	0.2	0	22	0.9	10	1.2	480	0	0.13	0.17	1.5	0	47.88
Prunes, dried	5 ea	61	146	1.6	0	0	0	38	4.3	31	1.5	2	1212	0.05	0.1	1.2	2	2.26
Pudding, choc, rte, 5oz can	5 oz	142	189	3.8	6	1	4	32	1.4	128	0.7	183	51	0.01	0.22	0.5	3	4.26
Pudding, tapioca, 5oz can	5 oz	142	169	2.8	5	0.9	1	28	0.1	119	0.3	226	0	0.03	0.14	0.4	1	4.26
Pudding, vanilla, 5oz can	5 oz	142	185	3.3	5	0.8	10	31	0.1	125	0.2	192	30	0.03	0.2	0.4	0	0
Raisins, seedless, unpacked	1 oz	28	84	0.9	1	0	0	22	1.1	14	0.6	3	2	0.04	0.02	0.2	1	0.92
Raspberries, fresh	1 cup	123	60	1.1	1	0	0	14	8.3	27	0.7	0	160	0.04	0.11	1.1	31	31.98
Raspberries, swtnd, fzn	1 cup	250	400	10	15	9.1	12	62	5.5	368	3.1	245	400	0.09	0.53	0.08	1	27.5
Rice, brown, ckd	½ cup	96	107	2.5	1	0.2	0	22	1.7	10	0.4	5	0	0.09	0.02	1.5	0	3.84
Rice, white, reg, ckd	½ cup	103	134	2.8	0	0.1	0	29	0.4	10	1.2	1	0	0.17	0.01	1.5	0	59.74
Rice, wild, ckd	½ cup	100	101	4	0	0	0	21	1.8	3	0.6	3	0	0.05	0.09	1.3	0	26
Rolls, hard, white	1 ea	50	146	4.9	2	0.3	0	26	1.1	48	1.6	272	0	0.24	0.17	2.1	0	47.5
Salad Dressing, blue cheese/roquefort	1 Tbs	15	76	0.7	8	1.5	3	1	0	12	0	164	32	0	0.02	0	0	1.21
Salad Dressing, French	1 Tbs	16	69	0.1	7	1.5	0	3	0	2	0.1	219	208	0	0	0	0	0.67
Salad Dressing, French, low cal	1 Tbs	15	20	0.1	1	0.1	0	3	0	2	0.1	118	195	0	0	0	0	0
Salad Dressing, Italian	1 Tbs	15	70	0.1	7	1.1	0	2	0	2	0	118	12	0	0	0	0	0.73
Salad Dressing, Italian, diet, 2cal/tsp, cmrcl	1 Tbs	15	16	0	1	0.2	1	1	0	0	0	118	0	0	0	0	0	0
Salad Dressing, ranch	1 Tbs	15	80	0	8	1.2	5	2	0	0	0	105	0	0	0	0	0	
Salad Dressing, thousand island	1 Tbs	15	57	0.1	5	0.9	4	2	0	2	0.1	105	48	0	0	0	0	0.94
Salad Dressing, thousand island, low cal	1 Tbs	15	24	0.1	2	0.2	2	2	0.2	2	0.1	150	48	0	0	0	0	0.84
Salad, chicken, w/celery	½ cup	78	268	10.6	25	3.1	48	1	0.2	16	0.6	201	155	0.03	0.07	3.3	1	8.46
Salad, pasta, garden primavera, prep f/dry	¾ cup	142	280	8	12	2.5	2	34	2	80	1.8	730	200	0.15	0.17	2	1	8.38
Salad, potato	½ cup	125	179	3.4	10	1.8	85	14	1.6	24	0.8	661	261	0.1	0.07	1.1	12	16.4
Salad, tuna	1 cup	205	383	32.9	19	3.2	27	19	0	35	2	824	199	0.06	0.14	13.7	5	0.56
Salami, beef & pork, dry	1 oz	28	117	6.4	10	3.4	22	1	0	2	0.4	521	0	0.17	0.08	1.4	0	13.09
Salmon, pink, w/bone, cnd, not drained	3 oz	85	118	16.8	5	1.3	47	0	0	181	0.7	471	47	0.02	0.16	5.6	0	4.25
Salmon, sockeye, fillet, bkd/brld	3 oz	85	184	23.2	9	1.6	74	0	0	6	0.5	56	178	0.18	0.15	5.7	2	1.74
Salsa, homemade, Mexican sauce	1 Tbs	15	3	0.1	0	0	0	1	0.2	1	0	1	57	0.01	0	0.1	2	
Sandwich, bacon, lettuce & tomato, on soft white	1 ea	130	323	10.8	18	4.7	22	30	1.7	54	2.1	619	271	0.36	0.2	3.4	12	15.5
Sandwich, egg salad, on soft white	1 ea	111	361	9.1	24	4.2	149	29	1.2	67	2.1	499	239	0.25	0.3	1.9	0	35.39
Sandwich, peanut butter & jam, on soft white, unsalted	1 ea	100	348	11.5	15	3.1	2	46	3	60	2.2	290	2	0.27	0.17	5.3	0	40.04
Sandwiches, reuben, grilled	1 ea	237	458	27.6	29	9.8	80	25	2.2	286	4.2	1933	453	0.21	0.34	2.8	13	37.79
Sardines, Atlantic, w/bones, cnd in oil, drained	1 oz	28	58	6.9	3	0.4	40	0	0	107	0.8	141	63	0.02	0.06	1.5	0	3.3

Food	Amount	Weight (g)	Calories	Protein (g)	Fat (g)	Sat. Fat (g)	Choles-terol (g)	Carbo-hydrate (g)	Fiber (g)	Calcium (mg)	Iron (mg)	Sodium (mg)	Vit A (IU)	Thiamin (Vit B₁) (mg)	Riboflavin (Vit B₂) (mg)	Niacin (mg)	Vit C (mg)	Folate (mcg)
Sauce, soy, made f/soy & wheat	1 Tbs	16	9	1.3	0	0	0	1	0.1	3	0.3	871	0	0.01	0.03	0.4	0	2.56
Sauce, teriyaki, rts	1 Tbs	18	15	1.1	0	0	0	3	0	4	0.3	690	0	0.01	0.01	0.2	0	3.6
Sauerkraut, w/liquid, cnd	½ cup	118	22	1.1	0	0	0	5	2.9	35	1.7	780	21	0.02	0.03	0.2	17	27.97
Sausage, pork, smkd, link	1 ea	68	265	15.1	22	7.7	46	1	0	20	0.8	1020	0	0.48	0.17	3.1	1	3.4
Scallops, brd, fried, mixed species, lrg	2 ea	31	67	5.6	3	0.8	19	3	0	13	0.3	144	23	0.01	0.03	0.5	1	11.47
Seaweed, spirulina, dried	1 cup	119	345	68.4	9	3.2	0	28	4.3	143	33.9	1247	678	2.83	4.37	15.3	12	111.8
Shrimp/Prawns brd, fried, lrg	7 ea	85	206	18.2	10	1.8	150	10	0.3	57	1.1	292	161	0.11	0.13	2.6	1	6.89
Shrimp/Prawns, ckd, lrg	3 oz	85	84	17.8	1	0.2	166	0	0	33	2.6	190	186	0.03	0.03	2.2	2	2.98
Soda, cola	12 fl-oz	369	151	0	0	0	0	38	0	11	0.1	15	0	0	0	0	0	0
Soda cola/Coke, diet w/sacc, low sod	12 fl-oz	340	0	0	0	0	0	0	0	14	0.1	54	0	0	0	0	0	0
Soda, ginger ale	12 fl-oz	366	124	0	0	0	0	32	0	11	0.7	26	0	0	0	0	0	0
Soda, lemon lime	12 fl-oz	340	136	0	0	0	0	35	0	7	0.2	37	0	0	0	0.1	0	0
Soda, root beer	12 fl-oz	340	139	0	0	0	0	36	0	17	0.2	44	0	0	0	0	0	0
Sole/Flounder, fillet, bkd/brld	3 oz	85	99	20.5	1	0.3	58	0	0	15	0.3	89	32	0.07	0.1	1.9	0	7.82
Soup, beef bouillon/broth, cnd, prep w/water	1 cup	240	17	2.7	1	0.3	0	0	0	14	0.4	782	0	0	0.05	1.9	0	4.8
Soup, chicken noodle, prep w/water	1 cup	241	75	4	2	0.7	7	9	0.7	17	0.8	1106	711	0.05	0.06	1.4	0	21.69
Soup, clam chowder, Manhattan, prep f/cnd	1 cup	244	112	12.3	2	0	10	11	3.1	4	1.8	725	2297				4	
Soup clam chowder, New England, prep w/milk	1 cup	248	164	9.5	7	3	22	17	1.5	186	1.5	992	164	0.07	0.24	1	3	9.67
Soup, cream of chicken, prep w/milk	1 cup	248	191	7.5	11	4.6	27	15	0.2	181	0.7	1047	714	0.07	0.26	0.9	1	7.69
Soup, cream of mushroom, prep w/milk	1 cup	245	201	6	13	5.1	20	15	0.5	176	0.6	906	152	0.08	0.28	0.9	2	9.8
Soup, minestrone, prep w/water	1 cup	241	82	4.3	3	0.6	2	11	1	34	0.9	911	2338	0.05	0.04	0.9	1	36.15
Soup, pea, split, w/ham, prep w/water	1 cup	245	184	10	4	1.7	7	27	2.2	22	2.2	975	431	0.14	0.07	1.4	1	2.45
Soup, tomato, prep w/milk	1 cup	248	161	6.1	6	2.9	17	22	2.7	159	1.8	744	848	0.13	0.25	1.5	68	20.83
Soup, tomato, prep w/water	1 cup	245	86	2.1	2	0.4	0	17	0.5	12	1.8	698	691	0.09	0.05	1.4	67	14.7
Soup, vegetable beef, prep w/water	1 cup	245	78	5.6	2	0.9	5	10	0.5	17	1.1	794	1899	0.04	0.05	1	2	10.54
Soup, vegetable, vegetarian, prep w/water	1 cup	250	75	2.2	2	0.3	0	12	0.5	22	1.1	852	3118	0.05	0.05	0.9	2	11
Sour Cream, cultured	1 Tbs	14	30	0.4	3	1.8	6	1	0	16	0	7	111	0.01	0.02	0	0	1.51
Spinach, ckd w/o add salt, drained	½ cup	103	24	3.1	0	0	0	4	2.5	140	3.7	72	8436	0.1	0.24	0.5	10	150.1
Spinach, raw chpd	1 cup	55	12	1.6	0	0	0	2	1.5	54	1.5	43	3693	0.04	0.1	0.4	15	106.9
Spinach, w/o add salt, cnd, drained	½ cup	103	24	2.9	1	0	0	4	2.5	131	2.4	28	9039	0.02	0.14	0.4	15	100.7
Squash, acorn, ckd	1 cup	245	83	1.6	0	0	0	22	6.4	64	1.4	7	632	0.25	0.02	1.3	16	27.69
Squash, summer, ckd w/o add salt, drained	½ cup	90	18	0.8	0	0	0	4	1.3	24	0.3	1	258	0.04	0.04	0.5	5	18.09
Squash, winter, avg, bkd, mashed	½ cup	103	40	0.9	1	0.1	0	9	2.9	14	0.3	1	3664	0.09	0.02	0.7	10	28.84
Strawberries, fresh, whole	1 cup	149	45	0.9	1	0	0	10	3.4	21	0.6	1	40	0.03	0.1	0.3	34	26.37
Strawberries, slices, swtnd, fzn	1 cup	250	240	1.3	0	0	0	65	4.8	28	1.5	8	60	0.04	0.13	1	104	37.25
Stuffing, bread, prep f/dry mix	½ cup	70	125	2.2	6	1.2	0	15	2	22	0.8	380	219	0.1	0.07	1	0	70.7
Sugar, beet/cane, brown, packed	1 tsp	5	19	0	0	0	0	5	0	4	0.1	0	0	0	0	0	0	0.05
Sugar, white, granulated	1 tsp	4	15	0	0	0	0	4	0	0	0	0	0	0	0	0	0	0
Syrup, maple	1 Tbs	20	52	0	0	0	0	13	0	13	0.2	2	0	0	0	0	0	0
Taco Shells	1 ea	10	47	0.7	2	0.3	0	7	0.7	20	0.2	67	33	0	0	0	0	0
Tangerines/Mandarin oranges, fresh, med	1 ea	116	51	0.7	0	0	0	13	2.7	16	0.1	1	1067	0.12	0.03	0.2	36	23.66
Tea, brewed	¾ cup	180	2	0	0	0	0	1	0	0	0	5	0	0	0.03	0	0	9.36
Tempeh	1 cup	166	320	30.8	18	3.7	0	16	9	184	4.5	15	0	0.13	0.59	4.4	0	39.67
Tofu, firm, silken	½ cup	126	78	8.7	3	0.5	0	3	0.1	40	1.3	45	0	0.13	0.05	0.3	0	15
Tomatoes, red, ripe, raw, med, whole	1 ea	100	21	0.9	0	0	0	5	1.1	5	0.4	9	623	0.06	0.05	0.6	19	
Tomatoes, red, ripe, w/o add salt, cnd, in liquid	½ cup	121	23	1.1	0	0	0	5	1.2	36	0.7	179	720	0.05	0.04	0.3	17	9.44
Tortilla/Taco/Tostada Shell, corn	1 ea	148	693	10.7	33	5	0	92	11.1	237	3.7	543	518	0.34	0.08	2	0	8.88
Trout, rainbow, fillet, bkd/brld, wild	3 oz	85	128	19.5	5	1.4	59	0	0	73	0.3	48	42	0.13	0.08	4.9	2	16.15

Food	Amount	Weight (g)	Calories	Protein (g)	Fat (g)	Sat. Fat (g)	Cholesterol (g)	Carbohydrate (g)	Fiber (g)	Calcium (mg)	Iron (mg)	Sodium (mg)	Vit A (IU)	Thiamin (Vit B_1) (mg)	Riboflavin (Vit B_2) (mg)	Niacin (mg)	Vit C (mg)	Folate (mcg)
Tuna, light, cnd in oil, drained	3 oz	85	168	24.8	7	1.3	15	0	0	11	1.2	301	66	0.03	0.1	10.5	0	4.51
Tuna, light cnd in water, drained	3½ oz	99	115	25.3	1	0.2	30	0	0	11	1.5	335	55	0.03	0.07	13.1	0	3.96
Turkey, average, w/o skin, rstd	3 oz	85	144	24.9	4	1.4	65	0	0	21	1.5	60	0	0.05	0.15	4.6	0	5.95
Turnip Greens, ckd f/fzn, drained	½ cup	73	22	2.4	0	0.1	0	4	2.5	111	1.4	11	5822	0.04	0.05	0.3	16	28.76
Turnips, ckd w/add salt, raw, cubes	½ cup	78	16	0.6	0	0	0	4	1.6	17	0.2	39	0	0.02	0.02	0.2	9	7.18
Veal, loin, brsd	3 oz	85	241	25.7	15	5.7	100	0	0	24	0.9	68	0	0.03	0.26	7.7	0	11.9
Veal, loin, lean, brsd	3 oz	85	192	28.5	8	2.2	106	0	0	27	0.9	71	0	0.04	0.29	8.5	0	12.75
Vinegar, balsamic, 60 grain	1 Tbs	15	21	0	1	0.1		5	0	0.1	3	0		0.08	0.1	0.3		
Watermelon, fresh, diced	1 cup	160	51	1	1	0.1		11	0.8	13	0.3	3	586	0.13	0.03	0	15	3.52
Wheat, bulgur, ckd	1 cup	135	112	4.2	0	0		6.1	14	1.3	7	3		0.04	1.4	1.4	24.3	
Wheat, flakes, rolled, dry	1 cup	30	97	3.5	1	0.1		21	4.4	18	1	0	0	0.13	0.03	0.3	0	21.12
Wheat, germ, tstd	1 Tbs	6	23	1.7	0	0		3	0.8	3	0.5	0	0	0.1	0.05	0.1	0	
Whiskey, 90 proof	2 fl-oz	42	110	0	0	0		0	0	0	0	0	0	0				0
Wine, cooler	4 oz	113	56	0.1	0	0		7	0	6	0.3	9	1	0.01	0.01	0.1	2	1.34
Wine, red	1/8 cup	30	22	0.1	0	0		1	0	2	0.1	2	0	0	0.01	0	0	0.6
Wine, Rose	2 fl-oz	59	42	0.1	0	0		1	0	5	0.2	3	0	0	0.01	0	0	0.65
Wine, white, med	2 fl-oz	59	40	0.1	0	0		0	0	5	0.2	3	0	0		0	0	0.12
Yogurt, fruit, low fat, 10g prot/8 oz	1 cup	227	231	9.9	2	1.6	10	43	0	345	0.2	133	104	0.08	0.4	0.2	1	21.11
Yogurt, plain, low fat, 12g prot/8 oz	8 oz	226	143	11.9	4	2.3	14	16	0	413	0.2	159	149	0.1	0.48	0.3	2	25.31
FAST FOOD RESTAURANTS																		
General																		
Burrito, bean	1 ea	166	342	10.8	10	5.3	3	55	6.3	86	3.5	754	254	0.48	0.46	3.1	1	66.4
Chili, con carne	1 cup	255	258	24.8	8	3.5	135	22	4	69	5.2	1015	1675	0.13	1.15	2.5	2	45.9
Cole Slaw, fast food	1 cup	120	178	1.8	13	1.9	6	15	2	41	0.9	324	409	0.05	0.04	0.1	10	46.8
English Muffin, w/butter	1 ea	63	189	4.9	6	2.4	13	30	1.9	103	1.6	386	136	0.25	0.31	2.6	1	56.7
Entree, enchilada, cheese	1 ea	230	451	13.6	27	14.9	62	40		458	1.9	1106	1638	0.12	0.6	2.7	1	92
Hot Dog, plain	1 ea	98	242	10.4	15	5.1	44	18		24	2.3	670		0.24	0.27	3.6		48.02
Pancake, w/butter & syrup	2 ea	232	520	8.3	14	5.9	58	91	1.2	128	2.6	1104	281	0.39	0.56	3.4	3	51.04
Sandwich, chicken, fillet, plain	1 ea	157	444	20.8	25	7.4	52	33	1.1	52	4	826	86	0.28	0.2	5.9	8	86.35
Sundae, hot fudge, fast food	1 ea	164	295	5.9	9	5.2	21	49	0	215	0.6	189	230	0.07	0.31	1.1	2	9.84
Arby's																		
Salad, chef	1 ea	273	136	12.3	6	2.6	84	9		113	3.3	529	3321	0.26	0.25	4.6	35	
Sandwich, beef, Arby Q	1 ea	190	389	17.6	15	5.4	29	48		70	9.2	1268		0.27	0.39	9.2		
Sandwich, beef, French dip	1 ea	154	369	24.7	16	7.5	58	31	0.9	232	3.6	1237	0	0.18	0.47	7.4	0	16.35
Sandwich, beef 'n cheddar	1 ea	194	508	24.6	26	7.7	52	43		150	6.1	1166		0.42	0.63	9.8	1	
Sandwich, chicken, grilled, deluxe	1 ea	195	365	20	17	3	37	35		59	2.1	764	339	0.27	0.25	11.5	7	
Sandwich, roast beef, regular	1 ea	155	383	22	18	6.9	43	35	1.1	60	4.9	936	0	0.28	0.48	11	1	14
Sauce, Arby's	½ oz	14	15	0.1	0	0	0	3			0.4	113						
Sauce, horsey	½ oz	14	110	0.1	5	1.2	0	3		20		105						
Burger King Corporation																		
Cheeseburger, Whopper	1 ea	294	730	33	46	16	115	46	3	250	4.5	1350	750	0.34	0.48	7	9	
Croissant, w/egg, saugage & cheese	1 ea	110	375	13.8	29	10	162	16	0.6	94	2.2	712	250		0.41	7	9	
Hamburger, Whopper	1 ea	270	640	27	39	11	90	45	3	80	4.5	870	500	0.33		7	9	
Onion Rings, reg svg	3 ea	30	75	1	3	0.5	0	10	1.5	24	0.3	196	0				0	
Potatoes, french fries, salted, med svg	1 ea	116	370	5	20	5	0	43	3	0	1.1	240	0				4	
Sandwich, chicken, broiler	1 ea	168	373	20.3	20	4.1	54	28	1.4	41	3.7	325	203				4	
Sandwich, fish, big	1 ea	255	700	26	41	6	90	56	3	60	2.7	980	100				1	
Dunkin Donuts, Inc.																		
Croissant, plain	1 ea	18	81	1.2	5	1.2	2	8	0	6	0.5	78	0				0	
Hidden Valley																		
Salad Dressing, ranch, reduced fat & cal	2 Tbs	28	58	0.5	5	0.9	10	2	0	11	0.1	237	15				0	

Food	Amount	Weight (g)	Calories	Protein (g)	Fat (g)	Sat. Fat (g)	Cholesterol (g)	Carbohydrate (g)	Fiber (g)	Calcium (mg)	Iron (mg)	Sodium (mg)	Vit A (IU)	Thiamin (Vit B_1) (mg)	Ribo flavin (Vit B_2) (mg)	Niacin (mg)	Vit C (mg)	Folate (mcg)
International Dairy Queen Inc.																		
Frozen Yogurt Cone, med	4 oz	113	148	5.1	1	0.3	3	32	0	143	1	91	0	0.05	0.2		1	
Frozen Yogurt, nonfat	4 oz	113	133	4	0	0		28	0	133	1	93	0				0	
Hamburger, homestyle	1 ea	138	290	17	12	5	45	29	2	60	2.7	630	200	0.29	0.25	3.9	4	
Ice Cream Cone, vanilla, med	1 ea	142	237	5.7	6	4.3	22	38	0	179	1.3	115	538	0.06	0.26	0.1	2	
Milk Shake, vanilla, med	1 ea	397	520	12	14	8	45	88	0.3	400	1.4	230	400	0.12	0.6	0.8	0	
Onion Rings, svg	3 oz	85	241	3.8	12	3	0	29	2.3	15	1.1	135	0	0.09	0.05	0.4	0	
Sandwich, fish, fillet	1 ea	182	396	17.1	17	3.7	48	42	2.1	43	1.9	674	0	0.32	0.24	3.2	0	
Sundae, chocolate, med	1 ea	184	315	6.3	8	4.7	24	56	0	197	1.1	165	590	0.06	0.27	0.3	0	
Jack in the Box																		
Bowl, chicken, terriyaki	1 ea	502	670	26	4	1	15	128	3	100	4.5	1730	6500	0.44	0.54	2	24	
Cheeseburger, Jumbo Jack	1 ea	296	640	31	38	15	105	44	3	250	4.5	1340	750	0.16	0.28	2.1	9	
Hamburger	1 ea	104	250	12	9	3.5	30	30	2	100	3.6	610					0	
Hamburger, sourdough, jack	1 ea	233	690	34	45	15	105	37	2	200	4.5	1180	750	0.68	0.5	8.4	9	
Sandwich, chicken, supreme	1 ea	305	830	33	49	7	65	66	3	200	3.6	2140	500	0.49	0.4	13.7	9	
Kentucky Fried Chicken Corporation																		
Chicken, leg, original recipe	1 ea	54	124	11.5	8	1.8	66	4	0	18	0.6	374	89				1	
Chicken, wing, hot & spicy	1 ea	55	210	10	15	4	55	9	1	20	0.7	350	100				1	
Chicken, wing, original recipe	1 ea	45	134	8.6	10	2.4	53	5	0	19	0.3	396	95				1	
Long John Silver's																		
Dinner, fish & fries, batter fried, 2pce	1 ea	261	610	27	37	7.9	60	52		40	1.8	1480		0.38	0.34	8	9	
McDonald's Nutrition Information Center																		
Biscuit, sausage & egg	1 ea	175	541	17.7	36	9.8	241	34	1	98	2.7	1140	295	0.53	0.57	4.1	0	27.73
Cheeseburger	1 ea	115	304	14.3	12	5.7	38	33	1.9	190	2.6	779	285	0.31	0.29	3.6	2	22.37
Cheeseburger, Quarter Pounder	1 ea	186	493	26	28	12.1	88	35	1.9	279	4.2	1200	465	0.37	0.4	6.3	2	31.06
Chicken, nuggets, McNuggets, 4 pce. svg	1 ea	71	190	12	11	2.5	40	10	0	9	0.7	340	0	0.08	0.11	5	0	
Danish, apple	1 ea	115	394	5.5	18	5.5	44	56	1.1	88	1.2	318	548	0.33	0.19	2.2	1	
Frozen Yogurt Cone, vanilla, low fat	3 oz	85	142	3.8	4	2.8	19	22	0	94	0.3	71	283				1	
Hamburger, Big Mac	1 ea	204	529	24.6	29	9.4	80	42	2.8	236	4.2	1011	283	0.46	0.42	5.7	3	46.53
Hamburger, Quarter Pounder	1 ea	160	391	21.4	20	7.4	65	34	1.9	140	4.2	763	93	0.37	0.3	6.3	2	25.63
McMuffin, egg	1 ea	138	294	17.2	12	4.6	238	27	1	203	2.7	802	507	0.5	0.45	3.3	1	33.47
McMuffin, sausage	1 ea	135	434	15.7	28	9.6	54	31	1.2	241	2.2	892	241	0.68	0.33	4.5	0	18.95
Milk Shake, vanilla, sml	1 ea	289	355	10.8	9	5.9	39	58	0	345	0.4	246	296	0.12	0.5	0.3	1	
Muffin, apple bran, fat free	1 ea	75	197	3.9	2	0.3	0	40	2	66	0.9	250	0	0.14	0.14	1.3	1	5.03
Pie, apple	1 ea	307	1037	12	52	14	0	136	4	80	4.3	797		0.71	0.43	5.6	96	33.16
Potatoes, french fries, sml svg	1 ea	68	210	3	10	1.5	0	26	2	9	0.4	135	0	0.05	0	1.9	9	25.57
Potatoes, hash browns	1 ea	55	135	1	8	1.6	0	15	1	7	0.4	342	0	0.08	0.02	0.9	2	8.64
Salad, garden, shaker	1 ea	149	100	7	6	3	75	4	2	150	1.1	120	1500				15	
Sandwich, Fillet O Fish	1 ea	131	378	13.4	21	3.8	42	35	1.7	126	1.5	731	168	0.29	0.21	2.3	0	26.73
Sauce, sweet & sour, pkt 1	1 1/8 oz	32	57	0	0	0	0	13		2	0.2	160	343	0	0.01	0.1	0	
Pizza Hut, Inc.																		
Pizza, cheese, pan, med, 12"	2 pce	205	495	22.8	21	9.5	47	53	3.8	273	2.8	951	1000	0.57	0.61	5.2	7	
Pizza, cheese, thin n' crispy, med, 12"	2 pce	148	350	18.8	14	6.8	43	36	3.4	247	1.8	911	922	0.39	0.39	4.8	5	
Pizza, pepperoni, pan, med, 12"	2 pce	211	539	22.4	24	8.1	49	57	4.1	209	3.3	1157	966	0.63	0.49	5.4	8	0
Pizza, pepperoni, personal pan	1 ea	255	637	27	28	10	55	69	5	250	4	1339	1164	0.56	0.66	8.2	10	
Pizza, supreme, pan, med, 12"	2 pce	255	581	28	28	11.2	56	52	5.6	219	4.3	1428	912	0.8	0.79	6	10	
Subway International																		
Sandwich, chicken breast, rstd, on white, 6"	1 ea	246	332	26	6	1	48	41	3	35	3	967	617				15	
Sandwich, Italian bmt, on white, 6"	1 ea	246	445	21	21	8	56	39	3	44	4	1652	753				15	
Sandwich, meatball, on white, 6"	1 ea	260	404	18	16	6	33	44	3	32	4	1035	712				16	
Sandwich, roast beef, deli style	1 ea	180	245	13	4	1	13	38	2	23	3	638	565				14	

Ribo

Food	Amount	Weight (g)	Calories	Protein (g)	Fat (g)	Sat. Fat (g)	Cholesterol (g)	Carbohydrate (g)	Fiber (g)	Calcium (mg)	Iron (mg)	Sodium (mg)	Vit A (IU)	Thiamin (Vit B₁) (mg)	flavin (Vit B₂) (mg)	Niacin (mg)	Vit C (mg)	Folate (mcg)
Sandwich, tuna, w/lt mayonnaise, on wheat, 6"	1 ea	253	391	19	15	2	32	46	3	38	3	940	729				15	
Sandwich, turkey, on white, 6"	1 ea	232	273	17	4	1	19	40	3	30	4	1391	601				15	
Taco Bell Inc.																		
Burrito, beef, big supreme	1 ea	298	520	24	23	10	55	54	11	150	2.7	1520	3000				5	
Burrito, seven layer	1 ea	234	438	13.2	19	5.8	21	55	10.7	165	3	1058	1240				5	
Burrito, supreme	1 ea	255	440	17	19	8	35	51	10	150	9	1230	2500	0.4	2.1	2.9	5	
Taco	1 ea	83	192	9.6	11	4.3	27	13	3.2	85	1.1	351	532	0.05	0.15	1.3	0	
Taco, soft	1 ea	92	225	9.2	10	4.1	26	12	3.1	82	1.1	337	511	0.39	0.22	2.7	0	
Wendy's Foods International																		
Cheeseburger, w/bacon, jr	1 ea	170	393	20.5	19	7.5	58	35	1.9	171	3.6	895	390	0.31	0.32	6.6	9	28.85
Chicken, nuggets	6 pce	94	292	13.9	20	3.6	37	14	0	24	0.5	589	0	0.15	0.14	0.9	1	
Frosty, dairy dessert, med	1 ea	298	440	11	11	7	50	73	0	410	1.4	260	1000	0.14	0.62	0.4	0	22.9
Hamburger, bacon classic, big	1 ea	251	517	30.1	26	10.7	88	41	2.4	206	4.5	1298	622	0.4	1.36	5.3	13	
Salad, caesar, w/o dressing, side	1 ea	130	151	12.4	8	3.4	25	9	2	190	1.6	538	2501				22	
Salad, chicken, grilled, w/o dressing	1 ea	338	195	22.1	8	1.7	46	10	4	188	2.1	676	5872				35	
Salad, garden, deluxe, w/o dressing	1 ea	271	110	6.7	6	1	1	10	3.9	189	1.5	319	5883				35	
Salad, taco, w/o chips	1 ea	510	411	28.7	20	10.5	69	31	8.7	403	4.5	1132	2582	0.29	0.5	3.2	28	88.27
Sandwich, chicken, brd	1 ea	208	433	27.4	16	3.1	54	47	1.8	93	2.7	754	217	0.43	0.32	13.3	13	
Sandwich, chicken, club	1 ea	220	483	30.6	20	4.4	64	48	1.9	95	2.9	957	222				14	
Sandwich, chicken, grilled	1 ea	177	283	22.6	7	1.5	61	34	1.8	84	2.7	698	201				9	
CONVENIENCE FOODS & MEALS																		
El Charrito																		
Entree, enchilada, beef, family size, 6 pack	1 ea	200	353	11.8	17	6.5	33	39	5.2	196	2.4	837	1961	0.22	0.19	1.5	3	
Healthy Choice																		
Dinner, fish, herb baked, fzn	1 ea	273	300	14.1	6	1.3	31	48	4.4	35	0.6	424	2650				0	
Dinner, meatloaf, traditional, fzn	1 ea	340	316	15.3	5	2.5	37	52	6.1	48	2.2	459	745				55	
Entree, burrito, chicken, con queso, fzn	1 ea	216	253	10.1	4	1.8	25	43	4.3	29	1.3	426	1084				4	
Entree, lasagna, roma, fzn	1 ea	284	311	19.3	7	2.2	26	44	4.4	111	2.7	430	371				4	
Entree, spaghetti, bolognese, fzn	1 ea	284	280	14	6	2	30	43	5	40	3.6	470	500				15	
Lean Cuisine																		
Entree, chow mein, chicken, w/rice	1 ea	241	198	12.3	5	0.9	33	26	1.9	19	0.3	482	95	0.14	0.16	4.7	6	
Entree, lasagna, w/meat sauce	1 ea	291	270	19	6	2.5	25	34	5	150	1.8	560	500	0.15	0.25	3	12	
Entree, ravioli, cheese	1 ea	241	250	12	8	3	55	32	4	200	1.1	500	750	0.06	0.25	1.2	6	
Entree, spaghetti, w/meatballs, fzn	1 ea	290	322	19.4	8	2.2	6	43	4.9	102	2.6	502	0					
The Budget Gourmet																		
Dinner, chicken, teriyaki, 3 dish	1 ea	340	360	20	12		55	44		80	1.4	610	1500	0.15	0.34	6	12	
Dinner, veal, parmigiana, 3 dish	1 ea	340	440	26	20		165	39		30	4.5	1160	5000	0.45	0.6	6	6	48
Entree, beef, sirloin tips, w/country gravy	1 ea	334	365	18.8	21		47	25		71	0.4	670	882	0.18	0.2	4.7	3	
Entree, linguini, w/shrimp	1 ea	284	330	15	15		75	33		10	3.6	1250	5000	0.3	0.17	3	2	
The Budget Gourmet-Slim Select																		
Entree, stroganoff, beef	1 ea	238	269	17.3	10		58	28		58	2.6	537	288				9	
Weight Watchers																		
Entree, chow mein, chicken	1 ea	255	200	12	2	0.5	25	34	3	40	0.7	430	1499	0.25	0.33	3.8	36	

Index